# THE OSAGE TRIBE

## TWO VERSIONS OF THE CHILD-NAMING RITE

BY

FRANCIS LA FLESCHE

EXTRACT FROM THE FORTY-THIRD ANNUAL REPORT OF THE
BUREAU OF AMERICAN ETHNOLOGY

UNITED STATES
GOVERNMENT PRINTING OFFICE
WASHINGTON
1928

## Printing Statement:

Due to the very old age and scarcity of this book,
many of the pages may be hard to read due to the
blurring of the original text, possible missing pages,
missing text and other issues beyond our control.

Because this is such an important and rare work, we
believe it is best to reproduce this book regardless of
its original condition.

Thank you for your understanding.

# CONTENTS

| | Page |
|---|---|
| Introduction | 29 |
| Child-naming rituals | 31 |
| Birth names of the Puma gens | 31 |
| The first three sons | 31 |
| The first three daughters | 32 |
| Sky names | 32 |
| Child-naming ritual of the Puma gens | 33 |
| Ceremony of decorating the Xo'-ḳa | 33 |
| Ḳi'-noⁿ Wi'-gi-e | 34 |
| Wa'-ṭse-ṭsi and the Ṭsi'-zhu Wa-shta-ge gentes | 35 |
| Ṭsi Ṭa'-pe (approach to the house) | 36 |
| The Wa-the'-the ceremony | 38 |
| Zha'-zhe Ḳi-ṭoⁿ Wi'-gi-e (name taking) | 40 |
| Old-age Wi'-gi-e | 45 |
| Wi'-gi-e of the Wa'-ṭse-ṭsi gens | 47 |
| Wi'-gi-e of the Bow people | 47 |
| Earth names and wi'-gi-es | 48 |
| Wi'-gi-e of the Wa'-ṭse-gi-ṭsi (Wa-ṭse'-moⁿ-iⁿ) | 51 |
| Special instructions to the mother | 54 |
| Origin Wi'-gi-e of the Tho'-xe gens | 56 |
| Child-naming ritual of the Ṭsi'-zhu Wa-shta-ge gens | 59 |
| Certain gentes called to take part in the ceremony | 59 |
| Wa-zho'-i-ga-the (Life symbol) Wi'-gi-e | 60 |
| The Xo'-ḳa ceremonially conducted to the child's house | 67 |
| A life symbol sent to each of the officiating gentes | 68 |
| Gentes recite their wi'-gi-es simultaneously | 68 |
| The child is passed from gens to gens to be blessed | 71 |
| First child-naming wi'-gi-e of the Ṭsi'-zhu Wa-noⁿ gens | 75 |
| The gentile hair cut of children | 87 |
| Hair cut of the Ṭsi'-zhu Wa-shta-ge gens | 89 |
| Paraphrase of the wi'-gi-e of the Red Eagle gens | 90 |
| Wi'-gi-e of the Ni'-ḳa Wa-ḳoⁿ-da-gi and the Tho'-xe gentes | 93 |
| Fondness of personal adornment | 95 |
| Ear perforating | 95 |
| Ḳi'-noⁿ Wi'-gi-e in Osage | 96 |
| Ṭsi Ṭa'-pe Wa-thoⁿ and Wi'-gi-e in Osage | 97 |
| Zha'-zhe Ḳi-ṭoⁿ Wi'-gi-e in Osage | 97 |
| U'-noⁿ Wi-gi-e in Osage | 101 |
| Wa-zho'-i-ga-the Wi'-gi-e in Osage | 103 |
| Zha'-zhe Ḳi-ṭoⁿ Wi'-gi-e in Osage | 110 |
| Wa-zho'-i-ga-the Wi'-gi-e in Osage | 113 |
| Native names of Osage full bloods | 122 |
| Names of the gentes and subgentes | 122 |
| Wa'-ṭse-ṭsi or Poⁿ'-ḳa Wa-shta-ge | 124 |
| Ṭa' I-ni-ḳa-shi-ga | 128 |

Native names of Osage full bloods—Continued.

| | Page |
|---|---|
| Ho' I-ni-ḳa-shi-ga | 130 |
| Hoⁿ'-ga U-ṭa-noⁿ-dsi | 132 |
| Wa-ça'-be | 133 |
| Iⁿ-ghoⁿ'-ga | 135 |
| Hoⁿ'-ga Gthe-zhe | 136 |
| Hoⁿ'-ga U-thu-ha-ge | 139 |
| O'-poⁿ | 141 |
| I'-ba-ṭse | 142 |
| Ṭsi'-zhu Wa-noⁿ | 144 |
| Çiⁿ'-dse-a-gthe | 146 |
| Ṭsi'-zhu Wa-shta-ge | 146 |
| Ṭse-do'-ga Iⁿ-dse | 152 |
| Ṭse Thoⁿ'-ḳa | 153 |
| Mi-ḳ'iⁿ' | 153 |
| Hoⁿ' I-ni-ḳa-shi-ga | 155 |
| Ni'-ḳa Wa-ḳoⁿ-da-gi | 157 |
| Tho'-xe | 160 |
| Index | 821 |

# ILLUSTRATIONS

PLATES

Page

1. Wa-xthi'-zhi (I$^n$-gtho$^{n'}$-ga (Puma) gens) _____ 30
2. Sho$^{n'}$-ge-mo$^n$-i$^n$ (Ṭsi'-zhu Wa-shta-ge gens) _____ 30
3. Shell gorget and downy plume (Life symbols) _____ 44
4. Wa-sho'-she (Ho$^{n'}$-ga A-hiu-ṭo$^n$ (Eagle) gens) _____ 44
5. Wa-ṭse'-mo$^n$-i$^n$ (Wa-ça'-be (Black Bear) gens) _____ 54
6. a, War standard (Symbolizes the white swan).  b, Ṭse'-wa-the root
   (Nelumbo lutea) used for food _____ 54
7. Xu-tha'-wa-ṭo$^n$-i$^n$ (Ṭsi'-zhu Wa-no$^n$ gens) _____ 84
8. Straps for tying captives _____ 84
9. Four Osage children _____ 92
10. Child's hair cut of the Tho-xe and Ni'-ka Wa-ko$^n$-da-gi gentes _____ 92
11. Men, showing hair cut of adult Osages _____ 92
12. Bone ear perforators and expanders _____ 92

TEXT FIGURES

1. Diagram showing places of gentes in the lodge _____ 36
2. Symbolic robe prepared for children _____ 54
3. Chart of constellation Wa'-ba-ha (Ursa Major) _____ 74
4. Chart of Ṭa Tha'-bthi$^n$, Three Deer (in Orion) _____ 74
5. Totemic cut of the Omaha boys' hair _____ 87
6. Symbolic hair cut of the Ho$^{n'}$-ga gens _____ 89
7. Symbolic hair cut of the Ṭsi'-zhu Wa-shta-ge gens _____ 89
8. Hair cut of the Ṭsi'-zhu Wa-no$^n$ and the Wa-ça'-be (Black Bear) gentes _ 92

27

# THE OSAGE TRIBE: TWO VERSIONS OF THE CHILD-NAMING RITE

By Francis La Flesche

## INTRODUCTION

The two versions of the Osage Child-naming Rite recorded in this volume were obtained with considerable difficulty, owing to the reluctance of the people to speak of the sacred rites that were formulated by the Ni'-ḳa Xu-be, Holy Men, of long ago. This unwillingness to speak of the tribal rites, excepting in the prescribed ceremonial way, arose from a sense of reverence for things sacred and from the belief that within the rites, and in the articles dedicated to religious use, there resides a mystic power which could punish, by supernatural means, the persons who speak irreverently of the rites and put to profane use the symbolic articles.

In the early part of the life of the Osage, according to tradition, the people kept together for protection and moved about without tribal or gentile organizations, a condition which they termed "ga-ni'-tha," which may be freely translated as, without law or order.

It was in those days that a group of men fell into the habit of gathering together, from time to time, to exchange ideas concerning the actions of the sun, moon, and stars which they observed move within the sky with marvelous precision, each in its own given path. They also noticed, in the course of their observations, that the travelers in the upper world move from one side of the sky to the other without making any disturbances in their relative positions, and that with these great movements four changes take place in the vegetal life of the earth which they agreed was effected by the actions of some of the heavenly travelers. These seasonal changes they named Be, Do-ge', Ṭoⁿ, and Ba'-the (Spring, Summer, Autumn and Winter).

The delving into the mysteries of the universe by this group of men, which was carried on for a long period of time, was primarily for the purpose of finding, if possible, the place from which comes all life.

The seasonal changes upon the earth which appear to accompany the movements of the sun and other cosmic bodies suggested to these men the existence between sky and earth of a procreative relationship, an idea which fixed itself firmly in their minds. It fitted their

29

notion that the earth was related to and influenced by all of the great bodies that move around within the sky. However, they were not satisfied that these celestial bodies move without the guidance of some governing power, and they continued their search and their discussions. Then, in course of time, there crept into the minds of these men, who became known as the "Little Old Men," the thought that a silent, invisible creative power pervades the sun, moon and stars and the earth, gives to them life, and keeps them eternally in motion and perfect order. This creative power which to their minds was the source of life they named Wa-ḳoⁿ'-da, Mysterious Power, and sometimes E-a'-wa-woⁿ a-ka, The Causer of Our Being.

These ideas are given expression in that part of the child-naming rite where the initiated members of two gentes are first called to enter the house in which the ceremonies are to take place. One of these gentes, the Ṭsi'-zhu Wa-shta-ge, Peaceful Ṭsi'-zhu, represents the sky with its sun, moon, and stars, and the other, the Wa'-ṭse-ṭsi Wa-shta-ge, Peaceful Wa'-ṭse-ṭsi, represents the earth with its waters and dry land. The house itself then becomes a symbol of the sky which encompasses the sun, moon, stars, and the earth. Thus the house, the two gentes and all the others who enter it to take part in the rite become, collectively, a symbol of the universe wherein life manifests itself by taking on an infinite variety of bodily forms. The whole ceremony is an expression of a longing desire that Wa-ḳoⁿ'-da who dwells in the universe will favor the little one who is to be named with a long life and an endless line of descendants.

The men who recorded the two versions of the Osage child-naming rite were typical full-blood Indians, neither of them spoke the English language, and nothing in all that they have given suggests foreign influence. Wa-xthi'-zhi (pl. 1) was a man of an inquiring mind. He did not hesitate to ask of his initiators the meaning of the parts of the rituals which he did not fully understand. He learned much from his father, who was well versed in the ancient tribal rites.

Shoⁿ'-ge-moⁿ-iⁿ (pl. 2) did not have these advantages, but he had a retentive mind and what he committed to memory of the rites was sufficient to him. He did not insist upon being informed as to the meaning of the parts of the rites that were obscure to him.

I am indebted to Mr. Vince Dillon, of Fairfax, Okla., for permitting me to use a photograph he had made of two little Osages showing symbolic hair cut of one of them. Also to Joe Shoⁿ'-ge-moⁿ-iⁿ for the loan of a photograph of his two daughters. Joe is the son of Shoⁿ'-ge-moⁿ-iⁿ, who recorded the second version of the child-naming ceremony.

WA-XTHI'-ZHI (I$^{N}$-GTHO$^{N'}$-GA (PUMA) GENS)

SHON'-GE-MON-IN (TSI'-ZHU WA-SHTA-GE GENS)

## CHILD-NAMING RITUALS

To a self-respecting Osage husband and wife, the ceremonial naming of their first three sons and their first three daughters is of the utmost importance. The couple regard the performing of the ceremony as a sacred duty to their children which must never be neglected.

Each of these sons and daughters must be named according to the rites prescribed by the ancient $No^{n\prime}$-$ho^n$-$zhi^n$-ga. Until the ceremonial naming the child has no place in the gentile organization, and it is not even regarded as a person.

Every one of these three sons and three daughters has a special kinship term which can be used only by the father, the mother, and the nearest relatives. These special kinship terms, as observed in their sequence, are as follows:

| Sons | Daughters |
|---|---|
| $I^n$-gtho$^{n\prime}$. | Mi′-no$^n$. |
| Ksho$^{n\prime}$-ga. | Wi′-he. |
| Ḳa′-zhi$^n$-ga. | Çi′-ge or A-çi$^{n\prime}$-ga. |

All the sons born after the third one are Ḳa′-zhi$^n$-ga, and all the daughters born after the third one, Çi-ge or A-çi$^{n\prime}$-ga.

To each of the first six children belongs a distinctive gentile personal name, spoken of as: i$^n$-gtho$^{n\prime}$ zha-zhe (I$^n$-gtho$^{n\prime}$ name), mi′-no$^n$ zha-zhe (Mi′-no$^n$ name), etc. These names must always be ceremonially conferred upon the newly born child. All the other sons and daughters are named without any formality because the ceremony performed for the Ḳa′-zhi$^n$-ga and the Çi′-ge serves for the other children that may follow. These destinctive gentile names may be designated as gentile birth names.

## BIRTH NAMES OF THE PUMA GENS

The gentile birth names of the Puma gens, as given by Wa-xthi′-zhi, are as follows:

### The First Three Sons

1. Mi′-wa-ga-xe, Child-of-the-sun. This name is commemorative of the talk that took place between the "Little Ones" and the Sun when they went to him to ask for aid as they were about to come to the earth, their future home. In asking for aid, the "Little Ones" addressed the Sun as grandfather, and the Sun, in reply, said to them: "It is true that you are my children." Hence the name, Mi′-wa-ga-xe, Child-of-the-sun. The name is mentioned in the Naming Ritual of the Puma gens. (See p. 41, lines 24 to 27.)

2. I′-e-çka-wa-the, Giver-of-speech. The Sun also gave to the "Little Ones" the power of expressing their thoughts by speech, and the skill in arranging their words so that they can be clearly understood. When a person speaks intelligently he is spoken of

as i'-e-wa-çka, a clear speaker.  The children are given the name
I'-e-çka-wa-the as a recognition of this great gift from the Sun.
The name is mentioned in the Naming Ritual of the Puma gens.
(See p. 41, line 34.)

The story of the introduction of this name, as told by the Black
Bear gens in their Ni'-ḳi Ritual, differs from the Puma version of the
story.  (See p. 228, 36th Ann. Rept. Bur. Amer. Ethn., lines 238 to
304.)

3. Mon'-ga-xe, Arrow-maker.  At the same time that the Sun
gave to the "Little Ones" the gift of speech he gave to them a finished arrow so that when they came to dwell upon the earth they
could make arrows like it and use them for defending themselves
against enemies and for killing animals to use for food.  The name
is mentioned in the Puma Naming Ritual.  (See p. 42, line 44.)

### The First Three Daughters

1. Mon'-ça-ṭse-xi, Sacred Arrowshaft.  The name Mon'-ca-ṭse-xi
refers to the ray of light which was given by the Sun to the "Little
Ones" for use as an arrowshaft.  This shaft had the quality of un-
erring precision which excited the wonder of the "Little Ones."  It
was to them a mysterious arrowshaft.  The name is mentioned in
the Naming Ritual of the Puma gens.  (See p. 41, line 29.)

2. Mon-zhon'-op-she-win, Woman-who-travels-over-the-earth.
This name refers to the ever recurring westward movement of the
moon over the earth.  The name is mentioned in the Naming Ritual
of the Puma gens.  (See p. 41, line 39.)

3. Non'-mi-ṭse-xi, Beloved-child-of-the-sun.  This name is mentioned in the Naming Ritual of the Puma gens.  (See p. 42, line 49.)

Another name follows that of the third son in the ritual, In-shta'-
sha-be, Dark-eyes, and is a Ḳa'-zhin-ga name.  The name is mentioned
in the Naming Ritual of the Puma gens.  (See p. 42, line 54.)

The name E-non'-gi-tha-bi, The Favorite, follows that of the third
daughter, and is a Çi'-ge name.  This name is not mentioned in the
ritual.  Wa-xthi'-zhi said the fourth daughter is the favored one
because if the first three should fail to bring forth children the parents
would cherish the hope that their fourth daughter will give them
grandchildren.

### Sky Names

The distinctive birth names of the Puma gens, mentioned above,
are spoken of as sky names, to distinguish them from the common
gentile names.  These birth names are said to have originated in the
sky when the "Little Ones" were about to descend to the earth to
take upon themselves bodily form.  Some of these names refer to
important events that came to pass before the descent from the sky

to the earth.  Earth names were also used by both the Puma and the Black Bear gentes.  These names will be referred to later.

Every Osage gens has its own version of the tribal Child-naming Ritual.  The versions belonging to the I$^n$-gtho$^{n\prime}$-ga (Puma) gens of the Ho$^{n\prime}$-ga great division and that belonging to the Ṭsi′-zhu great division have been secured and are given below in detail.

## CHILD-NAMING RITUAL OF THE PUMA GENS

### (Wa-xthi′-zhi)

When a man of the Puma gens is prepared for the ceremonial naming of his newly born son he sends for the Sho′-ḳa (official messenger) of his gens.  On the arrival of the Sho′-ḳa the father puts before him his customary fee of a blanket or blue cloth and a little pipe which he must carry as his official badge.  The father of the child then orders the Sho′-ḳa to go and call the No$^{n\prime}$-ho$^n$-zhi$^n$-ga of the Puma, the Ṭsi′-zhu Wa-shta-ge, and the Wa′-ṭse-ṭsi Wa-shta-ge gentes.  The Ṭsi′-zhu Wa-shta-ge is the Peace gens of the Ṭsi′-zhu great tribal division, and the Wa′-ṭse-ṭsi Wa-shta-ge the Peace gens of the Ho$^{n\prime}$-ga great tribal division.  Prominence was given, in this ceremony, to these two gentes because they are the favored people of the sun and the unclouded sky, the most sacred of the cosmic forces.  Through these two favored gentes the blessings of peace and long life are invoked for the child to be named and formally given its place in the tribal unit.

The No$^{n\prime}$-ho$^n$-zhi$^n$-ga of these three gentes assemble in the evening at the house of the father who, in a formal speech, makes known to them the purpose of the summons.  Then the heads of the Ṭsi′-zhu Wa-shta-ge and the Wa′-ṭse-ṭsi Wa-shta-ge gentes direct the Sho′-ḳa to go and call the No$^{n\prime}$-ho$^n$-zhi$^n$-ga of the following gentes to assemble at the house of the father on the next morning:

Ho$^{n\prime}$-ga A-hiu-ṭo$^n$, Wa-ça′-be-ṭo$^n$ and  the O′-po$^n$, of the Ho$^{n\prime}$-ga subdivision; Wa′-ṭse-ṭsi Wa-shta-ge, Ho′ I-ni-ḳa-shi-ga, Wa-zha′-zhe Çka and the Ṭa′ I-ni-ḳa-shi-ga of the Wa-zha′-zhe subdivision; Ṭsi′-zhu Wa-shta-ge, Ṭsi′-zhu Wa-no$^n$, Mi-k′i$^{n\prime}$ Wa-no$^n$ and the Tho′-xe of the Ṭsi′-zhu great division.

The Sho′-ḳa, as he goes on this errand, does not neglect the little pipe, his official badge.

### Ḳi′-no$^N$—Ceremony of Decorating the Xo′-ḳa

Before sunrise of the following day the No$^{n\prime}$-ho$^n$-zhi$^n$-ga of the Puma gens assemble at the house of the member who had been appointed by the father to act as Xo′-ḳa in the ceremony.  When all the members had taken their places the A′-ḳi-ho$^n$ Xo′-ḳa (master of ceremonies) recites the wi′-gi-e relating to the symbolic articles with which the

Xo'-ḳa is to be decorated. The wi'-gi-e is accompanied by certain ceremonial acts performed by an assistant. The first section of the wi'-gi-e relates to the red dawn, the beginning of the life of day. The assistant, who has put red paint on the palms of his hands, spreads them out toward the dawn that is reddening the eastern sky. When the A'-ḳi-hoⁿ Xo'-ḳa reaches the fourth line the assistant paints red the face of the Xo'-ḳa. Then, as the A'-ḳi-hoⁿ Xo'-ḳa goes on to the second section the assistant takes up a white, downy feather (pl. 3, b), taken from the under covert of an eagle's tail, and holds it poised over the Xo'-ḳa's head. When the twelfth line of the wi'-gi-e is reached the assistant quickly fastens the feather to the scalplock of the Xo'-ḳa. This feather symbolizes one of the two white shafts of light that may be seen at either side of the sun as it rises through the fading color of the dawn. Each of these two shafts symbolizes a never-ending life. The one at the right belongs to the Hoⁿ'-ga great division and the one at the left to the Ṭsi'-zhu great division. At the beginning of the third section of the wi'-gi-e the assistant rubs in the palms of his hands a bit of buffalo fat, then holds his outspread hands poised over the Xo'-ḳa's head. When the twentieth line is reached he anoints the Xo'-ḳa's hair with the oil, an act by which is expressed the wish that the child whom the Xo'-ḳa represents shall always be abundantly supplied with food of all kinds.

At the fourth section of the wi'-gi-e the assistant takes up a necklace of beads, or a narrow woven band, to which is attached a shell gorget (pl. 3, a) and holds it in readiness. When the twenty-sixth line is reached he puts the necklace upon the neck of the Xo'-ḳa so that the gorget hangs upon his breast. This gorget typifies the Sun, whose life endures forever.

### Ḳi'-noⁿ Wi'-gi-e

(FREE TRANSLATION)

1

1. Verily, at that time and place, it has been said, in this house,
2. The people spake to one another, saying: With what shall the little ones decorate their faces, as they travel the path of life?
3. With the symbol of the god who never fails to appear at the beginning of day,
4. The little ones shall decorate their faces, as they travel the path of life.
5. When they decorate their faces with this symbol,
6. They shall be difficult to overcome by death, as they travel the path of life, O, younger brothers.

2

7. Verily, at that time and place, it has been said, in this house,
8. They spake to one another, saying: What shall they use as a plume?
9. There is a god who never fails to appear at the beginning of day (the sun),
10. At whose right side
11. There stands a plume-like shaft,
12. Which the little ones shall use as a plume,
13. And they shall become difficult to overcome by death.
14. When the little ones use this plume,
15. They shall have a plume that will forever stand, as they travel the path of life.

3

16. Verily, at that time and place, it has been said, in this house,
17. They spake to one another, saying: With what shall the little ones anoint their hair?
18. The young male buffalo
19. Has fat adhering to the muscle on the right side of his spine.
20. The little ones shall use the oil of this fat to anoint their hair.
21. When they use this fat
22. They shall always live to see old age, as they travel the path of life, O, younger brothers.

4

23. Verily, at that time and place, it has been said, in this house,
24. They spake to one another, saying: What neck ornament shall they put upon him? (the Xo'-ḳa).
25. The mussel who sitteth upon the earth
26. They shall always put upon him, O, younger brothers.
27. The God of Day who sitteth in the heavens,
28. He shall bring to us,
29. They shall put upon him the sun as a neck ornament, O, younger brothers.
30. When they make of him (the sun) the means by which to reach old age,
31. They shall always live to see old age, as they travel the path of life.

### Wa'-ṭse-ṭsi and the Ṭsi'-zhu Wa-shta-ge Gentes

As the ceremony of decorating the Xo'-ḳa goes on, the Non-hon-zhin-ga members of the Wa'-ṭse-ṭsi Wa-shta-ge gens, followed by those of the Ṭsi'-zhu Wa-shta-ge gens, go to the house of the father of the child to be named, and enter to take their places, those of the Wa'-ṭse-ṭsi at the east end on the south side and those of the Ṭsi'-zhu at the east end on the north side. (Fig. 1.) The house then becomes the home of these two gentes for the time being and for the purposes of the ceremony. The Wa'-ṭse-ṭsi is the Peace gens of the Hoⁿ'-ga great tribal division, its life symbol is the water portion of the earth. The hereditary chief of the Hoⁿ'-ga division was chosen from this gens. The Ṭsi'-zhu is the Peace gens of the Ṭsi'-zhu great division. Its life symbol is the clear blue sky. The hereditary chief of the Ṭsi'-zhu great division was chosen from this gens.

### Ṭsi Ṭa'-ᵽe (Approach to the House)

The purpose of the Ḳi'-noⁿ ceremony is to prepare the Xo'-ḳa who represents the child to be named to approach in the prescribed manner the house wherein sit the Noⁿ'-hoⁿ-zhiⁿ-ga of the Wa'-ṭse-ṭsi and the Ṭsi'-zhu gentes, the first representing the life-giving power of water and the latter the life-giving power of the sun whose abode is in the great blue sky. The Xo'-ḳa is to come to the sacred house as a suppliant for a full and complete life, uninterrupted by diseases

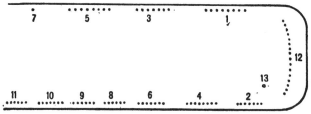

Fig. 1.—Diagram showing places of gentes in the lodge. 1. Ṭsi'-zhu Wa-shta-ge; 2. Wa-ṭse-tsi Wa-shta-ge; 3. Ṭsi'zhu Wa-noⁿ; 4. Hoⁿ'-ga A-hiu-ṭoⁿ; 5. Mi-ḳ'iⁿ' Wa-noⁿ; 6. Wa-ça'-be; 7. Tho'-xe; 8. O'poⁿ; 9. Ho' I-ni-ḳa-shi-ga; 10. Wa-zha'-zhe çka; 11. Ṭa' I-ni-ḳa-shi-ga; 12. Iⁿ-gthoⁿ'-ga; 13. Sho'-ḳa.

or accidents, and for an endless line of descendants. The ceremonial approach of the Xo'-ḳa to the sacred house is called Ṭsi Ṭa'-ᵽe (Ṭsi, house; Ṭa'-ᵽe, approach), as to a place of refuge.

At the close of the Ḳi'-noⁿ ceremony the Xo'-ḳa wraps about his body a buffalo robe, hair outside, and thus clothed in his sacerdotal attire he goes out of his own house to make his processional approach to the sacred house, following his Sho'-ḳa who precedes him in the march. After the manner of all suppliants who approach Wa-ḳoⁿ'-da, the Xo'-ḳa carries with him a little pipe with which to make a smoke offering to that mysterious power that controls all life. The Xo'-ḳa and the Sho'-ḳa, on their solemn approach to the House of Mystery, keep a certain distance apart. When they have gone some 40 or 50 paces they make a pause and the Xo'-ḳa sings the following song, after which he recites the first section of the wi'-gi-e called Wa'-çi-thu-çe Wi'-gi-e (Footstep Wi'-gi-e). The song precedes each of the four sections of the wi'-gi-e:

FOOTSTEP SONG AND WI'-GI-E

Wa-ṭse wiⁿ u-tha-ḳi-oⁿ stse,
Wa-ṭse wiⁿ u-tha-ḳi-oⁿ stse he
Wa-ṭse wiⁿ u-tha-ḳi-oⁿ stse,
E the he wi-ṭa doⁿ u-tha-ḳi-oⁿ stse he,
Wa-ṭse wiⁿ u-tha-ḳi-oⁿ stse.

WI'-GI-E

1

1. Toward what shall the little ones take their footsteps? they asked of one another.
2. It is the Male Star (the sun) who sitteth in the heavens,
3. Toward which the little ones shall take their footsteps
4. When the little ones take their footsteps toward the Male Star,
5. They shall always live to see old age, O, younger brothers, they said to one another.

2

6. Toward what shall the little ones take their footsteps? they asked of one another.
7. It is the Female Star (the moon) who sitteth in the heavens,
8. Toward which the little ones shall take their footsteps.
9. When the little ones take their footsteps toward the Female Star,
10. They shall always live to see old age, O, younger brothers, they said to one another.

3

11. Toward what shall the little ones take their footsteps? they asked of one another.
12. It is the Male Star (the sun) who sitteth in the heavens,
13. Toward which the little ones shall take their footsteps.
14. When the little ones take their footsteps toward the Male Star,
15. They shall always live to see old age, O, younger brothers, they said to one another.

4

16. Toward what shall the little ones take their footsteps? they said to one another.
17. It is the Female Star (the moon) who sitteth in the heavens,
18. Toward which the little ones shall take their footsteps.
19. When the little ones take their footsteps toward the Female Star,
20. They shall always live to see old age, O, younger brothers, they said to one another.

The words of the processional song:

Into a star you have cast yourself,
Into my star you have cast yourself, etc.

are addressed to the child upon whom is to be conferred his personal, gentile name, and who is to be given his place in the Puma gens into which he was born. The star referred to in the song is the sun, the greatest life symbol of the Puma gens.

In the first section of the "Footstep Wi'-gi-e," which the Xo'-ḳa recites as he makes his processional approach to the House of Mystery, the sun is referred to as the "Male Star." The first line of the wi'-gi-e, "Toward what shall the little ones take their footsteps," implies that much thought was given by the ancient No$^n$'-ho$^n$-zhi$^n$-ga to the question as to the places where prayers for aid for the attainment of long life should be directed. The lines that follow imply that the No$^n$'-ho$^n$-zhi$^n$-ga had finally arrived at the belief that if the "Little Ones" go with their prayers to the "Male Star," the sun, they would find the way by which they could reach old age. The authors of these peculiar rites in speaking of long life did not only mean the attainment of old age by the child but they also meant the continuity of its life by procreation.

In the second section of the wi'-gi-e the moon is referred to as the "Female Star." The same form that is used for the sun is also used for the moon. The pairing of these two great cosmic bodies in this wi'-gi-e suggests a procreative relationship between the two. The last two sections of the wi'-gi-e are repetitions of the first two. These repetitions are made in order to complete the mystic number four. The moon, referred to in the second section as the female star, is the life symbol of the Wa-ça'-be, or the Black Bear gens.

When he Xo'-ḳa have finished reciting the first section of the Footstep Wi'-gi-e, which speaks of the approach of the little ones to the sun, he and the Sho'-ḳa continue their march. Again they pause and the Xo'-ḳa recites the second section which tells of the approach of the little ones toward the moon seeking for long life. The fourth pause brings them to the door of the House of Mystery, which they enter, followed by the A'-ḳi-ho$^n$ Xo'-ḳa and the No$^n$'-ho$^n$-zhi$^n$-ga of the Puma gens who are to give their child a place in the visible universe. They take their place at the east end of the lodge where sit the father and mother with the child. The No$^n$'-ho$^n$-zhi$^n$-ga who had been called to take part in the ceremony also enter and take their fixed places, those belonging to the Ho$^n$'-ga great division at the south side and those of the Ṭsi'-zhu great division at the north side of the lodge. (Fig. 1.)

## THE WA-THE'-THE CEREMONY

When all the No$^n$'-ho$^n$-zhi$^n$-ga have become settled in their places, according to gentes, the A'-ḳi-ho$^n$ Xo'-ḳa proceeds with the ceremonial acts called Wa-the'-the, which, translated literally, means, The Sending; that is, the sending of a fee of a blanket or other article of value to each head of the gentes taking part in the child-naming ceremony. It is understood by these ceremonial acts that the members of the gens to whose head is sent a fee are requested to recite the wi'-gi-e relating to the Life Symbol of their gens. Each article is received from the hands of the A'-ḳi-hoⁿ Xo'-ḳa by the Sho'-ḳa who delivers it to the head of the gens for whom it is sent.

Wa-xthi'-zhi, who gives this child-naming ritual of his gens, the Puma, when acting as A'-ḳi-hoⁿ Xo'-ḳa, sends the fees in the following order:

Ṭsi'-zhu Wa-shta-ge: Fee, with a red downy eagle feather, symbolizing the sun. The members of the gens will recite their wi'-gi-e relating to the life-giving power of the sun. (See 36th Ann. Rept. Bur. Amer. Ethn., p. 124, lines 1 to 177.)

Wa-ça'-be: Fee; will recite the Zha'-zhe Ḳi-ṭoⁿ Wi'-gi-e, Name Wi'-gi-e of the gens. (See 36th Ann. Rept. Bur. Amer. Ethn., p. 228, lines 238 to 304.) The Wa-ça'-be and the Iⁿ-gthoⁿ'-ga gentes are closely related and one acts as Sho'-ḳa for the other in their ceremonies of initiation into the mysteries of the tribal rites.

Ṭsi'-zhu Wa-noⁿ: Fee; will recite their wi'-gi-e relating to the life-giving power of the sun, their life symbol. (See 36th Ann. Rept. Bur. Amer. Ethn., p. 118, lines 1 to 36.)

Hoⁿ'-ga A-hiu-ṭoⁿ: Fee; will recite wi'-gi-e relating to the mottled eagle, the "stainless" bird that led the people down from the sky to the earth. (See 36th Ann. Rept. Bur. Amer. Ethn., p. 162, lines 177 to 311.)

Mi-k'iⁿ' Wa-noⁿ: Fee; the members of this gens will recite their wi'-gi-e relating to the moon and all the stars and to their power to aid the "little ones" to reach old age. (See 36th Ann. Rept. Bur. Amer. Ethn., p. 122, lines 1 to 44.)

O'-poⁿ: Fee; the members of the gens will recite the Wa-dsu-ṭa I-hi-thoⁿ-be Wi'-gi-e which tells of the various places of the earth where the little ones may find the animals on which to live. (See 36th Ann. Rept. Bur. Amer. Ethn., p. 112, lines 1 to 109.)

Tho'-xe: Fee; some grains of maize are also sent. The members of this gens will recite the wi'-gi-e relating to the bringing of the maize to the people by a buffalo bull, and to his offer to aid the little ones to reach old age. (See 36th Ann. Rept. Bur. Amer. Ethn., p. 280, lines 83 to 110; also p. 134, lines 1 to 162.)

Wa'-ṭse-ṭsi Wa-shta-ge: Fee, with cedar fronds. Members of this gens will recite their wi'-gi-e relating to the red cedar, an evergreen tree which has power to resist death, and to its offer to aid the little ones to reach old age. (See 36th Ann. Rept. Bur. Amer. Ethn., p. 95, lines 1 to 34.)

Ho' I-ni-ḳa-shi-ga: Fee, with a kettle of water. The members of this gens will recite their wi'-gi-e relating to the everflowing water which has power to help the little ones to reach old age. These are the Fish people. (See 36th Ann. Rept. Bur. Amer. Ethn., p. 98, lines 1 to 35.)

Wa-zha'-zhe çka: Fee, with a mussel shell. The mussel is the life symbol of this gens. The members of the gens will recite their wi'-gi-e relating to the power of the mussel to resist death, and to its consent to aid the little ones to reach old age. The Wa-zha'-zhe çka are a water people. (See 36th Ann. Rept. Bur. Amer. Ethn., p. 94, lines 1 to 29.)

Ṭa I-ni-ḳa-shi-ga, the Deer People: Only a fee is sent to them. The members will recite their Wa-dsu'-ṭa I-hi-tho$^n$-be Wi'-gi-e, which tells of the various places of the earth where the deer will reveal themselves to the little ones to give them help to reach old age. (See 36th Ann. Rept. Bur. Amer. Ethn., p. 97, lines 44 to 103.)

When the Sho'-ḳa had delivered the last fee every No$^{n'}$-ho$^n$-zhi$^n$-ga who knows his wi'-gi-e begins to recite it in a loud voice. None of the wi'-gi-es are alike and none of the members of a gens recite in unison, consequently there would be a volume of sounds most bewildering to the uninitiated.

## ZHA'-ZHE ḲI-ṬO$^N$ WI'-GI-E

The wi'-gi-e recited by the members of the I$^n$-gtho$^{n'}$-ga gens at this time is called Zha'-zhe Ḳi-ṭo$^n$ Wi'-gi-e, freely translated, the Name Wi'-gi-e. It is in three parts. The first, which includes sections 1 to 8, is called Zha'-zhe Ḳi-ṭo$^n$, the taking of names; the second, which includes sections 9 and 10, is called U'-no$^n$ U-tha-ge, the telling of the means by which to reach old age; the third, which includes sections 11 and 12, is called U'-no$^n$-bthe U-gi-dse, the story of the search for the life-giving foods.

### NAME-TAKING WI'-GI-E

#### (FREE TRANSLATION)

#### 1

1. Verily, at that time and place, it has been said, in this house,
2. The Ho$^{n'}$-ga, a people who possess seven fireplaces,
3. Spake to one another, saying: O, younger brothers,
4. The little ones have become persons,
5. Should not the little ones go below to become a people? they
    said to one another.
6. Then, at that very time,
7. They said: There are four great gods
8. To whom we shall appeal for aid.
9. Verily at that time,
10. They spake to the god of day (the sun) saying:

11. O, my grandfather,
12. Our little ones have become persons,
13. Should they not go below (to the earth) to become a people?
14. At that very time
15. The god of day replied: You say the little ones should go below to become a people,
16. When the little ones go below to become a people,
17. They shall always live to see old age, as they travel the path of life.

2

18. Verily, at that time and place, it has been said, in this house,
19. They said: The little ones shall go below to become a people.
20. Then again they spake to the god of day, saying: The little ones have no names, O, grandfather.
21. The god of day replied: O, little ones,
22. You say your little ones have no names,
23. Your little ones shall be named after me,
24. Mi'-wa-ga-xe, Child-of-the-sun,
25. The little ones shall take, as they travel the path of life.
26. When they take this for a personal name,
27. They shall always live to see old age, as they travel the path of life.

3

28. What shall the little ones take for a personal name? it has been said,
29. $Mo^n$-çi'-tse-xi, Sacred-arrowshaft,
30. The little ones shall take for a name, as they travel the path of life.
31. When they take this for a personal name,
32. They shall always live to see old age, as they travel the path of life.

4

33. What shall the little ones take for a personal name?
34. I'-e-çka-wa-the, Giver-of-clear-speech
35. The little ones shall take for a name, as they travel the path of life.
36. When they take this for a personal name,
37. They shall always live to see old age, as they travel the path of life.

5

38. What shall the little ones take for a personal name?
39. $Mo^n$-zho$^{n\prime}$-op-she-wi$^n$, Woman-who-travels-over-the-earth,
40. The little ones shall take for a name, as they travel the path of life.

41. When they take this for a personal name,
42. They shall always live to see old age, as they travel the path of life.

6

43. What shall they take for a personal name?
44. Mo$^{n\prime}$-ga-xe, Arrow-maker,
45. The little ones shall take for a name, as they travel the path of life.
46. When they take this for a personal name,
47. They shall always live to see old age, as they travel the path of life.

7

48. What shall the little ones take for a personal name?
49. No$^{n\prime}$-mi-tse-xi, Beloved-child-of-the-sun,
50. The little ones shall take for a name, as they travel the path of life.
51. When they take this for a personal name,
52. They shall always live to see old age, as they travel the path of life.

8

53. What shall the little ones take for a personal name?
54. I$^{n}$-shta$^\prime$-sha-be, Dark-eyes,
55. The little ones shall take for a name, as they travel the path of life.
56. When they take this for a personal name,
57. They shall always live to see old age, as they travel the path of life.

9

58. Verily, at that time and place, it has been said, in this house,
59. They spake to one another, saying: O, younger brothers,
60. The little ones have nothing of which to make their bodies,
61. They went forth with hurrying footsteps,
62. To the soft stone that sitteth upon the earth.
63. Verily, at that time,
64. They spake to him, saying: O, my grandfather,
65. The little ones have nothing of which to make their bodies.
66. The soft stone replied: O, little ones,
67. You say your little ones have nothing of which to make their bodies.
68. The little ones shall make of me their bodies.
69. Verily, at that time and place,

70. He spake further, saying: When the little ones become ill and fretful,
71. They shall cling to me as one who can produce the heat by which they can be purified.

### 10

72. Verily, at that time and place, it has been said, in this house,
73. They spake to one another, saying: Give heed, my younger brothers,
74. You will go forth to make further search,
75. Then, even as these words were spoken, they hastened
76. To the friable stone,
77. And, standing close to him,
78. Spake, saying: O, grandfather, the little ones have nothing of which to make their bodies.
79. The friable stone replied: O, my little ones,
80. You say the little ones have nothing of which to make their bodies.
81. The little ones shall make of me their bodies.
82. When they make of me their bodies,
83. They shall cling to me as one who can produce the heat by which their bodies can be purified.

### 11

84. Verily, at that time and place, it has been said, in this house,
85. They spake to one another, saying: O, younger brothers,
86. The little ones have nothing which they can use for food at all times,
87. You will go and search for such food as they can use for all time.
88. A younger brother hastened
89. To the very center of a lake,
90. Where lay the root of the tse'-wa-the (*Nelumbo lutea*).
91. He hastened home with the root,
92. And spake, saying: O, elder brothers, how will this serve for food?
93. The elder brothers hastened to try the taste of the root,
94. Like milk the juice squirted in their mouths,
95. And they said to one another: O, younger brothers,
96. This will serve as food for the little ones.
97. When the little ones make use of this plant as food,
98. They shall always live to see old age, as they travel the path of life.

12

99. There lacks one more, O, younger brothers, they said to one
    another.
100. You will go forth and make further search.
101. Even as these words were spoken,
102. One hastened to the farther borders of the lake,
103. Where sat the do (*Apios apios*).
104. Close to it he stood,
105. Then he hastened home, carrying the plant with him.
106. Standing before his brothers, he spake, saying: O, elder brothers,
107. How will this serve for food?
108. They replied: O, younger brother,
109. That is the very object for which you have been searching.
110. The elder brothers hastened to try the taste of the root,
111. Like milk the juice squirted in their mouths.
112. Then they spake, saying: The little ones shall use this plant
    for food.
113. When the little ones use this plant for food,
114. They shall always live to see old age.
115. It shall make their limbs to stretch in growth, as they travel
    the path of life.

When Wa-xthi'-ʒhi made up his mind to give a description of the
Child-naming Ritual of his own gens, the Puma, he did not hesitate
to recite the wi'-gi-es and to tell of the ceremonial forms that accompany the entire ritual. But when asked to recite the wi'-gi-es
of the 11 gentes who were summoned to take part in the ceremony of
conferring a name upon a Puma child he declined to give them,
although he knew all of them, for the reason that they were not his
to give. He had not obtained from any of these gentes the right to
transfer them to strangers or to members of other gentes.

It so happened that when Wa-xthi'-zhi was describing the Child-naming Ritual of his own gens, which he had a perfect right to do, Wa-sho'-
she (pl. 4), a member of the $Ho^{n'}$-ga A-hiu-ṭo$^n$ gens, was present.
This man, when asked if he would be willing to give the U'-no$^n$
Wi'-gi-e (Old-age Wi'-gi-e) of his gens for a fee, promptly replied that
he would. He had obtained by purchase from his father the wi'-gi-e
and so had acquired the right to transfer it to anybody, but the transfer must always be made for a fee. The fee was provided and Wa-
sho'-she sat down and recorded the Old-age Wi'-gi-e of his own gens,
the $Ho^{n'}$-ga A-hiu-ṭo$^n$. This name refers to the "Stainless Bird," the
mottled eagle, who conducted the $Ho^{n'}$-ga people to earth from mid-
heaven. (See 36th Ann. Rept. Bur. Amer. Ethn., p. 162, lines 177
to 199.)

SHELL GORGET AND DOWNY PLUME (LIFE SYMBOLS)

WA-SHO'-SHE (HO$^{\text{N}}$'-GA A-HIU-TO$^{\text{N}}$ (EAGLE) GENS)

The first seven lines of the wi'-gi-e refer back to the time when "the Ho$^n$'-ga who possess seven fireplaces" chose for one of their life symbols the "Stainless Bird," the mottled eagle. The people who are here spoken of as the Ho$^n$'-ga having seven fireplaces are those who compose the seven gentile groups that represent the land portion of the earth in the two great tribal divisions symbolizing the cosmos. These seven gentile groups (seven fireplaces) are, as given by Black-dog. (See 36th Ann. Rept. Bur. Amer. Ethn., pp. 52–53.)

1. Wa-ça'-be-ṭo$^n$, They-who-own-the-black-bear.
2. I$^n$-gtho$^n$'-ga, Puma.
3. O-po$^n$, Elk.
4. Mo$^n$-i$^n$-ḳa-ga-xe, Makers-of-the-earth.
5. Ho$^n$'-ga gthe-zhe, The-mottled-sacred-one.
6. Xu-tha', Eagle (the adult golden eagle).
7. Ho$^n$'-ga zhi$^n$-ga, The-little-sacred-one.

When the "Ho$^n$'-ga, a people who possess seven fireplaces" went to the "Stainless Bird" and said to him (lines 5, 6, and 7): "The little ones have nothing of which to make their bodies," meaning that they have no symbol for the long life which they crave, he replied in the words as given in the wi'-gi-e, from line 10 to the end:

### OLD-AGE WI'-GI-E

#### FREE TRANSLATION

1. Verily, at that time and place, it has been said, in this house,
2. The Ho$^n$'-ga, a people who possess seven fireplaces,
3. Spake to one another, saying: Lo, we have nothing of which to make our bodies.
4. Then, at that very time,
5. They spake to the bird that has no stains (evil disposition),
6. Saying: O, grandfather,
7. The little ones have nothing of which to make their bodies.
8. Then, at that very time,
9. The bird that has no stains (evil disposition)
10. Spake, saying: When the little ones make of me their bodies,
11. They shall always live to see old age, as they travel the path of life.
12. Again the bird spake:
13. Behold my toes that are gathered together in folds,
14. Which I have made to be the sign of my old age.
15. When the little ones make of me the means of reaching old age,
16. They shall always live to see old age, as they travel the path of life.

17. Behold, also, the wrinkles upon my shins,
18. Which I have made to be the sign of my old age.
19. When the little ones make of me the means of reaching old age,
20. They shall always live to see old age, as they travel the path of life.
21. The bird that has no stain
22. Again spake, saying: Behold the wrinkles upon my knees,
23. Which I have made to be the sign of my old age.
24. When the little ones make of me the means of reaching old age,
25. They shall always live to see old age, as they travel the path of life.

26. Behold the flaccid muscles of my inner thigh,
27. Which I have made to be the sign of my old age.
28. When the little ones make of me the means of reaching old age,
29. They shall always live to see old age, as they travel the path of life.

30. Behold the muscles of my breast, gathered together as in a fold,
31. Which I have made to be the sign of my old age.
32. When the little ones make of me the means of reaching old age,
33. They shall always live to see old age, as they travel the path of life.

34. Behold the flaccid muscles of my arms,
35. Which I have made to be the sign of my old age.
36. When the little ones make of me the means of reaching old age,
37. They shall always live to see old age, as they travel the path of life.

38. Behold the bend of my shoulders,
39. Which I have made to be the sign of my old age.
40. When the little ones make of me the means of reaching old age,
41. They shall always live to see their shoulders bent with age, as they travel the path of life.

42. Behold the flaccid muscles of my throat,
43. Which I have made to be the sign of my old age.
44. When the little ones make of me the means of reaching old age,
45. They shall always live to see old age, as they travel the path of life.

46. Behold the folds in the corners of my eyelids,
47. Which I have made to be the signs of my old age.
48. When the little ones make of me the means of reaching old age,
49. They shall always live to see the corners of their eyelids folded with age, as they travel the path of life.

50. Behold my eyelids that are gathered into folds,
51. Which I have made to be the signs of my old age.
52. When the little ones make of me the means of reaching old age,
53. They shall always live to see their eyelids gathered into folds
    with age, as they travel the path of life.

54. Behold the hair on the crown of my head, now grown thin,
55. Which I have made to be the sign of my old age.
56. When the little ones make of me the means of reaching old age,
57. They shall always live to see the hair on the crown of their heads
    grown thin with age, as they travel the path of life.

### Wi'-gi-e of the Wa'-ṭse-ṭsi Gens

At the close of the recital of the wi'-gi-es by all the Noⁿ'-hoⁿ-zhiⁿ-ga,
the Sho'-ḳa places before the head of the Ṭsi'-zhu Wa-shta-ge gens a
bowl of water into which had been put fronds of the red cedar. The
red cedar and the water are the life symbols of the Wa'-ṭse-ṭsi, the
people who came to earth from the stars. The following is an
epitome of their wi'-gi-e:

> I am a person who is fit for use as a symbol,
> Behold the female red cedar,
> Verily, I am a person who has made of that tree his body.
> When the little ones make of me their bodies,
> They shall always live to see old age.
> Behold the male red cedar,
> The little ones shall always use this tree as a symbol.
> When the little ones use it for a symbol,
> They shall always live to see old age.
> Behold these waters,
> That we shall make to be companions to the tree.
> When the little ones make use of these waters
> As the means of reaching old age,
> They shall always live to see old age.
>                     —(See 36th Ann. Rept. Bur. Amer. Ethn., p. 95.)

### Wi'-gi-e of the Bow People

The E-noⁿ' Miⁿ-dse-ṭoⁿ, a people who belong to the same great
tribal division as the Wa'-ṭse-ṭsi, use a similar wi'-gi-e, which is as
follows:

> I am a person who is fitted for use as a symbol.
> Verily, in the midst of the rushing waters
> Abides my being.
> Verily, I am a person who has made of the waters his body.
> Behold the right side of the river,
> Of which I have made the right side of my body.
> When the little ones make of me their bodies .
> And use the right side of the river
> To make their bodies,
> The right side of their bodies shall be free from all causes of death.

Behold the left side of the river,
Of which I have made the left side of my body.
When the little ones also make of it the left side of their bodies,
The left side of their bodies shall always be free from all causes of death.

Behold the channel of the river,
Of which I have made the hollow of my body.
When the little ones make of me their bodies,
The hollow of their bodies shall always be free from all causes of death.

A bowl of shelled corn, the life symbol of the Tho'-xe gens, was also placed before the head of the Ṭsi'-zhu Wa-shta-ge gens. (For the Maize Wi'-gi-e of the Tho'-xe gens, see 36th Ann. Rept. Bur. Amer. Ethn., p. 135, lines 57 to 113; also p. 277, lines 83 to 110.)

When the bowls of water and cedar fronds and shelled corn are placed before the Ṭsi'-zhu Wa-shta-ge, the Sho'-ḳa puts in his arms the child to be blessed and named. The head of the Ṭsi'-zhu Wa-shta-ge gens then passes the tips of the fingers of his right hand over the bowl of water and cedar fronds, and the bowl of the life-giving corn, then touches with the tips of his fingers the lips, head, arms and body of the child. The two bowls and the child are then passed on to the head of the Wa'-ṭse-ṭsi Wa-shta-ge gens, who goes through the same motions with the child. The child and the two bowls are then passed on to the heads of each of the other gentes who make the same motions over the child as were made by the heads of the first two gentes.

These ceremonial acts performed by the heads of the gentes officiating, by which the child is brought into touch with the ever-flowing waters, the red cedar, an everlasting tree, and the life-giving corn, are supplicatory acts by which the aid of Wa-ḳoⁿ'-da is sought for the child who is to go forth to take part in the great life activities. Not only is the attainment of old age desired for the child but also the continuity of its life by a never-ending line of descendants.

At the close of these ceremonial acts a sacred gentile name is conferred upon the child without further ceremony. If, however, there are two or more names to choose from, as is the case in some of the gentes, the mother of the child has the privilege of making a choice from two or three names. This privilege is given by the Xo'-ḳa, who offers to the mother two small sticks prepared for this purpose, each of which represents a name mentioned in the origin ritual of the gens naming the child. The mother usually chooses the stick representing the name which to her has the greater religious significance and is the most euphonious.

### Earth Names and Wi'-gi-es

It was stated (see p. 33) that earth names as well as sky names were used by both the Iⁿ-gthoⁿ'-ga and the Wa-ça'-be gentes as distinctive birth names for their children.

In the course of a conversation concerning the gentile names, classed as sky and earth names, Wa-xthi'-zhi, of the Puma gens, remarked that: When the Ho$^n$'-ga people were coming from the sky to the earth they chose two persons (gentes) to act as official messengers. One of these persons was called Ho$^n$-ga Wa'-ṭse-gi-ṭsi, The-sacred-one-from-the-stars, and the other Ho$^{n'}$-ga Wa-ṭse-ga-wa, The-sacred-radiant-star. These messengers were expected to find some way of dispersing the waters that submerged the earth and of exposing the ground beneath so as to make it habitable for all living creatures.

Wa'-ṭse-gi-ṭsi and Wa'-ṭse-ga-wa, the two messengers, found on the still waters the water spider, the water beetle, the white leech, and the dark leech, of whom they asked for aid which they could not give, but promised to help the people to reach old age. (See 36th Ann. Rept. Bur. Amer. Ethn., p. 163, lines 200 to 273.) The two messengers went on and they met O'-po$^n$-ṭo$^n$-ga, the Great Elk, and appealed to him for aid. The Great Elk threw himself upon the waters four times and splashed about until the ground was exposed and ready to receive men and animals. He then called to the four corners of the earth for the life-giving winds to come. Next he threw himself upon the ground and rolled about; then, as he arose, the hairs of his body clung to the soil and became the grasses of the earth. (See 36th Ann. Rept. Bur. Amer. Ethn., pp. 165–167, lines 274 to 354.)

The two messengers then led the people over the dry land of the earth, when suddenly Ho$^n$'-ga Wa'-ṭse-gi-ṭsi, The-one-from-the-stars, came upon I$^n$-gtho$^n$'-ga, the Puma. The messenger then changed his name from Wa'-ṭse-gi-ṭsi to I$^n$-gtho$^n$'-ga. In like manner the Ho$^n$'-ga Wa'-ṭse-ga-wa, the Radiant Star, came upon Wa-ça'-be, the Black Bear. The Radiant Star then changed his name from Wa'-ṭse-ga-wa to Wa-ça'-be, the Black Bear.

These were the first earth names of the two related gentes, the I$^n$-gtho$^n$'-ga and the Wa-ça'-be. Wa-xthi'-zhi mentioned several other personal earth names of these two gentes but he suggested that the parts of the rituals given by himself and Wa-ṭse'-mo$^n$-i$^n$ (pl. 5), in which are mentioned the earth names, be referred to as authoritative, and so the following paraphrases of those parts of the rituals are here given.

### EARTH NAME WI'-GI-ES

#### (WA-XTHI'-ZHI)

The people spake to one another, saying: The little ones have nothing to use as a symbol of courage.
Then, at that very time,
The Ho$^n$'-ga Wa'-ṭse-ga-wa (Ho$^{n'}$-ga-radiant-star),
Went forth with hurried footsteps

To the $I^n$-gtho$^n$'-ga do-ga, (male puma),

With whom he stood face to face and spake,

Saying: The little ones have nothing to use as a symbol of courage, O, grandfather.

The Male puma replied: I am a person whom the little ones may use as a symbol of courage.

The brothers spake in low tones,

Saying: He is a puma, O, younger brothers,

Let us take personal names from him;

$I^n$-gtho$^n$'-ga-to$^n$-ga, the Great-puma,

Shall be our name, O, younger brothers;

$I^n$-gtho$^n$'-ga-zhi$^n$-ga, the Young-puma,

Shall be our names, as we travel the path of life.

The Ho$^n$'-ga Wa'-tse-ga-wa, Radiant-star,

Went forth with hurried footsteps,

To the Wa-ça'-be, the Black-bear that is without blemish,

Who stood as in a flame of fire.

The Radiant-star spake to him, saying: The little ones have nothing to use as a symbol of their courage.

Wa-ça'-be replied: I am a person whom the little ones may use as a symbol of their courage.

The brothers spake to one another, saying: He is a black bear!

He is very dark in color!

Let us take from him personal names.

Sha'-be-tsi-gthe, the Dark-one,

Shall be our name henceforth, as we travel the path of life.

You have found the Dark-one, O, younger brothers,

Sha'-be-i-the, Finder-of-the-dark-one,

Shall be our name, henceforth, as we travel the path of life.

Look you, O, younger brothers, they said to one another,

The little ones have nothing to use as a symbol of courage.

Then they went forth in a body to an open prairie,

Where sat Mi'-xa-çka, the Great-white-swan.

Face to face they stood with him and spake,

Saying: The little ones have nothing to use as a symbol of courage, O, grandfather.

The brothers spake in low tones, saying: O, younger brothers,

We shall take from him personal names.

How white he is! the younger ones exclaimed,

He is a bird,

A white swan.

Mi'-xa-çka, the White-swan,

Shall be our name, O, younger brothers.

How white he is! they again exclaimed,

Wa-zhi$^n$'-çka, the White-bird, shall also

Be our name, O, younger brothers.

        —(36th Ann. Rept. Bur. Amer. Ethn., pp. 194–195, lines 1063 to 1115.)

Earth names mentioned in the origin wi'-gi-e given by Wa-tse'-mo$^n$-i$^n$.

## WI'-GI-E OF THE WA'ṬSE-GI-ṬSI

### HE-WHO-CAME-FROM-THE-STARS

What said they? it has been said, in this house,
The people spake, saying: O, younger brothers,
We are a people who give no mercy to the foe.
Then they spake to the one (gens) who had made of the Puma his body,
Saying: O, younger brother.
Hardly were these words spoken when the Puma hastened forth.
After a time the people said: There are signs that our brother is returning.
Then some of the brothers ran to meet him.

To their inquiry the Puma replied: O, elder brothers,
Yonder stands a man,
Verily, a man whose appearance inspires fear,
A man who is like us in form.
The people spake, saying: O, younger brother,
We are a people who show no mercy to the foe.
Whoever this man may be,
We shall send him to the abode of spirits,
We shall make him to lie low.

Then toward the man they hastened:
They made one ceremonial pause.
At the fourth pause,
The Puma exclaimed: There he stands!
It is well, the people replied,
We shall send him to the abode of spirits.
Then, at that very time,
The stranger spake, saying:
I am a sacred man, O, elder brothers.

The Puma spake, saying:
He speaks clearly our language!
I am Hon'-ga Wa'-ṭse-gi-ṭsi, a sacred person come from the stars, the stranger
　　continued.
I am Zhin-ga'-ga-hi-ge,[1] The-young-chief;
I am Wa'-ṭse-ga-hi-ge, The-star-chief;
I am Wa'-ṭse-ga-wa, The-star-radiant;
I am Wa'-ṭse-mon-in, The-traveling-star.

That pleases us! the people exclaimed.
Zhin-ga'-ga-hi-ge, The-young-chief, the stranger went on,
Shall be your name, as you travel the path of life;
Wa'-ṭse-ga-wa, The-star-radiant,
Shall also be your name, as you travel the path of life.
I have done much to make you contented and happy.
We are pleased! the people exclaimed,
We shall henceforth put away all anger and hatred,
We shall accept the names thus offered us.
Zhin-ga'-ga-hi-ge, The-young-chief,
Shall be our name,
Wa'-ṭse-ga-wa, The-star-radiant,

---

[1] The name Zhin-ga'-ga-hi-ge is still used in the Ṭa-pa' gens of the Omaha, a cognate tribe.

Shall be our name.
I'-e-çka-wa-the, He-speaks-clearly,
We shall also take as a name in his honor,
Pa'-thin-hon-ga, The-sacred-stranger,
We shall also take as a name in his honor.

Mi'-xa-çka, the white swan from whom personal names were taken, as mentioned in the following wi'-gi-e given by Wa-ṭse'-mon-in, is a warrior symbol. The black color on its feet and on the tip of its nose typifies the fire that knows no mercy. The standards (crooks), which were carried by an Osage war party (pl. 6, *a*), typify the neck of the white swan.

MI'-XA-ÇKA, THE WHITE SWAN

The people spake to one another, saying:
We have nothing of which to make a symbol (war standard).
They spake to the Puma (gens), saying:
Go thou and make search (for materials).
Even as these words were spoken the Puma went forth to search.

In time he hastened homeward,
And, standing before the elder brothers, he spake, saying:
O, elder brothers, what appears to be an animal,
Is in yonder place.
Make haste! the people said to one another,
We shall send him to the abode of spirits.
Verily, we are a people who give no mercy to the foe.

They made one ceremonial pause,
The fourth pause brought them close to the place.
Then the Puma spake, saying: There he stands! O, elder brothers.
An elder brother pointed with his index finger at the bird,
And it fell to the ground in death, its feathers strewing the earth.
They gathered around the fallen bird and stood.

Then one spake, saying: It is a swan! O, elder brothers,
A white swan!
Even from its white plumage
We shall take personal names,
Mi'-xa-çka, White-swan,
Wa-zhin'-ga-çka, White-bird,
And Mon'-shon-çka, White-feathers,
The little ones shall be named, as they travel the path of life.
                    —(36th Ann. Rept. Bur. Amer. Ethn., pp. 228–231, lines 238
                       to 358.)

The earth names given by Wa-xthi'-zhi, of the In-gthon'-ga (Puma) gens, in his wi'-gi-es are as follows:

1. In-gthon'-ga-ṭon-ga, the Great-puma.
2. Inn-gthon'-ga-zhin-ga, the Young-puma.
3. Sha'-be-ṭsi-gthe, the Dark-one.
4. Sha'-be-i-the, Finder-of-the-dark-one.
5. Mi'-xa-çka, the White-swan.
6. Wa-zhin'-çka, the White-bird.

The earth names given by Wa-ţse'-moⁿ-iⁿ of the Wa-ça'-be (Black Bear) gens in his wi'-gi-es:

1. Wa'-ţse-gi-ţsi, He-who-came-from-the-stars.
2. Zhiⁿ-ga'-ga-hi-ge, Young-chief.
3. Wa'-ţse-ga-hi-ge, Star-chief.
4. Wa-ţse'-ga-wa, Star-radiant.
5. Wa-ţse'-moⁿ-iⁿ, Traveling-star.
6. I'-e-çka-wa-the, He-speaks-clearly.
7. Pa'-thiⁿ-hoⁿ-ga, The-sacred-stranger.
8. Mi'-xa-çka, White-swan.
9. Wa-zhiⁿ'-ga-çka, White-bird.
10. Moⁿ-shoⁿ-çka, White-feather.

The following earth names, not specifically mentioned by Wa-xthi'-zhi, also appear in the wi'-gi-es recorded by himself and by Wa-ţse'-moⁿ-iⁿ. These names are also regarded as sacred and are ceremonially bestowed upon the children of the Puma and Black Bear gentes:

## WA-XTHI'-ZHI

1. Moⁿ'-hiⁿ-çi-i-ba-btho-ga, Round-handled-knife. (36th Ann. Rept. Bur. Amer. Ethn., p. 206, line 1399.)

2. Moⁿ'-hiⁿ-hoⁿ-ga, Sacred-knife. (36th Ann. Rept. Bur. Amer. Ethn., p. 207, line 1424.)

3. Moⁿ-hiⁿ-zhu-dse, Red-knife. (36th Ann. Rept. Bur. Amer. Ethn., p. 208, line 1439.)

4. The fourth name given by Wa-xthi'-zhi (Noⁿ-be'-wa-koⁿ-da, Mysterious-hand) does not appear in any of the wi'-gi-es given either by himself or by Wa-ţse'-moⁿ-iⁿ. However, the Mysterious-hand is spoken of by both of these men in their conversations concerning the rites, and is referred to in some of the wi'-gi-es. (See 36th Ann. Rept., p. 230, lines 323 to 340.) The story of the Mysterious-hand, as told colloquially, is that when the people came from the sky to the earth they had no weapons, but they killed animals by moistening the index finger of the right hand with saliva and pointing it at them. This name is also bestowed ceremonially.

## WA-TSE'-MOⁿ-Iⁿ

1. Miⁿ'-ţse-xi, Sacred-robe. (36th Ann. Rept. Bur. Amer. Ethn., p. 235, line 510.)

2. Noⁿ'-ḳa-dsi-wiⁿ, Spine-woman. (36th Ann. Rept. Bur. Amer. Ethn., p. 235, line 512.)

3. Ţse'-pa'-ga-xe, Buffalo-head-maker. (36th Ann. Rept. Bur. Amer. Ethn., p. 235, line 518.)

4. Moⁿ'-hiⁿ-zhu-dse, Red-knife. (36th Ann. Rept. Bur. Amer. Ethn., p. 237, line 573.)

5. Moⁿ'-hiⁿ-hoⁿ-ga, Sacred-knife. (36th Ann. Rept. Bur. Amer. Ethn., p. 237, line 576.)

## Special Instructions to the Mother

At the close of the ceremony of blessing the child by the various gentes officiating, the Sho'-ḳa conducts the mother to a seat prepared for her in front of the Xo'-ḳa, who gives her special instructions in the ceremonies to be observed by her to complete the child-naming rite. Between the two is spread a buffalo robe which had been decorated with certain symbolic designs. (Fig. 2.) This formal talk to the mother is called "Ḳi'-noⁿ U-tha-ge," Telling of the Symbolic Painting. Extra fees are required for the special instruction, which, with the help of friends and relatives, the mother is enabled to pay.

If the mother is skilled with her awl and thread in ornamental work she would decorate with porcupine quills the symbolic robe to be used in this special ceremony; if not skilled, she would content herself with painting the symbolic designs on the robe.

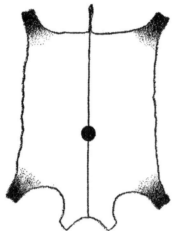

FIG. 2.—Symbolic robe prepared for children

When the robe has been spread before the Xo'-ḳa he begins to talk, as follows:

Wi-ṭsi-ni-e', My daughter-in-law, I see you have brought with you a robe which you have dressed and decorated for the comfort of your little one. It is a sacred robe which should be put to use with proper ceremony. This ceremony you will observe for a period of four days, during which you will paint red the parting of your hair. It will be a sign that you appeal for a long and fruitful life for yourself and child, to the god of day whose path lies over the middle of the earth.

You have reddened the head and the forelegs of the robe. The head and forelegs of the robe typify that part of the earth whence rises the god of day to take his westward journey. Red is the color of the day when it is young, the time when you will rise and go forth to prepare food for the little one whose tender life is wholly dependent upon your efforts. A narrow line runs from the head of the robe along the middle of the back to the tail. This line typifies the path of the god of day who ever travels from east to west. Midway of the path is a round spot which represents the god of day when it has reached the middle of heaven. Here he marks the time when you will turn your thoughts from other things to the feeding of the little one so that the nourishing of its life may be continuous. The god of day continues his journey and in time reaches the edge of the earth, behind which he finally disappears. The hind legs and

WA-ṬSE'-MOⁿ-Iⁿ (WA-ÇA'-BE (BLACK BEAR) GENS)

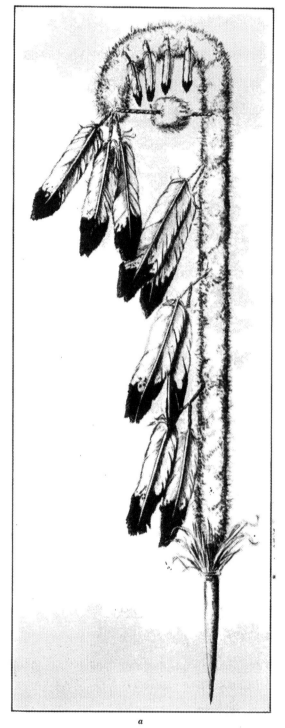

*a*

*b*

*a*, WAR STANDARD (SYMBOLIZES THE WHITE SWAN)
*b*, ṬSE'-WA-THE ROOT (NELUMBO LUTEA), USED FOR FOOD

the tail of the robe are reddened to typify the glow that warns us of the ending of the day when your thoughts will again turn to the care of the little one. When you put these symbolic marks upon this sacred robe your thoughts reached out in appeal to Wa-ko$^n$'-da for yourself and child.

As the shadow of night spreads over the land you will take your little one in your arms, draw this robe over you, then rest in sleep. The robe which you draw over yourself and child typifies the heaven, whence comes all life, and the act is an appeal to heaven for protection.

The procuring of food for the little one should always be done with a feeling of gratitude toward the Mysterious Power that brings forth life in all forms. There is a plant which is dedicated to use as a sacred food in the bringing up of the little ones, known as ţse'-wa-the (*Nelumbo lutea*) (pl. 6, *b*). (36th Ann. Rept. Bur. Amer. Ethn., p. 183, lines 910 to 923.) You will at times go to the lake to gather the roots of this plant for use in feeding your little one. When about to go to the lake you will paint red the parting of your hair, as a sign of your gratitude to the god of day who passes over your head and over the plant you go to seek, shedding his life-giving power upon you as he goes upon his journey.

When you come to the edge of the lake you will look about for a staff to support you as you work in the water. You will choose the willow for your staff, for it is a tree that clings persistently to life. By this act you will make an appeal to the great Life-giving Power for a long and fruitful life for yourself and the little one. With the willow staff in your hands you will step into the water and take up from the soft earth beneath a root of the sacred plant, the ţse'-wa-the. You will find clinging to the root some of the soft earth from which the plant draws nourishment and strength. Take this bit of soil and touch your forehead and body with it, an act which will be as a sign that you appeal to the earth wherein there is Life-giving Power. When you have performed this act return the root to the earth beneath the water, with the wish that the plant shall forever be plentiful. Then gather enough of the roots to satisfy the little one and yourself.

The maize is another sacred life-giving plant. You raise this plant from year to year. When you prepare the ground for planting the seed you will take one grain and put it in a hill, you will press down upon it the soil with your foot, and say: "My father-in-law bade me do this, as an expression of my faith that the sky and the earth will yield to me not only one ear of maize but one animal as well, or even one herd of animals." In the next hill you will put two grains, in the next three, the next four, the next five, the next six, and in the seventh seven, always repeating the words at each planting.

The ceremony closes with the end of the special instructions given to the mother of the child blessed and named, and as each member of the gentes who had taken part in the rite rises to go he makes some pleasant remarks to the father and the mother.

When the mother goes to her field to plant the seeds of the maize she remembers the instructions and follows them in every detail. As the maize matures and the ears are still green and tender the mother cuts the stalks from the hills she had ceremonially made, leaving the ears on the stalks. She ties the stalks in bundles, and, with the aid of friends, carries them home to her house. She then prepares a feast to which she invites the man who had acted as Xo'-ḳa at the ceremonial naming of her child. He in turn invites some of his friends who had acted as Xo'-ḳa in child-naming ceremonies to come and share in the feast prepared for him.

If among the invited guests there happens to be a member of the Tho'-xe gens, learned in the rituals, he is requested by the honored guest to recite the maize wi'-gi-e of his gens.

A paraphrase is here given of the wi'-gi-e which the Tho'-xe recite to give pleasure to the host and to the guests. The mythical story points to mid-heaven as the region of the conception of life forms, and as the starting point of the Osage people in their journey to earth, the region of actual birth into bodily existence.

### ORIGIN WI'-GI-E OF THE THO'-XE GENS

The people spake to one another, saying: Lo, the little ones are not a people,
Let search be made by the younger brothers for a place where the little ones may
  become a people.
Even as these words were being spoken, a younger brother
Hastened to the first division of heaven,
Close to which he came and paused,
When, returning to the elder brothers, he spake, saying:
Verily, nothing of importance has come to my notice.
Make further search, O, younger brothers, the people said,
The little ones are not a people.

Then, a younger brother,
Even as these words were being spoken,
Hastened to the second division of heaven, where he paused,
When, as the god of darkness cast a shadow upon the heavens,
He returned to the eldest brothers and stood.
They looked up and spake, saying: How has it fared with you?  It was not your
  wont to suffer so, O, younger brother.
He replied: I have been to the second division of heaven.
It is not possible for the little ones to become a people there.

O, Younger brother,
We bid you make further search, the people said.
Even as these words were being spoken,
One hastened to the third division of heaven,
He drew near and paused.

The younger brother,
As the god of darkness cast a shadow upon the heavens,
Returned to the elder brothers and stood.
The elder brothers spake: How has it fared with you? It was not your wont to
   suffer so.
The younger brother replied: It is impossible!

O, younger brother, the people said,
We bid you make further search.
Then a younger brother
Hastened to the
Fourth division of heaven.
Close to it he came and paused.
Then the Man of Mystery, the god of the clouds,
Drew near and stood before him.

The younger brother turned to the elder brothers and said: Here stands a man!
A fear-inspiring man!
His name, I verily believe, is Fear-inspiring.
The people spake to him, saying: O, grandfather!
The Man of Mystery replied: I am a person of whom your little ones may make
   their bodies.
When they make of me their bodies,
They shall cause themselves to be deathless.

Little-hawk
They shall take for their personal name,
Then shall they always live to see old age.
Hawk-maiden, also,
Is a name that is mine.
That name also
Your little ones shall take to be their name,
Then shall they always live to see old age.

O, younger brother! the people said,
And the younger brother went in haste
To the Tho'-xe (the Buffalo-bull),
Close to whom he stood and spake, saying:
O, grandfather!

Then to the elder brothers he said: Here stands a man!
A fear-inspiring man!
The Tho'-xe spake: I am a person of whom the little ones may make their bodies.
Whereupon he threw himself to the ground,
Then up sprang the blazing star,
From the earth where it stood in all its beauty, pleasing to look upon.
Tho'-xe spake, saying: Of this plant also the little ones may make their bodies.
The people tasted the root of the plant,
And exclaimed: It is bitter to the taste!
Tho'-xe spake, saying: This plant shall be medicine to the little ones.
When they use it as medicine,
Their arms shall lengthen in growth,
And they shall live to see old age.

19078°—28——5

Again Tho'-xe threw himself upon the ground,
And the poppy mallow
Sprang from the earth and stood resplendent in its reddened blossoms.
Of this plant also Tho'-xe said,
The little ones shall make their bodies.
When they use it as medicine,
Their arms shall lengthen in growth.
The root is astringent,
And, referring thereto, your little ones shall take the name Astringent.
When the little ones make of this plant their bodies,
They shall always live to see old age.

Tho'-xe (the Buffalo-bull),
Threw himself to the ground,
And a red ear of maize
He tossed in the air,
As he exclaimed: The little ones shall make of this their bodies!
Then shall they always live to see old age.

Again Tho'-xe threw himself to the ground,
And a blue ear of maize,
Together with a blue squash,
He tossed in the air as he said,
These plants, also,
Shall be food for the little ones,
Then shall they live to see old age.

A third time he threw himself to the ground,
And a white ear of maize,
Together with a white squash he tossed in the air,
As he exclaimed: These plants also shall be food for the little ones!
Then shall they be difficult for death to overcome them,
And they shall always live to see old age.

A fourth time he threw himself to the ground,
And a speckled ear of maize,
Together with a speckled squash,
He tossed in the air as he exclaimed:
What creature is there that would be without a mate!
And he wedded together the maize and the squash,
Then exclaimed: These also shall be food for the little ones!
And they shall be difficult for death to overcome them.

The feasting of the Non'-hon-zhin-ga upon the fruits of the seeds of the maize planted by the mother with religious care in the seven sacred hills completes the rite of the naming of her child, by which its right to a place in its gens is formally recognized; the child has a place, not only in its gens, but also in the sky and the earth which the two great tribal divisions, the Hon'-ga and the Tsi'-zhu, represent.

# CHILD-NAMING RITUAL OF THE ȚSI'-ZHU WA-SHTA-GE GENS

(SHO[N]'-GE-MO[N]-I[N])

The Child-naming ritual of the Ṭsi'-zhu Wa-shta-ge gens of the Osage tribe, here recorded, was given by Sho[n]'-ge-mo[n]-i[n], a member of the Ba'-po subgens of the Ṭsi'-zhu Wa-shta-ge gens. The name Ba'-po (Popper in English), Sho[n]'-ge-mo[n]-i[n] explained, is the name of the elder tree, the trunk of which boys, from time reaching beyond memory, used for making poppers. The name refers to a mythical story and to a ceremonial office. The mythical story is as follows: When the people of the Ṭsi'-zhu great division descended from the sky to make the earth their home they came down as eagles, and they alighted on a great red oak tree. The shock of their alighting caused the acorns to drop from the tree in great profusion, which was taken as a prophecy that the Ṭsi'-zhu would become a numerous people. One eagle was crowded off the tree, but as he dropped down he alighted upon a blossoming elder tree. This eagle was a peace bird and his alighting on the ba'-po tree made it to become a peace symbol. The Ba'-po subgens was given the office of furnishing a pipestem for the peace pipe in the keeping of the Ṭsi'-zhu Wa-shta-ge gens, and the Ba'-po made the stem of an elder sapling a symbol of peace.

When Sho[n]'-ge-mo[n]-i[n] is called by a member of the Ṭsi'-zhu Wa-shta-ge gens to act as Xo'-ḳa (instructor) in the ceremonial naming of his child he goes to the house of the father without any formality. Usually the call is made when the sun is traveling downward (afternoon); when he receives the message he promptly responds to the call. On his arrival at the house the father, in a formal speech, informs him that his summons was for the purpose of asking him to conduct the ceremonies to be performed at the naming of his child. When Sho[n]'-ge-mo[n]-i[n] gives his consent to officiate at the ceremony the fees for the men who are to take part are placed before him. These he examines to make sure that there are enough articles to go around, and to see if the man had also provided a pipe for the Sho'-ḳa or Official Messenger.

### CERTAIN GENTES CALLED TO TAKE PART IN THE CEREMONY

Being satisfied that the man had supplied all the necessary articles, he places in the hands of the father the ceremonial pipe and bids him go after the Sho'-ḳa of the gens. The father returns with the messenger who was already invested with the little pipe, the badge of his authority. When the two men had taken their seats Sho[n]'-ge-mo[n]-i[n] directs the Sho'-ḳa to go and call the heads of the following gentes, with their No[n]'-ho[n]-zhi[n]-ga members, to come to the house of the father, at sunrise the next morning, to take part in the ceremonies of naming his child:

1. Wa'-ṭse-ṭsi, of the Wa-zha'-zhe subdivision, to recite their wi'-gi-e relating to their life symbol, the red cedar. (36th Ann. Rept. Bur. Amer. Ethn., p. 95, lines 1 to 34.)

2. No$^{n\prime}$-po$^{n}$-da, Deer gens, of the Wa-zha'-zhe subdivision, to recite their wi'-gi-e relating to one of their life symbols, the water. (36th Ann. Rept. Bur. Amer. Ethn., p. 98, lines 1 to 25.)

3. I'-ba-ṭse Ṭa-dse, Wind People, of the Ho$^{n\prime}$-ga subdivision, to recite their wi'-gi-e relating to one of their life symbols, the maize.

4. Tho'-xe, Buffalo-bull gens of the Ṭsi-zhu great division, to recite their wi'-gi-e relating to the maize. Tho'-xe is the gens that gave to the people the maize and the squashes. (36th Ann. Rept. Bur. Amer. Ethn., p. 279, lines 54 to 110.) The Tho'-xe authorized the I'-ba-ṭse and certain other gentes to use the Maize ritual in their child-naming ceremonies.

5. Çi$^{n\prime}$-dse-a-gthe, Wolf gens of the Ṭsi'-zhu great division, to recite their wi'-gi-e relating to their life symbol, the sun. The Dogstar is also one of their life symbols. (36th Ann. Rept. Bur. Amer. Ethn., p. 118, lines 1 to 36.)

### Wa-zho'-i-ga-the (Life Symbol) Wi'-gi-e

The Sho'-ḳa returns to the house of the father and reports that he has given notice to all the gentes named to attend the ceremony. Then Sho$^{n\prime}$-ge-mo$^{n}$-i$^{n}$ proceeds to recite the Wa-zho'-i-ga-the Wi'-gi-e of his gens, a name which means, The Taking of Bodies; that is, The Taking of Life Symbols. The reciting of this wi'-gi-e is for the benefit of the father and the child.

#### THE TAKING OF LIFE SYMBOLS.

##### FREE TRANSLATION

1

1. The people spake to one another, saying: Lo, the little ones have nothing of which to make their bodies,
2. Take heed, O, younger brothers, and see what can be done.
3. Then to the youngest of the brothers they spake, saying:
4. The little ones have nothing of which to make their bodies, O, younger brother.
5. Hardly were these words spoken,
6. When the young messenger stood before the God of Day (the sun), to whom he spake, saying:
7. O, my grandfather!
8. The God of Day replied: My grandchild!
9. The messenger spake: The little ones have nothing of which to make their bodies, O, grandfather.

10. The God of Day spake: I am a person of whom the little ones
　　may well make their bodies,
11. I am a god who has power to resist death.
12. When the little ones make of me their bodies,
13. They also shall have power to resist death, as they travel the
　　path of life.
14. Even among the gods
15. There is not one who is able to see my path.
16. When the little ones make of me their bodies,
17. Even the gods
18. Shall not be able to see their path, as they travel the path of life.

2

19. Again the people spake, saying: O, younger brothers,
20. Take heed and see what can be done,
21. The little ones have nothing of which to make their bodies.
22. They spake to the youngest of the brothers, saying:
23. O, younger brother,
24. The little ones have nothing of which to make their bodies,
25. Take heed and see what can be done.
26. Hardly were these words spoken
27. When the young messenger stood before the Goddess of Night
　　(the moon),
28. To whom he spake, saying: O, my grandmother!
29. The Goddess of Night replied: My grandchild!
30. The messenger spake: The little ones have nothing of which to
　　make their bodies.
31. Then spake the Goddess of Night: I am a person of whom the
　　little ones may well make their bodies,
32. I am a goddess who has power to resist death.
33. When the little ones make of me their bodies,
34. They also shall have power to resist death, as they travel the
　　path of life.
35. Even among the gods
36. There is not one who is able to see my path.
37. When the little ones make of me their bodies,
38. Even the gods
39. Shall not be able to see their path, as they travel the path of
　　life.
40. Even among the gods
41. There is not one of them who can stand in my way to prevent
　　my going.
42. When the little ones make of me their bodies,
43. Even the gods
44. Shall not be able to stand in their way, as they travel the path
　　of life.

45. Moreover, I have been able to bring myself to see old age.
46. When the little ones make of me their bodies,
47. They also shall bring themselves to see old age, as they travel the path of life.
48. I have brought myself to the days that are calm and peaceful.
49. When the little ones make of me their bodies,
50. They also shall bring themselves to the calm and peaceful days, as they travel the path of life.

### 3

51. Again the people spake, saying: Lo, the little ones have nothing of which to make their bodies,
52. Take heed and see what can be done, O, younger brothers.
53. Then they spake to the youngest of the brothers,
54. Saying: O, younger brother!
55. The little ones have nothing of which to make their bodies,
56. Take heed and see what can be done.
57. Even as these words were being spoken,
58. He stood before the Male Star (Morning Star) who sitteth in the heavens,
59. And spake to him, saying: O, grandfather!
60. The Male Star replied: My grandchild!
61. The messenger spake: The little ones have nothing of which to make their bodies.
62. The Male Star replied: I am a person of whom the little ones may well make their bodies.
63. I am a god who has power to resist death.
64. When the little ones make of me their bodies,
65. They also shall have power to resist death, as they travel the path of life.
66. Even among the gods
67. There is not one who is able to see my path.
68. When the little ones make of me their bodies,
69. Even the gods
70. Shall not be able to see their path, as they travel the path of life.
71. Even among the gods
72. There is not one who can stand in my way to prevent my going,
73. When the little ones make of me their bodies.
74. Even the gods
75. Shall not be able to stand in their way to prevent their going.
76. Moreover, I have been able to bring myself to see old age.
77. When the little ones make of me their bodies,
78. They also shall be able to bring themselves to see old age, as they travel the path of life.

79. They shall also live to see the days that are calm and peaceful.
80. When the little ones make of me their bodies,
81. They shall be able to bring themselves to the calm and peaceful days, as they travel the path of life.

### 4

82. The people spake, saying: O, younger brothers,
83. The little ones have nothing of which to make their bodies,
84. Take heed and see what can be done.
85. Then they spake to the youngest of the brothers,
86. Saying: O, younger brother,
87. The little ones have nothing of which to make their bodies,
88. Take heed and see what can be done.
89. Even as these words were being spoken,
90. The messenger stood before the Female Star (Evening Star) who sitteth in the heavens,
91. And spake to her, saying: O, my grandmother!
92. The Female Star replied: My grandchild!
93. The messenger spake: The little ones have nothing of which to make their bodies.
94. The Female Star replied: I am a person of whom the little ones may well make their bodies.
95. I am a god who has power to resist death.
96. When the little ones make of me their bodies,
97. They also shall have power to resist death, as they travel the path of life.
98. Even among the gods
99. There is not one who can stand in my way to prevent my going.
100. When the little ones make of me their bodies,
101. Even the gods
102. Shall not be able to stand in their way to stop their going.
103. Moreover, I have been able to bring myself to see old age.
104. When the little ones make of me their bodies,
105. They also shall be able to bring themselves to see old age, as they travel the path of life.
106. I have been able to bring myself to the calm and peaceful days.
107. When the little ones make of me their bodies,
108. They also shall be able to bring themselves to the calm and peaceful days, as they travel the path of life.

### 5

109. The people spake, saying: O, younger brothers,
110. The little ones have nothing of which to make their bodies.
111. Then to the youngest of the brothers
112. They spake, saying: O, younger brother,

113. Take heed and see what can be done.
114. Even as these words were being spoken,
115. The messenger stood before the Litter (Ursa Major), who stands in the heavens,
116. To whom he spake, saying, O, grandfather!
117. The little ones have nothing of which to make their bodies.
118. The Litter replied: I am a person of whom the little ones may well make their bodies.
119. I am a god who has power to resist death.
120. When the little ones make of me their bodies,
121. They also shall have power to resist death, as they travel the path of life.
122. Even among the gods
123. There is not one who is able to see my path.
124. When the little ones make of me their bodies,
125. Even the gods
126. Shall not be able to see their path, as they travel the path of life.
127. Even among the gods
128. There is not one who can stand in my way to prevent my going.
129. When the little ones make of me their bodies,
130. Even the gods
131. Shall not be able to stand in their way to prevent their going.
132. Moreover, I have been able to bring myself to see old age.
133. When the little ones make of me their bodies,
134. They also shall be able to bring themselves to see old age.
135. I have been able to bring myself to the calm and peaceful days.
136. When the little ones make of me their bodies,
137. They also shall be able to bring themselves to the calm and peaceful days, as they travel the path of life.

6

138. The people spake, saying: The little ones have nothing of which to make their bodies,
139. Give heed, younger brothers, and see what can be done.
140. Then to the youngest of the brothers,
141. They spake, saying: O, younger brother,
142. The little ones have nothing of which to make their bodies.
143. Even as these words were being spoken,
144. The messenger stood before Deer-head (Pleiades), who sitteth in the heavens,
145. To whom he spake, saying: O, my grandmother!
146. She replied: My grandchild!
147. The messenger spake: The little ones have nothing of which to make their bodies.
148. Deer-head replied: I am a person of whom the little ones may well make their bodies,

149. I am a god who has power to resist death.
150. When the little ones make of me their bodies,
151. They also shall have power to resist death, as they travel the path of life.
152. Even among the gods
153. There is not one who is able to see my path.
154. When the little ones make of me their bodies,
155. Even the gods
156. Shall not be able to see their path, as they travel the path of life.
157. Even among the gods
158. There is not one who can stand in my way to prevent my going.
159. When the little ones make of me their bodies,
160. Even the gods
161. Shall not be able to stand in their way to prevent their going.
162. Moreover, I have been able to bring myself to see old age.
163. When the little ones make of me their bodies,
164. They also shall be able to bring themselves to see old age.
165. I have been able to bring myself to the calm and peaceful days.
166. When the little ones make of me their bodies,
167. They also shall be able to bring themselves to the calm and peaceful days, as they travel the path of life.

7

168. The people spake, saying: The little ones have nothing of which to make their bodies,
169. Give heed, O, younger brothers, and see what can be done.
170. Then to the youngest of the brothers,
171. They spake, saying: O, younger brother,
172. The little ones have nothing of which to make their bodies,
173. Take heed and see what can be done.
174. Even as these words were being spoken,
175. The messenger stood before Three-deer (Orion's belt), who stands in the heavens,
176. To whom he spake, saying: O, grandfather!
177. The little ones have nothing of which to make their bodies.
178. Three-deer replied: I am a person of whom the little ones may well make their bodies,
179. I am a god who has power to resist death.
180. When the little ones make of me their bodies,
181. They also shall have power to resist death, as they travel the path of life.
182. Even among the gods
183. There is not one who is able to see my path.
184. When the little ones make of me their bodies,

185. Even the gods
186. Shall not be able to see their path, as they travel the path of
     life.
187. Even among the gods
188. There is not one who can stand in my way to prevent my going.
189. When the little ones make of me their bodies,
190. Even the gods
191. Shall not be able to stand in their way to prevent their going.
192. Moreover, I have been able to bring myself to see old age.
193. When the little ones make of me their bodies,
194. They also shall have the power to bring themselves to see old
     age.
195. I have been able to bring myself to the calm and peaceful days.
196. When the little ones make of me their bodies,
197. They also shall be able to bring themselves to the calm and
     peaceful days, as they travel the path of life.

8

198. The people spake, saying: The little ones have nothing of
     which to make their bodies, O, younger brothers,
199. Take heed and see what can be done.
200. Then to the youngest of the brothers
201. They spake, saying: O, younger brother,
202. The little ones have nothing of which to make their bodies,
203. Take heed and see what can be done.
204. Even as these words were being spoken,
205. The messenger stood before Double-star (Theta and Iota in
     Orion) who sitteth in the heavens,
206. To whom he spake, saying: O, grandmother!
207. The little ones have nothing of which to make their bodies.
208. Double-star replied: I am a person of whom the little ones may
     well make their bodies.
209. I am a god who has power to resist death.
210. When the little ones make of me their bodies,
211. They also shall have power to resist death, as they travel the
     path of life.
212. Even among the gods
213. There is not one who is able to see my path.
214. When the little ones make of me their bodies,
215. Even the gods
216. Shall not be able to see their path, as they travel the path of
     life.
217. Even among the gods
218. There is not one who can stand in my way to prevent my going.
219. When the little ones make of me their bodies,

220. Even the gods
221. Shall not be able to stand in their way to prevent their going.
222. Moreover, I have been able to bring myself to see old age.
223. When the little ones make of me their bodies,
224. They also shall be able to bring themselves to see old age.
225. I have been able to bring myself to the calm and peaceful days.
226. When the little ones make of me their bodies,
227. They also shall be able to bring themselves to the calm and peaceful days, as they travel the path of life.

At the close of the wi'-gi-e Sho$^{n'}$-ge-mo$^n$-i$^n$ and the Sho'-ķa are invited by the family to join them in the evening meal, after which the two men go home.

## The Xo'-ķa Ceremonially Conducted to the Child's House

Before sunrise the next morning the Sho'-ķa, carrying his little pipe, the badge of his office, goes to Sho$^{n'}$-ge-mo$^n$-i$^n$'s house to conduct him to the house of the child to be named. Upon receiving the formal message from the Sho'-ķa, Sho$^{n'}$-ge-mo$^n$-i$^n$ takes his paint pouch from a bag containing his personal belongings and puts some red paint on the inner surface of his hands. Then as the eastern clouds take from the rising sun a crimson tinge, he lifts his hands, palms outward, toward them and the sun itself. After a silent pause he withdraws his hands and reddens his face with the paint on them, as though with the color of the sun, and his messengers, the reddened clouds. When he has put upon his face the sacred color he takes from a package in which he keeps his ornamental feathers a red downy eagle feather which he fastens to his scalplock so that the red feather, the life symbol of his gens, stands firm and upright. In the days when buffalo were plentiful the No$^{n'}$-ho$^n$-zhi$^n$-ga who is to act as Xo'-ķa at the child-naming ceremony wore a buffalo robe with the hair outside, but since the extinction of that animal he substituted for the robe a woven blanket obtained from traders.

Having thus decorated himself with red paint and the red feather, symbols of the sky, and the substitute of the buffalo robe, an earth symbol, Sho$^{n'}$-ge-mo$^n$-i$^n$, now actual Xo'-ķa, goes forth to the house of the child to be named, following the Sho'-ķa, who leads the way. It was explained by the old man that the manner of approach of his gens, the Ţsi'-zhu Wa-shta-ge, to the house of the child was very simple, that it did not have the elaborate ceremonial forms described by Wa-xthi'-zhi that were followed by his gens, the Puma, and the other war gentes of the Ho$^{n'}$-ga great division.

Arriving at the house, the Sho'-ķa enters without pause and leads the Xo'-ķa to his place at the left of the father, who sits with his wife and child at the east end of the house. When the Xo'-ķa has taken his seat the No$^{n'}$-ho$^n$-zhi$^n$-ga of his gens, the Ţsi-zhu Wa-shta-ge, enter and take their places back of the Xo'-ḳa and the parents and sit in a row occupying the entire width of the house. Then the Noⁿ'-hoⁿ-zhiⁿ-ga of the other gentes who are to take part in the ceremony enter, those of the Hoⁿ'-ga great division taking their accustomed places at the south side and those of the Ṭsi'-zhu great division at the north side of the house. (Fig. 1.) Except for the blankets of various colors, the Noⁿ'-hoⁿ-zhiⁿ-ga were decorated alike, their faces painted red, the color of the sun and the dawn, and a red downy feather fastened to the scalplock of each one.

## A Life Symbol Sent to Each of the Officiating Gentes

When all the Noⁿ'-hoⁿ-zhiⁿ-ga had settled down in their places, and had exchanged with each other the usual social greetings, Shoⁿ'-ge-moⁿ-iⁿ opens the proceedings with a formal statement, setting forth the purpose of the gathering and adding some pertinent remarks concerning the ancient rite of naming the children and their formal recognition as members of the tribe. He then goes on to the ceremony of distributing the fees and the symbolic articles to be used in the rite. The distribution was made in the following order:

1. To the Wa'-ṭse-ṭsi, Star gens of the Wa-zha'-zhe subdivision of the Hoⁿ'-ga great division, he sent, by the Sho'-ḳa, cedar fronds with fee. The cedar is a life symbol of the Wa'-ṭse-ṭsi gens.

2. To the Tho'-xe, Buffalo-bull gens, of the Ṭsi'-zhu great division, a bowl of shelled corn with fee. The maize is one of the life symbols of the Tho'-xe.

3. To the Noⁿ'-poⁿ-da, Deer gens of the Wa-zha'-zhe subdivion of the Hoⁿ'-ga great division, a bowl of water with fee. Water is one of the life symbols of the Noⁿ'-poⁿ-da.

4. To the Çiⁿ'-dse-a-gthe, Wolf-tail gens, of the Ṭsi'-zhu great division, fee only. The sun is one of the life symbols of this gens. The Dog-star is also one of its symbols.

5. I'-ba-ṭse Ṭa-dse, Wind gens of the Hoⁿ'-ga subdivision of the Hoⁿ'-ga great division, a bowl of shelled corn. The Tho'-xe authorized the I'-ba-ṭse to use the maize ritual. This gens also has the office of performing the ceremonies by which the souls of warriors slain in battle are sent direct to the spirit land.

## Members of the Officiating Gentes Recite Their Wi'-gi-es Simultaneously

When the Sho'-ḳa, the Ceremonial Messenger, had made the last delivery of the symbolic articles and fees to the gentes above named, each Noⁿ'-hoⁿ-zhiⁿ-ga begins to recite the wi'-gi-e of his gens relating to its life symbol, such as the cedar fronds, the corn or water. As each Noⁿ'-hoⁿ-zhiⁿ-ga recites the wi'-gi-e of his gens, old Shoⁿ'-ge-moⁿ-iⁿ recites the Name Wi'-gi-e of his own gens, the Ṭsi-zhu Wa-shta-ge, which is as follows:

THE NAME WI'-GI-E

FREE TRANSLATION

1

1. The people spake to one another, saying: O, younger brothers,
2. The little ones have nothing of which to make their bodies,
3. Take heed and see what can be done.
4. Then to the youngest of the brothers they spake,
5. Saying: O, younger brother,
6. The little ones have nothing of which to make their bodies,
7. You will give heed and see what can be done.
8. Even as these words were being spoken
9. To the first division of heaven,
10. The messenger verily descended,
11. Where the little ones had not yet become a people.

2

12. Again the people spake, saying: O, younger brothers,
13. The little ones have nothing of which to make their bodies,
14. Take heed and see what can be done.
15. Then to the youngest of the brothers they spake,
16. Saying: O, younger brother,
17. You will give heed and see what can be done.
18. To the second division of heaven the messenger descended,
19. When he cried out:
20. It can not be, it is impossible:
21. The little ones have not yet become a people.

3

22. Again the people spake, saying: O, younger brothers,
23. The little ones have nothing of which to make their bodies,
24. Take heed and see what can be done.
25. Then to the youngest of the brothers they spake,
26. Saying: O, younger brother,
27. The little ones have nothing of which to make their bodies,
28. You will give heed and see what can be done.
29. Even as these words were being spoken,
30. The messenger descended to the third division of heaven,
31. Where the little ones had not yet become a people.

4

32. Verily, at that time and place,
33. The people spake, saying: O, younger brothers, the little ones
have nothing of which to make their bodies,

34. Take heed and see what can be done.
35. Then to the youngest of the brothers they spake,
36. Saying: O, younger brother,
37. The little ones have nothing of which to make their bodies,
38. You will give heed and see what can be done.
39. Even as these words were being spoken,
40. The messenger descended to the fourth division of heaven,
41. Where lay the bird (the female eagle) that has no stains (evil disposition).
42. Verily, a person who is ever present upon her nest.
43. Upon the center of the earth, that sat in all her greatness,[2]
44. There stood a person (the male eagle).
45. From him we shall take the name, $Mo^n$-$zho^{n\prime}$, Earth,
46. Verily, he is a person who travels far and wide, above the earth.
47. We shall take from him the name, $Mo^n$-$zho^{n\prime}$-ga-$sho^n$, Travels-above-the-earth.
48. Verily, he is a person whose home is upon the center of the earth.
49. We will take from him the name, $Mo^n$-$zho^{n\prime}$-u-çko$^n$-çka, Center-of-the-earth.

### 5

50. The little ones are now a people.
51. We shall also take the name, Xi-tha$^\prime$-da-wi$^n$, Good-eagle-woman,
52. Also the name, Hi$^{n\prime}$-i-ḳi$^n$-da-bi, Feathers-fought-over,
53. Hi$^{n\prime}$-ga-mo$^n$-ge, Feathers-scattered-by-the-winds, shall also be our name,
54. As also, No$^n$-be$^\prime$-çi, Yellow-hands.
55. And Wa-zhi$^{n\prime}$-ga-hi$^n$, Feathers-of-the-bird, shall be our name.

### 6

56. Verily, at that time and place,
57. The eagle spake, saying: Behold the hollow of my foot,
58. Which I have made to be the sign of old age.
59. When the little ones make of me their bodies,
60. They shall live to see the sign of old age in the hollow of their foot.

61. The wrinkles upon my shin,
62. I have made to be the sign of old age.
63. When the little ones make of me their bodies,
64. They shall live to see wrinkles upon their shin.

---

[1] The words of this line are figurative and mean the earth when she displays her greatness by her blossoming flowers and her ripening fruit.

65. The folds of the skin on my knee,
66. I have made to be the sign of old age.
67. When the little ones make of me their bodies,
68. They shall live to see the skin of their knee gathered in folds.

69. The stripes on the feathers of my thigh,
70. I have made to be the sign of old age.
71. When the little ones make of me their bodies,
72. They shall live to see the sign of old age upon their thigh.
73. The stripes upon my breast,
74. I have made to be the sign of old age.
75. When the little ones make of me their bodies,
76. They shall live to see the sign of old age on their breast.

77. The stripes upon the corners of my mouth,
78. I have made to be the sign of old age.
79. When the little ones make of me their bodies,
80. They shall live to see the sign of old age in the corners of their mouth.

81. The stripes upon my forehead,
82. I have made to be the sign of old age.
83. When the little ones make of me their bodies,
84. They shall live to see the sign of old age on their forehead.

85. The folds of my eyelids,
86. I have made to be the sign of old age.
87. When the little ones make of me their bodies,
88. They shall live to see the sign of old age on their eyelids.

89. I have been able to bring myself to old age.
90. When the little ones make of me their bodies,
91. They also shall be able to bring themselves to old age.
92. I have been able to bring myself to the calm and peaceful days.
93. When the little ones make of me their bodies,
94. They also shall be able to bring themselves to the calm and peaceful days, as they travel the path of life.

### The Child is Passed from Gens to Gens to be Blessed

At the close of the simultaneous recital of the wi'-gi-es by the No$^n$'-ho$^n$-zhi$^n$-ga of the six gentes, namely, the Wa'-tse-tsi, Tho'-xe, No$^n$'-po$^n$-da, Çi$^n$'-dse-a-gthe, I'-ba-tse, and the Tsi'-zhu Wa-shta-ge, the Sho'-ka carries the infant to the head of the Wa'-tse-tsi gens, who takes it in his arms, then, dipping the tips of the fingers into a wooden vessel, in which had been put sacred water and red cedar fronds, he gently touches with his moistened fingertips the lips, head, arms, and body of the little one. This ceremonial act is an appeal to Wa-ko$^n$'-da to grant to the little one health and strength so that it may grow to maturity and old age without interruption by disease.

The child is next taken by the Sho'-ḳa to the head of the No[n]'-po[n]-da gens, who blesses it in the same manner with the symbolic water and cedar fronds.

Then the little one is taken to the head of the I'-ba-ṭse gens, who touches the lips, head, arms and body of the child with pounded corn, besides the sacred water and cedar fronds. The touching of the child with the life-giving corn is an act of appeal to Wa-ḳo[n]'-da that the child be not permitted to suffer for want of food during its life, so that it may reach maturity and old age without difficulty. The gentile symbol of the I'-ba-ṭse gens is the wind but it was authorized by the Tho'-xe gens to use the corn ritual in its child-naming ritual.

The Sho'-ḳa takes the little one from the I'-ba-ṭse to the head of the Tho'-xe, Buffalo-bull, gens. In the mythical story of the origin of the maize it was Tho'-xe, Buffalo-bull, who gave to the people the maize and the squash. (See 36th Ann. Rept. Bur. Amer. Ethn., pp. 279–281, lines 54 to 110.) The head of the Tho'-xe gens takes the little one in his arms and blesses it with the sacred water and cedar fronds as did the Wa'-ṭse-ṭsi, then, mixing some of his own pounded corn with that of the I'-ba-ṭse, he blesses the child with the sacred corn, the life symbol of his own gens. The ceremonial act of the Tho'-xe is an expression of the wish that the life-giving corn will aid the new member of the Ṭsi'-zhu Wa-shta-ge gens to successfully reach maturity and old age.

The next to take the child in his arms and bless it with the symbolic water, cedar fronds and corn is the head of the Çi[n]'-dse-a-gthe, Wolf, gens. His ceremonial acts do not differ from those of the Tho'-xe.

The Sho'-ḳa then brings the little one to its own gens, the Ṭsi'-zhu Wa-shta-ge, the People of Peace. The head of the gens takes the little one in his arms and blesses it in the same manner in which the Tho'-xe blessed it. This is the gens to whom the sick are brought that they might taste of the sacred food prepared by them and be strengthened. From this healing power the members of the gens like to take the name, Wa-stse'-e-do[n], Good-doctor.

When each of these gentes had blessed the child in turn the Sho'-ḳa brings the mother to the Xo'-ḳa, who places in her hands two little sticks, each of which represents a sacred name of the gens of which the little one has now become a member. The Xo'-ḳa bids her take one of the names represented by the sticks. The mother usually takes for her child the name that is most euphonious and which she thinks has the greater religious significance. The selection of a name for the new member of the gens closes the ceremony.

During the month of April, 1916, Sho[n]'-ge-mo[n]-i[n] was summoned to the house of Wa-xthi'-zhi to name his grandson, whose father is a member of the Ṭsi'-zhu Wa-shta-ge gens. Sho[n]'-ge-mo[n]-i[n] promptly responded to the call but Wa-xthi'-zhi became uncertain as to whether or not the ceremonial naming of a child according to the ancient tribal rites would come under the prohibition of the new religion which he had accepted against the practice of the ancient Osage ceremonies. The full ceremony was omitted, but the old man was asked to offer to the mother the choice of two sacred names: Mo$^n$-zho$^{n\prime}$, Earth (see p. 70, line 45), and Wa-stse'-e-do$^n$, Good-doctor. The mother, a member of the I$^n$-gtho$^{n\prime}$-ga (Puma) gens, chose for her son, a member of the Tsi'-zhu Wa-shta-ge gens, the name Wa-stse'-e-do$^n$. Although the full child-naming ceremony was omitted, Wa-xthi'-zhi gave as fees to Sho$^{n\prime}$-ge-mo$^n$-i$^n$ a horse, a blanket, and other articles of value, amounting to about one hundred and fifty dollars.

The first wi'-gi-e recited in the child-naming ritual given by Sho$^{n\prime}$-ge-mo$^n$-i$^n$ (pp. 60 to 67) is entitled Wa-zho'-i-ga-the Wi'-gi-e, literally, The Taking of Bodies, and freely translated, The Taking of Life Symbols. In this wi'-gi-e eight gods, in the forms of certain cosmic bodies, are adopted as Life Symbols. Sex is attributed to these gods and goddesses and they are addressed as "grandfather" and "grandmother" because of their great age and mysterious character. The wi'-gi-e is an expression by the ancient No$^{n\prime}$-ho$^n$-zhi$^n$-ga of their longing desire for a tribal life that will be as lasting as that of the gods and goddesses who forever travel in the heavens. These gods and goddesses are paired in this wi'-gi-e as follows:

1. Wa-ko$^{n\prime}$-da Ho$^{n\prime}$-ba do$^n$, God of Day (the Sun), grandfather,
2. Wa-ko$^{n\prime}$-da Ho$^n$ do$^n$, Goddess of Night (the Moon), grandmother.

3. Wa'-tse-do-ga, Male Star (the Morning star), grandfather,
4. Wa'-tse Mi-ga, Female Star (the Evening star), grandmother.

5. Wa'-ba-ha, Litter (the Dipper), grandfather,
6. Ta-pa', Deer-head (the Pleiades), grandmother.

7. Ta Tha'-bthi$^n$, Three-deer (the three great stars that form Orion's Belt), grandfather,
8. Mi-ka-k'e u-ki-tha-ç'i$^n$ (Stars-strung-together) (theta and iota in Orion), grandmother.

Xu'-tha-wa-to$^n$-i$^n$ of the Tsi'-zhu Wa-no$^n$ (Elder Tsi'-zhu), a war gens of the Tsi'-zhu great tribal division, was asked for the Child-naming Ritual of his gens, he being referred to as one versed in the rituals of the Tsi'-zhu war gentes, but he declined to give it in full. With some reluctance he consented to recite the first wi'-gi-e of his ritual which corresponds to and bears the same title as the one given by Sho$^{n\prime}$-ge-mo$^n$-i$^n$, a No$^{n\prime}$-ho$^n$-zhi$^n$-ga of the Tsi'-zhu Wa-shta-ge gens. (See pp. 60 to 67.)

19078°—28——6

In the Sho$^{n}$'-ge-mo$^{n}$-i$^{n}$ wi'-gi-e (The Taking of Life Symbols), the people of the Ṭsi'-zhu Wa-shta-ge gens implored four gods and four goddesses of the sky for permission to take from them "bodies" for

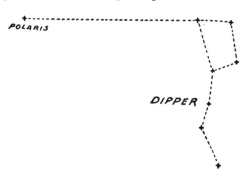

their little ones. The people of the Ṭsi'-zhu Wa-no$^{n}$, in the wi'-gi-e recorded by Xu-thu'-wa-ṭo$^{n}$-i$^{n}$, entreated six gods and four goddesses of the sky for permission to take "bodies" from them for their little ones. The following is the order in which the Ṭsi'-zhu Wa-no$^{n}$ people approached these ten sky deities, the

FIG. 3.—Chart of constellation Wa'-ba-ha (Ursa Major)

order in which they paired them according to sex, and the terms of relationship they used in addressing them:

1. Wa-ḳo$^{n}$'-da Ho$^{n}$'-ba do$^{n}$, the God of Day (the Sun), grandfather,
2. Wa-ḳo$^{n}$'-da Ho$^{n}$ do$^{n}$, the Goddess of Night (the Moon), grandmother.

3. Mi-ḳa'-ḳ'e Ho$^{n}$'-ba$^{n}$ do$^{n}$, the Day-star (Morning star), grandfather,
4. Mi-ḳa'-ḳ'e Ho$^{n}$' do$^{n}$, the Night-star (Evening star), grandmother.

5. Wa'-ba-ha, Litter, the Dipper (Great Bear), (fig. 3), grandfather,
6. Mi-ḳa'-ḳ'e u-ḳi-tha-ç' i$^{n}$, Double-star, grandmother.

7. Ṭa-pa', Deer-head, Pleiades, grandfather,
8. Ṭa Tha'-bthi$^{n}$, Three-deer, the three great stars in Orion's belt (fig. 4), grandmother.

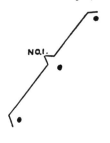

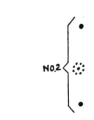

ORION

NO.1. ṬA THA-BTHI$^{n}$, THREE-DEER.
NO.2. MI-ḲA'-Ḳ'E U-ḲI'-THA-TS'I$^{n}$ = STARS-STRUNG-TOGETHER.

FIG. 4.—Chart of Ṭa Tha'-bthi$^{n}$, Three Deer (in Orion)

9. Mi-ḳa'-ḳ'e Zhu-dse, Red-star, the Pole star, grandfather,
10. Sho$^{n}$-ge A-ga-k'e e-go$^{n}$, Dog-star, Sirius, grandfather.

The two wi'-gi-es do not agree as to the sexes of two of the sky deities. In the Ṭsi'-zhu Wa-shta-ge wi'-gi-e, Ṭa-pa' (Pleiades) is addressed as grandmother and in that of the Ṭsi'-zhu Wa-no$^n$ as grandfather. Ṭa-tha'-bthi$^n$, Three-deer, is addressed as grandfather in the Ṭsi'-zhu Wa-shta-ge wi'-gi-e and in that of the Ṭsi'-zhu Wa-no$^n$ as grandmother.

The difference between the two wi'-gi-es in this respect was spoken of to Sho$^{n'}$-ge-mo$^n$-i$^n$ and he said: "We notice such mistakes in the tribal rites but controversy over them is always avoided by the No$^{n'}$-ho$^n$-zhi$^n$-ga. Xu-tha'-wa-ṭo$^n$-i$^n$ recited his wi'-gi-e correctly, and we recite ours as it was handed down to us. The Ṭsi'-zhu Wa-no$^n$, being a war people, mention in their wi'-gi-e their two war gods, the Red-star and the Dog-star; they address both as grandfather. We (the Ṭsi'-zhu Wa-shta-ge) are a peace people, therefore we do not mention those two gods in our child-naming ritual."

FIRST CHILD-NAMING WI'-GI-E OF THE ṬSI'-ZHU WA-NO$^N$ GENS

The following is the first wi'-gi-e in the Child-naming Ritual of the Ṭsi'-zhu Wa-no$^n$, war gens, of the Ṭsi'-zhu great tribal division, as recited by Xu-tha'-wa-ṭo$^n$-i$^n$.

TAKING OF LIFE SYMBOLS

1

1. Verily, at that time and place, it has been said, in this house,
2. The Ṭsi'-zhu, a people who have seven fireplaces, spake to one another,
3. Saying: O, younger brothers,
4. The little ones have nothing of which to make their bodies.
5. Then, at that very time they spake
6. To the Sho'-ḳa Wa-ba-xi (the Chief Messenger),
7. Saying: O, younger brother,
8. The little ones have nothing of which to make their bodies,
9. Take heed and see what can be done.
10. Then, at that very time,
11. The Chief Messenger
12. Hastened to the
13. God of Day (the Sun), who sitteth in the heavens,
14. And returned with him to the people.
15. They spake to the God of Day, saying: O, grandfather,
16. The little ones have nothing of which to make their bodies.
17. Then, at that very time,
18. The God of Day quickly replied: It is well you sent for me.
19. Of all the groups of gods,
20. I am a god by myself.
21. The little ones shall make of me their bodies.

22. Even among the gods,
23. There is not one who has power to see my path.
24. When the little ones make of me their bodies,
25. Even among the gods
26. There is not one who shall be able to see their path, in life's journey.
27. Even among the gods
28. There is not one who has power to cross my path.
29. When the little ones make of me their bodies,
30. Even among the gods
31. There is not one who shall be able to cross their path, in life's journey.
32. Even among the gods
33. What one is there who can stand in my way to prevent my going?
34. When the little ones make of me their bodies,
35. Even among the gods
36. There is not one who shall be able to stand in their way to prevent their going.
37. I am not the only god,
38. Take heed and make further search.

2

39. Verily, at that time and place, it has been said, in this house,
40. The Chief Messenger
41. Hastened to the
42. Goddess of Night (the Moon), who sitteth in the heavens,
43. And returned with her to the people.
44. They spake to her, saying: O, grandmother,
45. The little ones have nothing of which to make their bodies.
46. Then, at that very time,
47. The Goddess of Night replied: It is well you sent for me.
48. Of all the groups of gods,
49. I am a god by myself.
50. Even among the gods
51. There is not one who has power to see my path.
52. When the little ones make of me their bodies,
53. Even among the gods
54. There is not one who shall be able to see their path.
55. Even among the gods
56. There is not one who has power to cross my path.
57. When the little ones make of me their bodies,
58. Even among the gods
59. There is not one who shall be able to cross their path.
60. Even among the gods

61. What one is there who can stand in my way to prevent my
    going?
62. When the little ones make of me their bodies,
63. Even among the gods
64. There is not one who shall be able to stand in their way to
    prevent their going.
65. I am not the only god,
66. Take heed and make further search.

3

67. Verily, at that time and place, it has been said, in this house,
68. The Chief Messenger
69. Hastened to the
70. Star of Day (the Morning Star), who sitteth in the heavens,
71. And returned with him to the people.
72. They spake to the Star of Day, saying: O, grandfather,
73. The little ones have nothing of which to make their bodies.
74. Then, at that very time,
75. The Star of Day replied: It is well you sent for me.
76. The little ones shall make of me their bodies.
77. Of all the groups of gods,
78. I am a god by myself.
79. The little ones shall make of me their bodies.
80. Even among the gods
81. There is not one who has power to see my path.
82. When the little ones make of me their bodies,
83. Even among the gods
84. There is not one who shall be able to see their path.
85. Even among the gods
86. There is not one who has power to cross my path.
87. When the little ones make of me their bodies,
88. Even among the gods
89. There is not one who shall be able to cross their path.
90. Even among the gods
91. What one is there who can stand in my way to prevent my
    going?
92. When the little ones make of me their bodies,
93. Even among the gods
94. There is not one who shall be able to stand in their way to
    prevent their going.
95. I am not the only god,
96. Take heed and make further search.

4

97. The Chief Messenger
98. Hastened to the
99. Star of Night (the Evening Star), who sitteth in the heavens,
100. And returned with her to the people.
101. They spake to her, saying: O, grandmother,
102. The little ones have nothing of which to make their bodies.
103. Then, at that very time,
104. The Star of Night replied: It is well you sent for me.
105. Of all the groups of gods
106. I am a god by myself.
107. When the little ones make of me their bodies,
108. Even among the gods
109. There is not one who shall be able to see their path, in their
     life's journey.
110. Even among the gods
111. There is not one who has power to cross my path.
112. When the little ones make of me their bodies,
113. Even among the gods
114. There is not one who shall be able to cross their path, in their
     life's journey.
115. Even among the gods
116. What one is there who can stand in my way to prevent my
     going?
117. When the little ones make of me their bodies,
118. Even among the gods
119. There is not one who shall be able to stand in their way to prevent
     their going.
120. I am not the only god,
121. Take heed and make further search.

5

122. Verily, at that time and place, it has been said, in this house,
123. The Chief Messenger
124. Hastened to the
125. Litter (Great Bear), who stands in the midst of the heavens,
126. And returned with him to the people.
127. They spake to Litter, saying: O, grandfather,
128. The little ones have nothing of which to make their bodies.
129. Then, at that very time,
130. The Litter replied: It is well you sent for me.
131. Of all the groups of gods,
132. I am a god by myself.
133. The little ones shall make of me their bodies.

134. Even among the gods
135. There is not one who has power to see my path.
136. When the little ones make of me their bodies,
137. Even among the gods
138. There is not one who shall be able to see their path, in their life's journey.
139. Even among the gods
140. There is not one who has power to cross my path.
141. When the little ones make of me their bodies,
142. Even among the gods
143. There is not one who shall be able to cross their path.
144. Even among the gods
145. What one is there who can stand in my way to prevent my going?
146. When the little ones make of me their bodies,
147. Even among the gods
148. There is not one who shall be able to stand in their way to prevent their going.
149. I am not the only god,
150. Take heed and make further search.

6

151. Verily, at that time and place, it has been said, in this house,
152. The Chief Messenger
153. Hastened to
154. Ṭa-pa', Deer-head (Pleiades), who stands in the heavens,
155. And returned with her to the people.
156. They spake to her, saying: O, grandmother,
157. The little ones have nothing of which to make their bodies.
158. .Then, at that very time,
159. Deer-head replied: It is well you sent for me.
160. Of all the groups of gods
161. I am a god by myself.
162. Even among the gods
163. There is not one who has power to see my path.
164. When the little ones make of me their bodies,
165. Even among the gods
166. There is not one who shall be able to see their path.
167. Even among the gods
168. There is not one who has power to cross my path.
169. When the little ones make of me their bodies,
170. Even among the gods
171. There is not one who shall be able to cross their path.
172. Even among the gods
173. What one is there who can stand in my way to prevent my going?

174. When the little ones make of me their bodies,
175. Even among the gods
176. There is not one who shall be able to stand in their way to
     prevent their going.
177. I am not the only god,
178. Take heed and make further search.

7

179. Verily, at that time and place, it has been said, in this house,
180. The Chief Messenger
181. Hastened to
182. Ṭa Tha'-bthiⁿ, Three-deer (Orion's belt), who sitteth in the
     heavens,
183. And returned with him to the people.
184. They spake to him, saying: O, grandfather,
185. The little ones have nothing of which to make their bodies.
186. Then, at that very time,
187. Three-deer replied: Of all the groups of gods,
188. I am a god by myself.
189. The little ones shall make of me their bodies.
190. Even among the gods
191. There is not one who has power to see my path.
192. When the little ones make of me their bodies,
193. Even among the gods
194. There is not one who shall be able to see their path.
195. Even among the gods
196. There is not one who has power to cross my path.
197. When the little ones make of me their bodies,
198. Even among the gods
199. There is not one who shall be able to cross their path.
200. Even among the gods
201. What one is there who can stand in my way to prevent my
     going?
202. When the little ones make of me their bodies,
203. Even among the gods
204. There is not one who shall be able to stand in their way to
     prevent their going.
205. I am not the only god,
206. Take heed and make further search.

8

207. Verily, at that time and place, it has been said, in this house,
208. The Chief Messenger
209. Hastened to
210. Mi-ḳa'-ḳ'e U-ḳi-tha-ç'iⁿ, Double-star (theta and iota in Orion),
     who sitteth in the heavens,

211. And returned with her to the people.
212. They spake to her, saying: O, grandmother,
213. The little ones have nothing of which to make their bodies.
214. Then, at that very time,
215. Double-star replied: It is well you sent for me.
216. Of all the groups of gods
217. I am a god by myself.
218. Even among the gods
219. There is not one who has power to see my path.
220. When the little ones make of me their bodies,
221. Even among the gods
222. There is not one who shall be able to see their path.
223. Even among the gods
224. There is not one who has power to cross my path.
225. When the little ones make of me their bodies,
226. Even among the gods
227. There is not one who shall be able to cross their path.
228. Even among the gods
229. What one is there who can stand in my way to prevent my going?
230. When the little ones make of me their bodies,
231. Even among the gods
232. There is not one who shall be able to stand in their way to prevent their going.
233. I am not the only god,
234. Take heed and make further search.

### 9

235. Verily, at that time and place, it has been said, in this house,
236. The Chief Messenger
237. Hastened to
238. Mi-ḳa'-ḳ'e Zhu-dse, Red-star (Pole star), who sitteth in the heavens,
239. And returned with him to the people.
240. They spake to him, saying: O, grandfather,
241. The little ones have nothing of which to make their bodies.
242. Red-star replied: It is well you sent for me.
243. Of all the groups of gods
244. I am a god by myself.
245. The little ones shall make of me their bodies.
246. Even among the gods
247. There is not one who has power to see my path.
248. When the little ones make of me their bodies,
249. Even among the gods
250. There is not one who shall be able to see their path.

251. Even among the gods
252. There is not one who has power to cross my path.
253. When the little ones make of me their bodies,
254. Even among the gods
255. There is not one who shall be able to cross their path.
256. Even among the gods
257. What one is there who can stand in my way to prevent my going?
258. When the little ones make of me their bodies,
259. Even among the gods
260. There is not one who shall be able to stand in their way to prevent their going.
261. I am not the only god,
262. Take heed and make further search.

### 10

263. Verily, at that time and place, it has been said, in this house,
264. The Chief Messenger
265. Hastened to
266. The side of the heavens
267. Where lay Sho$^{n}$'-ge, the Dog (Sirius), as though suspended in the sky,
268. And returned with him to the people.
269. They spake to him, saying: O grandfather,
270. The little ones have nothing of which to make their bodies.
271. Then, at that very time,
272. The Dog replied: The little ones shall make of me their bodies.
273. Behold my toes, that are gathered closely together,
274. I have not folded them together without a purpose.
275. I have made them to be a sign of old age.
276. When the little ones make of me their bodies,
277. When they become aged men,
278. In their toes, closely folded together,
279. They shall see the sign of old age.
280. Behold the folds of skin on my ankle.
281. I have not put them there without a purpose.
282. I have made them to be a sign of old age.
283. When the little ones make of me their bodies,
284. When they become aged men,
285. In the skin of their ankles, gathered in folds,
286. They shall see the sign of old age.
287. Behold the flaccid muscles of my thigh.
288. They have not become flaccid without a purpose.
289. I have made them to be a sign of old age.
290. When the little ones make of me their bodies,

291. When they become aged men,
292. They shall see in the flaccid muscles of their thighs the sign of old age.

293. Behold my shoulders, that are drawn close together.
294. They are not drawn together without a purpose.
295. I have made them to be a sign of old age.
296. When the little ones make of me their bodies,
297. When they become aged men,
298. They shall see in their shoulders drawn together the sign of old age.

299. Behold the flaccid muscles of my throat.
300. They have not become flaccid without a purpose.
301. I have made them to be a sign of old age.
302. When the little ones make of me their bodies,
303. When they become aged men,
304. They shall see in the flaccid muscles of their throat the sign of old age.

305. Behold the folds of the corners of my mouth.
306. They are not put there without a purpose.
307. I have made them to be a sign of old age.
308. When the little ones make of me their bodies,
309. When they become aged men,
310. They shall see in the corners of their mouth the sign of old age.

311. Behold the folds in the corners of my eyes.
312. They are not put there without a purpose.
313. I have made them to be a sign of old age.
314. When the little ones make of me their bodies,
315. When they become aged men,
316. They shall see in the corners of their eyes the sign of old age.

317. Behold the tip of my nose.
318. It is not placed there without a purpose.
319. I have placed it there for chasing away other gods.
320. I use it for keeping other gods from entering my house.
321. When the little ones make of me their bodies,
322. They shall use it to chase away other gods, as they travel the path of life.

323. Behold the hair on the crown of my head grown thin.
324. It has not grown thin without a purpose.
325. I have made it to be a sign of old age.
326. When the little ones make of me their bodies,
327. When they become aged men,
328. They shall see in their whitened hair
329. The sign of old age, as they travel the path of life.

330. There comes a time
331. When a calm and peaceful day comes upon me,
332. So there shall come upon the little ones a calm and peaceful day,
        as they travel the path of life.

The most important wi'-gi-es (recited parts of a ritual) used in the child-naming rituals are those which relate to the life symbols of a gens, such as the sun, the moon, the morning and evening stars, night and day, deer, elk, bear, etc., which are called wa-zho'-i-ga-the, objects of which bodies are made; and those which relate to the personal, sacred names adopted by a gens to be used by its members for their children. The wi'-gi-e relating to the life symbols are usually recited at the beginning of the ceremony. (See wi'-gi-e of the Ṭsi'-zhu Wa-shta-ge gens, p. 60.) The name wi'-gi-es, called Zha'-zhe Ḳi-ṭoⁿ (Zha'-zhe, name; Ḳi-ṭoⁿ, the taking of), are recited when all the Noⁿ'-hoⁿ-zhiⁿ-ga who were invited to take part in the ceremony of the conferring of a name upon a child have assembled. The life-symbol and the name-taking wi'-gi-es are paraphrases of the mythical stories of the origin of the people of a gens. These mythical origin stories are called Ni'-ḳi-e, freely translated, Sayings of the Ancient Men.

Xu-tha'-wa-ṭoⁿ-iⁿ (pl. 7), of the Ṭsi'-zhu Wa-noⁿ gens of the Ṭsi'-zhu great tribal division, recorded the life symbol wi'-gi-e of his gens (see pp. 75–84) but he declined to give the wi'-gi-e of the sacred gens names. However, these names appear in the Wi'-gi-e Ṭoⁿ-ga, Great Wi'-gi-e (36th Ann. Rept. Bur. Amer. Ethn., pp. 254–269), which are here given in their order, as follows:

1. 'Iⁿ-çka', White Rock. In the origin story of this gens the people came down from the sky, as eagles, to the earth and alighted upon seven trees. Thence:

36. They moved onward over the earth.
32. They came to the top of a rocky cliff,
38. Close to it they came and paused,
40. They spake to one another, saying: White Rock
41. We shall make to be a personal name for ourselves.
            —(36th Ann. Rept. Bur. Amer. Ethn., p. 255.)

2. Moⁿ'-hiⁿ Wa-ḳoⁿ'-da, Mysterious Knife. From the White Rock the people went forth to wander over the earth. They thought to make for themselves a knife for ceremonial use. The Sho'-ḳa went again and again to find the right kind of stone of which to make the knife. He brought home the red flint, the blue flint, the flint streaked with yellow, the black flint and the white flint, one after the other, each of which was rejected as being unfit for use by the little ones as a knife. Finally he brought home a round-handled

XU-THA'-WA-ṬOᴺ-Iᴺ  (ṬSI'-ZHU  WA-NOᴺ  GENS)

STRAPS FOR TYING CAPTIVES

knife which was accepted as suitable for the purpose. Then followed the idea of the people of making a magical war club for ceremonial use. The Sho'-ḳa went in search for the right kind of tree out of which to make it. He brought to the elder brothers the hickory tree, the thick-barked hickory tree, the red oak tree, the red wood tree, the dark wood tree, each of which was rejected as being unsuitable for use as a club. Then he brought to them the willow tree, a tree that never dies. This the elder brothers accepted as eminently fitted for use as a club, and:

268. Their round-handled-knife
269. They quickly took from its resting place,
271. And spake, saying: It is a fear-inspiring knife,
272. Verily, it is a mysterious knife.
273. Mysterious-knife
274. The little ones shall take as their personal name.
276. They lifted the round-handled knife
277. And quickly stabbed with it the body of the willow tree.
278. Then from its wound its life-blood streamed forth.
                    —(36th Ann. Rept. Bur. Amer. Ethn., p. 261.)

3. We'-thiⁿ-ça-gi, Strong-strap. With the mysterious knife the people shaped out of the "tree-that-never-dies" a mystic club. Taking with them the knife and the club they went in search of a buffalo and found one. On coming in sight of the animal they brandished the magic weapon four times in the air and the buffalo fell lifeless to the ground:

511. The skin of the (left) hind leg
512. They cut into a narrow strip,
514. And said: Verily the skin stretches not,
515. We shall make use of it as we travel the path of life.
517. Verily, it is a strong strap,
519. We shall consecrate it for ceremonial use,
520. Therefore Strong-strap
521. We shall make to be our sacred personal name.
                    —(36th Ann. Rept. Bur. Amer. Ethn., pp. 267–268.)

4. We'-thiⁿ-ga-xe, Strap-maker. By the cutting of the first strap out of the skin of the left hind leg of the magically killed buffalo the people of the Ṭsi'-zhu Wa-noⁿ gens created for themselves the office of making the straps (pl. 8) for the warriors for the tying of captives when any are taken. As they continued to cut out the strap they said:

523. Strap-maker, also,
524. We shall make to be our sacred personal name.
                    —(36th Ann. Rept. Bur. Amer. Ethn., p. 268.)

5. We'-thiⁿ-zhiⁿ-ga, Slender-strap. The strap they made out of the skin of the left hind leg of the animal was long and slender, and when they had finished it,

526. They said: Slender-strap, also,
527. We shall make to be our sacred personal name.
549. The skin of the left side
550. They cut in a circle,
552. And seven slender straps
553. They made of it for the Ṭsi-zhu who possesses seven fireplaces,
554. One for each fireplace,
556. And they said: We shall consecrate these straps for ceremonial use.
                    —(36th Ann. Rept. Bur. Amer. Ethn., pp. 268–269.)

These seven straps cut from the left side of the buffalo were to serve as types for similar straps to be ceremonially made for each of the other gentes of the tribe when about to go to war, to use in tying captives.

6. He-thi'-shi-zhe, Curved-horn. As the people saw the horns of the buffalo they exclaimed:

558. Behold the left horn,
559. We shall consecrate it for ceremonial use,
561. Therefore Curved-horn, also,
562. We shall make to be our sacred personal name.
                    —(36th Ann. Rept. Bur. Amer. Ethn., p. 269.)

7. He-thi'-zha-ge, Outspread-horns. The people noticed that the horns of the buffalo stood wide apart and outspread and so they exclaimed:

564. Outspread-horns, also,
565. We shall make to be our sacred personal name.
566. And they said, again: Behold the left horn,
568. We consecrete it for ceremonial use.
                    —(36th Ann. Rept. Bur. Amer. Ethn., p. 269.)

Personal names relating to any of the life symbols of a gens serve to keep the members informed of their place in the gentile and tribal organization. For example: Men who were given such names as Ho-çoⁿ', White-fish; To'-ho-ho-e, Blue-fish; and Ho'-ḳi-e-çi, Wriggling-fish, know that they are members of the Ho'-i-ni-ḳa-shi-ga, Fish-people, gens whose life symbol is the Fish, and that the place of their gens is in the Wa-zha'-zhe, the first of the two subdivisions of the Hoⁿ'-ga great tribal division which symbolizes the earth. The Wa-zha'-zhe subdivision typifies the water portion of the earth.

Those who were given such names as O'-po$^n$-ṭo$^n$-ga, Great-elk; Mo$^{n'}$-thi$^n$-ḳa-ga-xe, Maker-of-the-land; and Mo$^n$-zho$^{n'}$-ga-xe, Maker-of-the-earth, know that they are members of the Elk gens whose life symbol is the male elk (36th Ann. Rept. Bur. Amer. Ethn., p. 165, lines 274 to 354) and that the place of their gens is with the Ho$^{n'}$-ga, the second of the two subdivisions of the Ho$^{n'}$-ga great tribal division which symbolizes the earth. The Ho$^{n'}$-ga subdivision typifies the land portion of the earth.

Men who bear the names Ṗi-çi', Acorn; U-bu'-dse, Profusion; and No$^n$-bu'-dse, Profusion (by the treading of the eagles on the branches of the red oak tree) know that they are members of the Ṭsi'-zhu Wa-shta-ge (Peacemaker) gens, that the life symbol of their gens is the red oak tree, the emblem of fruitfulness, and that

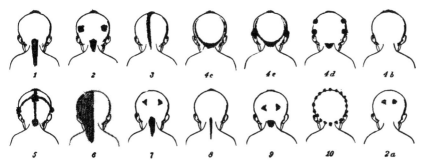

Fig. 5.—Totemic cut of the Omaha boys' hair. No. 1 is typical of the head and tail of the elk. No. 2 symbolizes the head, tail, and horns of the buffalo. No. 2a—the children of this subgens and those of the Ni-ni'-ba-to$^n$ subgens of other gentes have their hair cut alike; the locks on each side of the bared crown indicate the horns of the buffalo. No. 3 represents the line of the buffalo's back as seen against the sky. No. 4b stands for the head of the bear. No. 4c figures the head, tail, and body of small birds. No. 4d, the bare head, represents the shell of the turtle; and the tufts, the head, feet, and tail of the animal. No. 4e pictures the head, wings, and tail of the eagle. No. 5 symbolizes the four points of the compass connected by cross lines; the central tuft points to the zenith. No. 6 represents the shaggy side of the wolf. No. 7 indicates the horns and tail of the buffalo. No. 8 stands for the head and tail of the deer. No. 9 shows the head, tail, and knobs of the growing horn of the buffalo calf. No. 10 symbolizes reptile teeth. The children of this gens sometimes have the hair shaved off so as to represent the hairless body of snakes.

the place of their gens in the tribal organization is with the Ṭsi'-zhu, the second of the two great tribal divisions which symbolizes the sky, including the sun, moon and stars that move therein. (See 36th Ann. Rept. Bur. Amer. Ethn., p. 281, lines 111 to 120.)

## The Gentile Hair Cut of Children

Another custom, akin to the taking of personal gentile names, was originated by the ancient No$^{n'}$-ho$^n$-zhi$^n$-ga, that of the adoption by each of the various gentes of the tribe of a particular style of hair cut for the young children to typify one of the life symbols of the gens. (Fig. 5.) The style adopted by the Ho$^{n'}$-ga gens of the Ho$^{n'}$-ga tribal subdivision for their children was that of cutting nearly all the hair of the head close to the skin, leaving an unbroken fringe along the entire edge. (Fig. 6.) The story of its adoption is best told in the wi'-gi-e of the gens, a paraphrase of which is here given:

### THE WI'-GI-E

The Hon'-ga, a people who possess seven fireplaces, spake to one another,
Saying: O, younger brothers,
The little ones have nothing of which to make their bodies.
Then to the Hon'-ga A-hiu-ton (Winged Hon'-ga) they spake,
Saying: O, elder brother! and stood in mute appeal.
In quick response the Winged Hon'-ga set forth in haste
To a deep and miry marsh,
To the Little Rock who sitteth firmly upon the earth.
Close to the Little Rock he stood and spake,
Saying: O, Grandfather!
Our little ones have nothing of which to make their bodies.
The Little Rock spake in quick response:
I am a person of whom the little ones may well make their bodies.
Thereupon the Winged Hon'-ga hastened back to his brothers to whom he spake,
Saying: O, younger brothers, a Little Rock sits yonder.
Then, with heads bent thitherward,
The younger brothers set forth in haste
To the Little Rock who sitteth firmly upon the earth, in the marsh.
Around him they gathered, close to him they stood as they spake
To the Little Rock sitting with algae floating about him, like locks of hair blowing in the wind. (Fig. 6.)
O, Grandfather! they said to him,
Our little ones have nothing of which to make their bodies.
The Little Rock made reply:
I am a person who is difficult to be overcome by death.
When your little ones make of me their bodies,
They shall always be difficult to overcome by death.
Behold the locks that float about the edges of my head.
When the little ones reach old age,
Their locks shall float about the edges of their heads.
The little ones shall always live to see their locks grown scant with age.
The younger brothers spake, saying: Close to the God of Day who sitteth in the heavens,
We shall place the Little Rock.[3]
When our little ones make of the Little Rock their bodies,
Of the God of Day also
Our little ones shall make their bodies.
The four days,
The four great divisions of the days (the four stages of life),
The little ones shall always reach and enter,
They shall always live to see old age.

This style of hair cut is called kon'-ha-u-thi-stse (kon'-ha, along the edge; u-thi-stse, a line left uncut), meaning an unbroken line of hair left uncut along the entire edge.

---

[3] The Little Rock of the marsh is spoken of as the Gentle Rock because it is a special life symbol of the people for whom there must always be peace and happiness. As a memorial of the finding of the Little Rock of the marsh the members of the Hon'-ga gens in cutting the hair of their little ones leave a fringe around the entire edge.

At a festival being held at the Indian village near the town of Pawhuska, old Saucy-calf called the writer's attention to a little boy who was playing hide-and-seek with other youngsters and said: "Look at the way his hair is cut (fig. 6); that is the Ho$^n$-ga A-hiu-ṭo$^n$ hair cut.  That style is called ḳo$^n$-ha-u-thi-stse.  Xu-tha'-pa, Eagle-head, better known as Ben Wheeler, a young man who sat near us, looked up and said: "That's my little boy; I cut my children's hair like that."  Saucy-calf then explained that the act of the parents in cutting the hair of the child in that pre-scribed fashion was an implied petition to Wa-ḳo$^n$-da to permit the little one to live to see old age without obstruction of any kind.

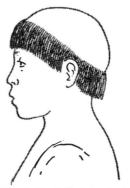

Fig. 6.—Symbolic hair cut of the Ho$^n$-ga gens

### Hair Cut of the Ṭsi'-zhu Wa-shta-ge Gens

The people of the Ṭsi'-zhu Wa-shta-ge (Peacemaker) gens, who occupied the most important and honored place in the great tribal division represent-ing the sky and all that it contains, adopted the ḳo$^n$-ha-u-thi-stse style of hair cut for their little ones, which varied slightly from the styles used by the Ho$^n$-ga.  In the Ṭsi'-zhu Wa-shta-ge symbolic hair cut the line of hair left uncut along the edge is divided into little locks to typify the petals of the cone-flower, which is the sacred flower of the gens (fig. 7).

Sho$^n$-g̣e-mo$^n$-i$^n$, in speaking of the symbolic hair cut of the children of his gens, the Ṭsi'-zhu Wa-shta-ge, told the fol-lowing mythical story of its origin:

In the beginning the Ṭsi'-zhu people came down, in the form of

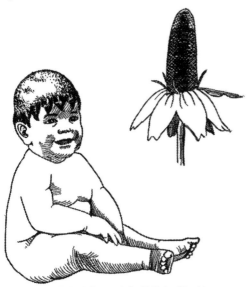

Fig. 7.—Symbolic hair cut of the Ṭsi'-zhu Wa-shta-ge gens

eagles, from the upper to the lower world.  As they came in sight of the earth they beheld a large red oak tree.  They soared down to it and alighted upon its topmost branches.  The shock of their weight

19078°—28——7

sent to the ground a shower of acorns which scattered around the foot of the tree, whereupon they said: We shall make of this tree our life symbol; our little ones shall multiply in numbers like the seeds of the oak that fall to the earth in countless numbers. The eagles that crowded upon the top branches of the oak became a people whose thoughts dwelt upon war, but two of the eagles found no resting place on the outspreading branches of the great oak and were obliged to drop to the earth. One alighted on a larger elder tree and his people became known as Ba'-po, people of the elder tree. The other eagle alighted upon the ground in the midst of a patch of little yellow flowers which his people made to be their life symbol and their emblem of peace. The people cut the hair of their children in such fashion as to make their heads resemble the little yellow flower, the emblem of peace. (Fig. 7.) This yellow flower is called Ba-shta', Hair-cut. It is the *Ratibida columnaris*.

A paraphrase of the wi'-gi-e of the Xu-tha'-zhu-dse, Red Eagle, gens in which the "little yellow flower," the emblem of peace, is mentioned, is here given.

### PARAPHRASE OF THE WI'-GI-E OF THE RED EAGLE GENS

#### PEACEFUL DAY IS MY NAME

Verily, my abode is in the days that are calm and peaceful.
When the little ones make of me their bodies (their life),
They shall become a people of the days that are ever serene.
From each of the great gods,
I verily remove all traces of anger and violence.
When the little ones make of me their bodies,
They shall have power to remove from the gods
All anger and the desire for destruction.
From the god of the lower world (the earth);
From the god of light who standeth in the midst of heaven;
From the god of the upper world (the over-arching sky),
I have power to remove all anger and violence.
When the little ones make of me their bodies,
They also shall have power to remove from the gods all anger.
When the little ones of the Wa-zha'-zhe (subdivision),
And those of the Hon'-ga (subdivision),
Make of me their bodies,
They shall have power to remove from all lands,
All anger, hatred and violence.

#### NO-ANGER IS ALSO MY NAME

I am a person of whom the little ones may well make their bodies.
My abode is in the midst of the earth's warm, quivering air.
When the little ones make of me their bodies,
They shall become a people of the earth's quivering air.
Verily, in the days that are gentle and peaceful,
I make my abode.
When the little ones make of me their bodies,

They shall become a people of the days that are gentle and peaceful.
Of a little yellow flower
I have made my body.
The little Ba-shta', that stands amidst the winds,
I have made to be my body.
When the little ones make of the Ba-shta' their bodies,
They shall ever live together without anger, without hatred.

Ṭon-won-i'-hi-zhin-ga, Little Ṭon-won-i'-hi, in speaking to Miss Fletcher in 1898 of the Osage gentile system, said that there are five subgentes in the Ṭsi'-zhu Wa-shta-ge gens, namely:

1. Ṭsi'-u-çkon-çka, House in the center, meaning the Sanctuary in the keeping of this gens which, figuratively, stands in the center of the earth.

2. Ba'-po, Elder, or, People of the elder trees.

3. Mon'-ça-hi, Arrow-tree, or, People of the arrow tree.

4. Zhon-çon', White-tree (Sycamore), or, People of the white tree.

5. Sho'-ḳa, Messengers, or, People from whom a ceremonial messenger is chosen for the gens. Sometimes this gens is called Ṭsi'-u-thu-ha-ge, Last group of houses.

It is from the people of the Ṭsi'-u-çkon-çka that the hereditary chief of the Ṭsi'-zhu great tribal division must always be chosen. The Ba'-po subgens has the office of making the stem for the ceremonial peace pipe of the Ṭsi'-zhu Wa-shta-ge. The stem must always be made of the Ba'-po, the elder tree. The people of the Arrow-tree and the Sycamore gentes have lost the significance of their life symbols. All of these five subgentes use the cone-flower symbolic hair cut.

There is something pathetic in the passing away of these ancient rites and customs which the Osage Indians had treasured from the earliest times of their tribal existence. Joe Shon'-ge-mon-in, like his father, had respect and reverence for the religious thoughts of his ancestors which they had expressed in symbols and rituals with ceremonial forms and handed down. Joe had two little daughters (pl. 9, *a*) upon whom he bestowed a large share of his affections. He not only gave to each of them a sacred name of his gens, but, from year to year, as they approached womanhood, he cut their hair to typify the sacred flower of peace and happiness, an act which implied a supplication to Wa-ḳon'-da to bless each little one with a long and fruitful life. At the last symbolic hair cut the children had reached school age and they willingly went to the house of learning. The white children with whom they mingled hooted and jeered at them for their strange hair cut and made them unhappy. When they came home they told their father of their unkind treatment at the school. The fond father quietly took a pair of shears and cut away from each little head the symbolic locks.

Little Ṭoⁿ-woⁿ'-i-hi also stated that there was another style of symbolic hair cut called çiⁿ'-dse-a-gthe, tails worn on the head, which belongs to the Ṭsi'-zhu Wa-noⁿ, the principal war gens of the Ṭsi'-zhu great tribal division, which he described as: All of the hair of the head cut close but leaving uncut a row of three locks, equidistant apart, beginning at the crown of the head and ending near the edge of the hair at the back of the head. (Fig. 8.) This style of hair cut symbolizes all animals of the dog family, including the gray wolf, the coyote, and the domestic dog. It also symbolizes a star called Shoⁿ'-ge a-ga-ḳ'e e-goⁿ, Dog that lies suspended in the sky (Sirius).

The Dog Star is mentioned in the Child-naming Wi'-gi-e of the Ṭsi'-zhu Wa-noⁿ gens, bearing the title Wa-zho'-i-ga-the Wi'-gi-e, Taking of Life Symbols, given by Xu-tha'-wa-ṭoⁿ-in. (See p. 82, sec. 10 of the wi'-gi-e.)

Little Ṭoⁿ-woⁿ'-i-hi said that the Wa-ça-be-ṭoⁿ, Black Bear gens of the Hoⁿ'-ga great division, had a similar style of hair cut as that

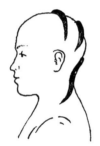

of the Ṭsi'-zhu Wa-noⁿ gens. Wa-xthi'-zhi said that the Puma gens also had the same style of hair cut.

The symbolic hair cut of the Ni'-ḳa Wa-ḳoⁿ-da-gi gens, Men of Mystery, is: hair of the head all cut close excepting a lock left uncut on the crown of the head (pl. 10, *a*) and a lock at the back of the head near the edge, which does not show in the picture. The life symbol of this gens is the hawk and the hair cut represents this raptorial bird which was adopted by all of the gentes of both the Hoⁿ'-ga and the Ṭsi'-zhu great tribal divisions as an emblem of courage for their warriors.

FIG. 8.—Hair cut of the Ṭsi'-zhu Wa-noⁿ and the Wa-ça'-be (Black Bear) gentes

The name of the boy whose picture shows the hair cut of his gens is Gthe-doⁿ'-çka, White-hawk (Gthe-doⁿ, hawk; çka, white). It is the name that belongs to the second son in a family of this gens. His father's name is Noⁿ'-ḳa-ṭo-ho, Blue-back (Noⁿ'-ḳa, back; ṭo-ho, blue), a name referring to the blue-backed hawk. White-hawk's mother is Xi-tha'-doⁿ-wiⁿ, Good-eagle-woman, daughter of Shoⁿ'-ge-moⁿ-iⁿ of the Ṭsi'-zhu Wa-shta-ge gens.

The style of symbolic hair cut adopted by the Tho'-xe gens is of the Çiⁿ'-dse A-gthe class and is described as, hair on entire head cut close excepting a little tuft left uncut just over the middle of the forehead, and a fringe running across the crown of the head from one ear to the other as shown in the picture (pl. 10, *b*); two tufts, one on either side of the head back of the fringe, and a tuft just above the nape of the neck, which do not show in the picture. This style of cut represents the buffalo bull, the principal life symbol of the gens.

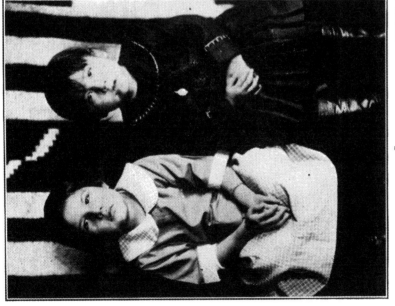

FOUR OSAGE CHILDREN

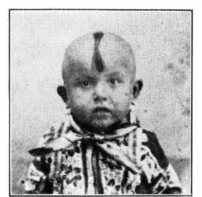

*a*

*b*

CHILD'S HAIR CUT OF THE THO-XE AND NI'-ḲA
WA-ḲOⁿ-DA-GI GENTES

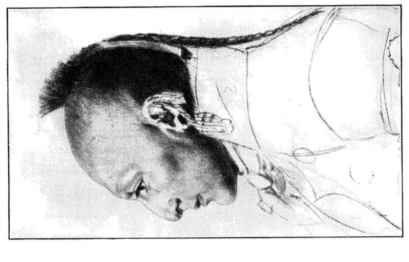

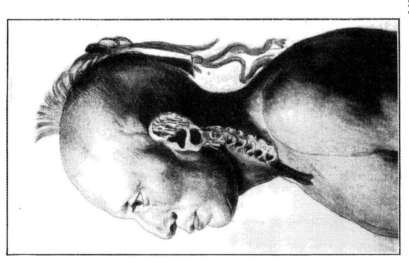

MEN, SHOWING HAIR CUT OF ADULT OSAGES

BONE EAR PERFORATORS AND EXPANDERS

The two gentes, the Ni'-ḳa Wa-ḳo$^n$-da-gi and the Tho'-xe, are closely related, being joint custodians of the rites pertaining to war. (See 36th Ann. Rept. Bur. Amer. Ethn., pp. 64–65.)  The symbolic hawks, each of which formed the central figure in the ceremonies of the war rites, were regarded as being in the special care of the Ni'-ḳa Wa-ḳo$^n$-da-gi, while all of the thirteen o-do$^{n\prime}$, military honors, to be won by each warrior of the tribe in order to secure ceremonial rank, belonged to the Tho'-xe.  The war honor must be won in a fight by a war party carrying a hawk, the tribal emblem of courage.  The places of these two gentes are on the Ṭsi'-zhu side of the two great tribal divisions, but they are not of the seven fireplaces of that great division.

In the Ṭsi'-zhu Wi'-gi-e recited by Mo$^n$-zho$^n$-a'-ḳi-da (36th Ann. Rept. Bur. Amer. Ethn., pp. 277–285), relating to the mythical story of the descent of the people from the upper to the lower world, these two gentes are mentioned.  A paraphrase of this part is here given:

## PARAPHRASE OF WI'-GI-E RELATING TO THE NI'-ḲA WA-ḲO$^N$-DA-GI AND THE THO'-XE GENTES

The Messenger
Then hastened down
To the fourth division of the heavens,
Close to it he stood and paused
And lo, Ni'-ḳa Wa-ḳo$^n$-da-gi, Man of Mysteries,
Appeared before him.
The Messenger turned and said to his followers: Here stands a man,
Verily, one who inspires fear.
I truly believe his name is, Fear-inspiring.
The Man of Mysteries spake, saying: I am a person of whom your little ones may
    well make their bodies.
When your little ones make of me their bodies,
They shall be free from all causes of death.
They shall take the name Little-hawk,
To use as their personal name,
Then shall they be able to live to see old age.
Woman-hawk
Is also a name that I have.
Your little ones shall use it as their personal name,
Then shall they be able to live to old age.

The Messenger quickly passed on
To Tho'-xe, who appeared in the form of a buffalo bull.
Close to him the Messenger stood and spake,
Saying: O, Grandfather!
Then, turning toward his followers, he said: Here stands a man,
Verily, a man who inspires fear.
Then Tho'-xe spake, saying: I am a person of whom your little ones may well
    make their bodies.
Thereupon he threw himself upon the earth,
And the blazing star, a purple flower,
Sprang up from the soil and stood, pleasing to the sense of sight.
And Tho'-xe spake, saying: This plant shall be medicine for your little ones,

It shall make their limbs to lengthen in growth,
And they shall be able to live to see old age.
Again Tho'-xe threw himself upon the earth
And the poppy mallow
Sprang from the soil and stood, beautiful, in its red blossoms.
Then Tho'-xe spake, saying: Of this plant also,
Your little ones shall make their bodies,
They shall use it as medicine
And it shall make their limbs to lengthen in growth.
It is astringent to the taste,
Therefore you shall name your little ones Astringent.
When the little ones make of this plant their bodies,
They shall be able to live to see old age.

At the time this work was begun the greater portion of the Osage people had practically ceased to observe the ancient custom of cutting the hair of their children in the prescribed symbolic fashion, and those who continued the practice were reluctant to speak of it on account of its sacred and mysterious character. For this reason it was not possible to make an exhaustive study of the hair cut of the various gentes of the tribe. In the days when the rite was generally and strictly observed the girl, when she had attained the age of ten, was permitted to let her hair grow long, and the boy was allowed to wear his hair in the same style as that of all the grown men; that is, all the hair of the head cut close excepting a crest beginning at the middle of the crown and terminating with a long braided tail called he-ga'-xa, horn, that hangs down the back of the head and on the shoulder. (Pl. 11.) The braided tail is called "a'-çku" by the Omaha and the Ponca Indians.

The Ponca and the Omaha, who were at one time a part of the Osage tribe, also had the same tribal custom of ceremonially cutting the hair of the children. The ritual used in the ceremony is a supplication to Wa-ko$^{n}$'-da to favor the child with a long and fruitful life.

In the course of her ethnological work among the Omahas in the years 1881–83, Miss Alice C. Fletcher undertook to gather information about the symbolic hair cut of the children of that tribe. At first she made slow progress because the Indians were unwilling to speak of matters that form a part of the tribal rites. One day, at the house of Xo'-ga, the members of the family and some visitors were speaking of Miss Fletcher's difficulty in gathering information about the hair cut, when the old man caught his little boy and, holding him fast between his knees, proceeded to cut his hair. The little fellow fought manfully but in a short time he stood with his head closely sheared, with locks left uncut here and there. The father swung the boy to his back and as he started to go he said: "That white woman is my friend and I am going to help her." He carried the child to Miss Fletcher and as he put him down before her he said, "That's the hair cut of our gens. (See fig. 5, No. 2.)

It is the picture of a bison; you can't see it [the bison] but we can. You may make a sketch of it and write about it as much as you like." The lady looked for a moment in silence at the locks and the little shorn head, then, with a hearty laugh and a handclap, she snatched up paper and pencil to make a sketch of the locks and the shorn head, to the delight of all the Indians present. Thereafter she had no trouble in getting information about the hair cut of all the gentes.

## Fondness of Personal Adornment

Like their relatives, the Omaha and the Ponca, the Osage people have a fondness for personal adornment. Much paint is used in decorating the face and body. Most of the lines and figures drawn upon the face and body are symbolic, as, for instance, a woman paints the parting of her hair almost daily. The red line symbolizes the path of the sun which forever passes over the earth and gives to it vitality. It is a sign of supplication for the continuity of life by procreation. Or, a man of the Life-giver gens paints his face all yellow with a narrow black line running diagonally across his face from one corner of his forehead down to the lower jaw on the opposite side. This is the life sign ceremonially put upon a captive when the word is passed by the Life-giver gens that the captive shall be permitted to live. A downy feather worn upright on the crown of the head by a man symbolizes the sun which brings life to the earth in material form. The white shell gorget which a man wears as a pendant on his necklace is also a symbol of the life-giving sun.

## Ear Perforating

Down to recent times the Osage men have been sacrificing the shapeliness of their external ears to the gratification of their fondness for adornment. In ordinary times, and particularly on festal days, the Osage men weighted their ears with strings of wampum or other ornaments made of bone or shells and silver earbobs which were introduced by traders. The weight of the earrings and the crowding of the holes in the ears with the rings enlarge the perforations to an extraordinary size. (Pl. 11.) The holes, which are bored along the rim of the pinna, were made by the same men who performed the ceremony connected with the perforating. These men provided themselves with perforating instruments made of sharpened bone, wooden expanders, and little blocks of wood against which the ear is pressed when performing the operation. (Pl. 12.) For a long time Wa'-thu-xa-ge and Tsi'-zhu-zhi$^n$-ga held this office. The former died a few years ago. Both of these men were members of the Peace gens of the Tsi'-zhu great tribal division. An Osage was asked why the ears of the children were bored and he replied that the children whose ears were bored were apt to be better behaved than those whose ears were not perforated.

## ḲI'-NO$^n$ WI'-GI-E

### 1

1. He'-dsi xtsi a', a bi$^n$ da, ṭsi ga,
2. Da'-do$^n$ ḳi-no$^n$ gi-the mo$^n$-thi$^n$ ṭa ba do$^n$ a', a bi$^n$ da, ṭsi ga,
3. Wa'-ḳo$^n$-da ṭse-ga xtsi e-tho$^n$-be hi no$^n$ no$^n$ a', a bi$^n$ da, ṭsi ga,
4. Ga' ḳi-no$^n$ gi-the mo$^n$-thi$^n$ bi a', a bi$^n$ da, ṭsi ga,
5. Ḳi'-no$^n$ gi-the mo$^n$-thi$^n$ bi do$^n$ shki a', a bi$^n$ da, ṭsi ga,
6. Ṭs'e wa-ṭse-xi ḳi-the mo$^n$-thi$^n$ ṭa bi a, wi-ço$^n$-ga, e-ḳi-a bi a, a bi$^n$ da, ṭsi ga.

### 2

7. He'-dsi xtsi a', a bi$^n$ da, ṭsi ga,
8. Da'-do$^n$ wa-gthe gi-the mo$^n$-thi$^n$ ṭa ba do$^n$ a', a bi$^n$ da, ṭsi ga,
9. Wa-ḳo$^n$-da ṭse-ga xtsi e-tho$^n$-be hi no$^n$ bi a, a bi$^n$ da, ṭsi ga,
10. Thi' u-ba-he i-sdu-ge dsi a', a bi$^n$ da, ṭsi ga,
11. Wa'-gthe ṭo$^n$ e-go$^n$ ṭo$^n$ no$^n$ a', a bi$^n$ da, ṭsi ga,
12. Ga'wa-gthe gi-the mo$^n$-thi$^n$ bi a', a bi$^n$ da, ṭsi ga,
13. Ṭs'e' wa-ṭse-xi ḳi-the mo$^n$-thi$^n$ ṭa bi$^n$ da', a bi$^n$ da, ṭsi ga,
14. Zhi$^{n'}$-ga wa-gthe gi-the mo$^n$-thi$^n$ bi do$^n$ a', a bi$^n$ da, ṭsi ga,
15. Wa'-gthe gi-xi-tha zhi ḳi-the mo$^n$-thi$^n$ ṭa bi$^n$ da', a bi$^n$ da, ṭsi ga.

### 3

16. He'-dsi xtsi a', a bi$^n$ da, ṭsi ga,
17. Da'-do$^n$ we-çda-the mo$^n$-thi$^n$ ṭa ba do$^n$ a', a bi$^n$ da, ṭsi ga,
18. Wa'-dsu-ṭa shi$^n$-ṭo-zhi$^n$-ga kshe no$^n$ a', a bi$^n$ da, ṭsi ga,
19. No$^{n'}$-ḳa o$^n$-he i-sdu-ge dsi a', a bi$^n$ da, ṭsi ga,
20. Ga' we-çda-the mo$^n$-thi$^n$ ṭa bi a', wi-ço$^n$-ga, e-ḳi-a bi a, a bi$^n$ da, ṭsi ga,
21. We-çda-the mo$^n$-thi$^n$ bi do$^n$ shki a, a bi$^n$ da, ṭsi ga,
22. U'-no$^n$ a bi i-the ḳi-the mo$^n$-thi$^n$ ṭa bi a', wi-ço$^n$-ga, e-ḳi-a bi a, a bi$^n$ da, ṭsi ga.
23. He'-dsi xtsi a', a bi$^n$ da, ṭsi ga,
24. Da'-do$^n$ wa-no$^n$-p'i$^n$ ṭo$^n$ kshi-the mo$^n$-thi$^n$ ṭa ba do$^n$ a', a bi$^n$ da, ṭsi ga,
25. Ṭsiu'-ge thi$^n$-kshe no$^n$ a', a bi$^n$ da, ṭsi ga,
26. Ga' wa-no$^n$-p'i$^n$ ṭo$^n$ kshi-the mo$^n$-thi$^n$ ṭa bi a',wi-ço$^n$-ga, e'-ḳi-a bi a', bi$^n$ da, ṭsi ga,
27. Wa'-ḳo$^n$-da Ho$^n$-ba do$^n$ thi$^n$-kshe a', a bi$^n$ da, ṭsi ga,
28. I'-tha-thu-çe ṭse a', a bi$^n$ da, ṭsi ga,
29. No$^{n'}$-p'i$^n$ ṭo$^n$ kshi-the ṭa bi a', wi-ço$^n$-ga, e-ḳi-a bi a,' a bi$^n$ da, ṭsi ga,
30. U'-no$^n$ tha bi do$^n$ shki a', a bi$^n$ da, ṭsi ga,
31. U'-no$^n$ a bi i-the ḳi-the mo$^n$-thi$^n$ ṭa bi a', wi-ço$^n$-ga, e'-ḳi-a, bi a, a bi$^n$ da, ṭsi ga.

## ṬSI TA'-ṖE WA-THOⁿ

Wa-ṭse wiⁿ u-tha-ḳi-oⁿ-stse,
Wa-ṭse wiⁿ u-tha-ḳi-oⁿ-stse he,
Wa-ṭse wiⁿ u-tha-ḳi-oⁿ-stse,
E the he wi-ta doⁿ u-tha-ḳi-oⁿ-stse he,
Wa-ṭse wiⁿ u-tha-ḳi-oⁿ-stse.

### WI'-GI-E

#### 1

1. Da'-doⁿ wa-çi-thi-çe moⁿ-thiⁿ ṭa ba doⁿ a', a biⁿ da, ṭsi ga,
2. Wa'-ṭse do-ga thiⁿ-kshe a', a biⁿ da, ṭsi ga,
3. Ga' wa-çi-thu-çe moⁿ-thiⁿ bi a', a biⁿ da, ṭsi ga,
4. Wa'-çi-thu-çe moⁿ-thiⁿ bi doⁿ a', a biⁿ da, ṭsi ga,
5. U'-noⁿ a bi i-the ḳi-the moⁿ-thiⁿ ṭa bi a', wi-çoⁿ-ge, e'-ḳi-a bi a, a biⁿ da, ṭsi ga.

#### 2

6. Da'-doⁿ wa-çi-thu-çe moⁿ-thiⁿ ṭa ba doⁿ a', a biⁿ da, ṭsi ga,
7. Wa'-ṭse mi-ga thiⁿ-kshe a', a biⁿ da, ṭsi ga,
8. Ga' wa-çi-thu-çe moⁿ-thiⁿ bi a', a biⁿ da ṭsi ga,
9. Wa'-çi-thu-çe moⁿ-thiⁿ bi doⁿ a', a biⁿ da, ṭsi ga,
10. U'-noⁿ a bi i-the ḳi-the moⁿ-thiⁿ ṭa bi a', wi-çoⁿ-ga, e-ḳi-a bi a', a biⁿ da, ṭsi ga.

#### 3

11. Da'-doⁿ wa-çi-thu-çe moⁿ-thiⁿ ṭa ba doⁿ a', a biⁿ da, ṭsi ga,
12. Wa'-tse do-ga thiⁿ-kshe a', a biⁿ da, ṭsi ga,
13. Ga' wa-çi-thu-çe moⁿ-thiⁿ bi a', a biⁿ da, ṭsi ga,
14. Wa'-çi-thu-çe moⁿ-thiⁿ bi doⁿ a', a biⁿ da, ṭsi ga,
15. U'-noⁿ a bi i-the ḳi-the moⁿ-thiⁿ ṭa bi a', wi-coⁿ-ga, e-ḳi-a, bi a, a biⁿ da, ṭsi ga.

#### 4

16. Da'-doⁿ wa-çi-thu-çe moⁿ-thiⁿ ṭa ba doⁿ a', a biⁿ da, ṭsi ga,
17. Wa'-ṭse mi-ga thiⁿ-kshe a', a biⁿ da, ṭsi ga,
18. Ga' wa-çi-thu-çe moⁿ-thiⁿ bi a', a biⁿ da, ṭsi ga,
19. Wa'-çi-thu-çe moⁿ-thiⁿ bi doⁿ a', a biⁿ da, ṭsi ga,
20. U'-noⁿ a bi i-the ḳi-the moⁿ-thiⁿ ṭa bi a', wi-çoⁿ-ga, e'-ḳi-a, bi a, a biⁿ da, ṭsi ga.

## ZHA'-ZHE ḲI-ṬOⁿ WI'-GI-E

#### 1

1. He'-dsi xtsi a', a biⁿ da, ṭsi ga,
2. Hoⁿ-ga u-dse-the ṗe-thoⁿ-ba ni-ḳa-shi-ga ba doⁿ a', a biⁿ da, ṭsi ga,
3. Ha'! wi-çoⁿ-ga, e-ḳi-a bi a', a biⁿ da, ṭsi ga,

4. Zhi$^n$'-ga ni-ḳa-shi-ga bi a', wi-ço$^n$-ga, e'-ḳi-a bi a', a bi$^n$ da,
   ṭsi ga,

5. Zhi$^n$'-ga hiu-dse ṭa ni-ḳa-shi-ga ba tho$^n$-ta zhi a', wi-ço$^n$-ga,
   e'-ḳi-a bi a', a bi$^n$ da, ṭsi ga,

6. He'-dsi xtsi a', a bi$^n$ da, ṭsi ga,

7. Wa'-ḳo$^n$-da gtho$^n$-the do-ba', a bi$^n$ da, ṭsi ga,

8. Gi'-ḳa ṭse a, wi-ço$^n$-ga, e-ḳi-a, bi a', a bi$^n$ da, ṭsi ga,

9. He'-dsi xtsi a', a bi$^n$ da, ṭsi ga,

10. Wa'-ḳo$^n$-da ho$^n$-ba do$^n$ thi$^n$-kshe a', a bi$^n$ da, ṭsi ga,

11. Ha'! wi-ṭsi-go-e', e-gi-a bi a', a bi$^n$ da, ṭsi ga,

12. Zhi$^n$'-ga ni-ḳa-shi-ga bi a', wi-ṭsi-go-e', e-gi-a bi a', a bi$^n$ da,
    ṭsi ga,

13. Zhi$^n$'-ga hiu-dse ṭa ni-ḳa-shi-ga ba tho$^n$-ṭa zhi a', wi-ṭsi-go-e',
    e-gi-a, bi a', a bi$^n$ da, ṭsi ga,

14. He'-dsi xtsi a', a bi$^n$ da, ṭsi ga,

15. Zhi$^n$'-ga hiu-dse ṭa ni-ḳa-shi-ga ṭa bi e'-she do$^n$ a', a bi$^n$ da,
    ṭsi ga,

16. Zhi$^n$'-ga hiu-dse ṭa ni-ḳa-shi-ga bi do$^n$ a', a bi$^n$ da, ṭsi ga,

17. U'-no$^n$ a bi i-the ḳi-the mo$^n$-thi$^n$ ṭa bi a', zhi$^n$-ga', a bi$^n$ da,
    ṭsi ga.

2

18. He'-dsi xtsi a', a bi$^n$ da, ṭsi ga,

19. Zhi$^n$'-ga hiu-dse ṭa ni-ḳa-shi-ga ṭa bi e'-she do$^n$ a', a bi$^n$ da,
    ṭsi ga,

20. Zhi$^n$'-ga zha-zhe ḳi-ṭo$^n$ ṭse thi$^n$-ge a-tha, wi-ṭsi-go-e', e-gi-a,
    bi a', a bi$^n$ da, ṭsi ga,

21. Ha'! zhi$^n$-ga e'-ṭsi-the a', a bi$^n$ da, ṭsi ga,

22. Zhi$^n$'-ga zha-zhe ḳi-ṭo$^n$ ṭse thi$^n$-ge e-she do$^n$ a', a bi$^n$ da, ṭsi ga,

23. Zhi$^n$'-ga zha-zhe ḳi-ṭo$^n$ ba-tho$^n$ ṭa-mi kshe i$^n$ da', a bi$^n$ da,
    ṭsi ga,

24. Mi'-wa-ga-xe a', a bi$^n$ da, ṭsi ga,

25. Zha'-zhe ḳi-ṭo$^n$ mo$^n$-thi$^n$ ṭa bi a', zhi$^n$-ga, e'-ṭsi-the a', a bi$^n$
    da, ṭsi ga,

26. Zha'-zhe ḳi-ṭo$^n$ mo$^n$-thi$^n$ bi do$^n$ shki a', a bi$^n$ da, ṭsi ga,

27. U'-no$^n$ a bi i-the ḳi-the mo$^n$-thi$^n$ ṭa bi$^n$ da', a bi$^n$ da, ṭsi ga.

3

28. Da'-do$^n$ zha-zhe ḳi-ṭo$^n$ ga no$^n$ shki a, hi$^n$ a', a bi$^n$ da, ṭsi ga,

29. Mo$^n$'-çi-ṭse-xi shki a', a bi$^n$ da, ṭsi ga,

30. Zha'-zhe ḳi-ṭo$^n$ mo$^n$-thi$^n$ ṭa bi a', zhi$^n$-ga', a bi$^n$ da, ṭsi ga,

31. Zha'-zhe ḳi-ṭo$^n$ mo$^n$-thi$^n$ bi do$^n$ shki a', a bi$^n$ da, ṭsi ga,

32. U'-no$^n$ a bi i-the ḳi-the mo$^n$-thi$^n$ ṭa bi a', zhi$^n$-ga, a bi$^n$ da,
    ṭsi ga.

4

33. Da'-do$^n$ zha-zhe ḳi-ṭo$^n$ ga no$^n$ shki a, hi$^n$ a', a bi$^n$ da, ṭsi ga,
34. I'-e-çka-wa-the shki a', a bi$^n$ da, ṭsi ga,
35. Zha'-zhe ḳi-ṭo$^n$ mo$^n$-thi$^n$ ṭa bi a', zhi$^n$-ga', a bi$^n$ da, ṭsi ga,
36. Zha'-zhe ḳi-ṭo$^n$ mo$^n$-thi$^n$ bi do$^n$ shki a', a bi$^n$ da, ṭsi ga,
37. U'-no$^n$ a bi i-the ḳi-the mo$^n$-thi$^n$ ṭa bi$^n$ da', a bi$^n$ da, ṭsi ga.

5

38. Da'-do$^n$ zha-zhe ḳi-ṭo$^n$ ga no$^n$ shki a, hi$^n$ a', a bi$^n$ da, ṭsi ga,
39. Mo$^n$'-zho$^n$-op-she-wi$^n$ a', a bi$^n$ da, ṭsi ga,
40. Zha'-zhe ḳi-ṭo$^n$ mo$^n$-thi$^n$ ṭa bi a', zhi$^n$-ga', a bi$^n$ da, ṭsi ga,
41. Zha'-zhe ḳi-ṭo$^n$ mo$^n$-thi$^n$ bi do$^n$ shki a', a bi$^n$ da, ṭsi ga,
42. U'-no$^n$ a bi i-the ḳi-the mo$^n$-thi$^n$ ṭa bi$^n$ da', a bi$^n$ da, ṭsi ga.

6

43. Da'-do$^n$ zha-zhe ḳi-ṭo$^n$ ga no$^n$ shki a, hi$^n$ a', a bi$^n$ da, ṭsi ga,
44. Mo$^n$'-ga-xe shki a', a bi$^n$ da, ṭsi ga,
45. Zha'-zhe ḳi-ṭo$^n$ mo$^n$-thi$^n$ ṭa bi a', zhi$^n$-ga', a bi$^n$ da, ṭsi ga,
46. Zha'-zhe ḳi-ṭo$^n$ mo$^n$-thi$^n$ bi do$^n$ shki a', a bi$^n$ da, ṭsi ga,
47. U'-no$^n$ a bi i-the ḳi-the mo$^n$-thi$^n$ ṭa bi$^n$ da', a bi$^n$ da, ṭsi ga.

7

48. Da'-do$^n$ zha-zhe ḳi-ṭo$^n$ ga no$^n$ shki a, hi$^n$ a', a bi$^n$ da, ṭsi ga,
49. No$^n$'-mi-ṭse-xi a', a bi$^n$ da, ṭsi ga,
50. Zha'-zhe ḳi-ṭo$^n$ mo$^n$-thi$^n$ ṭa bi a', zhi$^n$-ga', a bi$^n$ da, ṭsi ga,
51. Zha'-zhe ḳi-ṭo$^n$ mo$^n$-thi$^n$ bi do$^n$ shki a', a bi$^n$ da, ṭsi ga,
52. U'-no$^n$ a bi i-the ḳi-the mo$^n$-thi$^n$ ṭa bi$^n$ da, a bi$^n$ da, ṭsi ga.

8

53. Da'-do$^n$ zha-zhe ḳi-ṭo$^n$ ga no$^n$-shki a, hi$^n$ a', a bi$^n$ da, ṭsi ga,
54. I$^n$'-shta-sha-be shki a', a bi$^n$ da, ṭsi ga,
55. Zha'-zhe ḳi-ṭo$^n$ mo$^n$-thi$^n$ ṭa bi a, zhi$^n$-ga', a bi$^n$ da, ṭsi ga,
56. Zha'-zhe ḳi-ṭo$^n$ mo$^n$-thi$^n$ bi do$^n$ shki a', a bi$^n$ da, ṭsi ga,
57. U'-no$^n$ a bi i-the ḳi-the mo$^n$-thi$^n$ ṭa bi$^n$ da', a bi$^n$ da, ṭsi ga.

9

58. He'-dsi xtsi a', a bi$^n$ da, ṭsi ga,
59. Ha'! wi-ço$^n$-ga, e-ḳi-e no$^n$-zhi$^n$ bi a', a bi$^n$ da, ṭsi ga,
60. Zhi$^n$'-ga zhu-i-ga tha ba tho$^n$-ṭse thi$^n$-ge a-tha, wi-ço$^n$-ga,
    e'-ḳi-a bi a', a bi$^n$ da, ṭsi ga,
61. Thu-e' xtsi çi-thu-ça ba do$^n$ a', a bi$^n$ da, ṭsi ga,
62. 'I$^n$'-xe shto$^n$-ga thi$^n$-kshe no$^n$ a', a bi$^n$ da, ṭsi ga,
63. He'-dsi xtsi a', a bi$^n$ da, ṭsi ga,
64. Ha'! wi-ṭsi-go-e', e-gi-a bi a', a bi$^n$ da, ṭsi ga,
65. Zhi$^n$'-ga zhu-i-ga tha ba tho$^n$-ṭse thi$^n$-ge' a-tha, wi-ṭsi-go-e',
    e-ḳi-a bi a', a bi$^n$ da, ṭsi ga,

66. Ha'! zhi$^n$-ga, e-ṭsi-the_a', a bi$^n$ da, ṭsi ga,

67. Zhi$^{n'}$-ga zhu-i-ga tha ba tho$^n$-ṭse thi$^n$-ge' e-she do$^n$ a', a bi$^n$ da, ṭsi ga,

68. Zhi$^{n'}$-ga zhu-i-ga o$^n$-tha ba tho$^n$ ṭa mi kshi$^n$ da, a bi$^n$ da ṭsi ga,

69. He'-dsi xtsi a', a bi$^n$ da, ṭsi ga,

70. Zhi$^{n'}$-ga u-hu-shi-ga bi do$^n$ a', a bi$^n$ da, ṭsi ga,

71. U'-hu-shi-ge i-da-çi-ge o$^n$-ḳi-gtha-thi$^n$ mo$^n$-thi$^n$ ṭa bi a', zhi$^n$-ga, a bi$^n$ da, ṭsi ga.

10

72. He'-dsi xtsi a', a bi$^n$ da, ṭsi ga,

73. No$^{n'}$ wi-ço$^n$-ga, e-ḳi-a bi a', a bi$^n$ da, ṭsi ga,

74. O'-ṭo$^n$-be tha-the ṭse a, wi-ço$^n$-ga, e'-ḳi-a bi a', a bi$^n$ da, ṭsi ga,

75. Ga' xtsi hi-tha i do$^n$ a', a bi$^n$ da, ṭsi ga,

76. 'I$^{n'}$ sho-sho-dse thi$^n$-kshe no$^n$ a', a bi$^n$ da, ṭsi ga,

77. He'-dsi xtsi hi no$^n$-zhi$^n$-e do$^n$ a', a bi$^n$ da, ṭsi ga,

78. Zhi$^{n'}$-ga zhu-i-ga tha ba tho$^n$-ṭse thi$^n$-ge' a-tha, wi-ṭsi-go-e', e-gi-a bi a', a bi$^n$ da, ṭsi ga,

79. Ha'! zhi$^n$-ga e'-ṭsi-the a', a bi$^n$ da, ṭsi ga,

80. Zhi$^{n'}$-ga zhu-i-ga tha ba tho$^n$-ṭse thi$^n$ge' e-she do$^n$ a', a bi$^n$ da, ṭsi ga,

81. Zhi$^{n'}$-ga zhu-i-ga o$^n$-tha ba tho$^n$ ṭa mi kshi$^n$ da', a bi$^n$ da, a bi$^n$ da, ṭsi ga,

82. Zhi$^{n'}$-ga zhu-i-ga o$^n$-tha bi do$^n$ a', a bi$^n$ da, ṭsi ga,

83. U'-hu-shi-ga i-da-çi-ge o$^n$-ḳi-gtha-thi$^n$ mo$^n$-thi$^n$ ṭa bi a', zhi$^n$-ga, a bi$^n$ da, ṭsi ga.

11

84. He'-dsi xtsi a', a bi$^n$ da, ṭsi ga,

85. Ha'! wi-ço$^n$-ga, e-ḳi-a bi a', a bi$^n$ da, ṭsi ga,

86. Zhi$^{n'}$-ga no$^n$-bthe tha ba tho$^n$-ṭse thi$^n$-ge' a-tha, wi-ço$^n$-ga, e'-ḳi-a bi a', a bi$^n$ da, ṭsi ga,

87. O'-ṭo$^n$-be tha-the ṭse a, wi-ço$^n$-ga, e'-ḳi-a bi a', a bi$^n$ da, ṭsi ga,

88. Thu-e' xtsi çi-thu-çe the do$^n$ a', a bi$^n$ da, ṭsi ga,

89. Dse' u-çko$^n$-çka dsi xtsi a', a bi$^n$ da, ṭsi ga,

90. Ṭse'-wa-the kshe no$^n$ a', a bi$^n$ da, ṭsi ga,

91. E'-dsi-xtsi a-thi$^n$ gi-e do$^n$ a', a bi$^n$ da, ṭsi ga,

92. The ho$^{n'}$, wi-zhi$^n$-the, e-a-gthi no$^n$-zhi$^n$ a', a bi$^n$ da, ṭsi ga,

93. I'-k' u-ṭse a-ṭsi-a-tha bi do$^n$ a', a bi$^n$ da, ṭsi ga,

94. Ba'-çe-ni e-go$^n$ tha-dsu-zhe gtha bi a', a bi$^n$ da, ṭsi ga,

95. Ha'! wi-ço$^n$-ga, e-ḳi-a bi a', a bi$^n$ da, ṭsi ga,

96. Zhi$^{n'}$-ga no$^n$-bthe tha ba tho$^n$ ṭse a-ḳa', wi-ço$^n$-ga, e'-ḳi-a bi a', a bi$^n$ da, ṭsi ga,

97. Zhi$^{n'}$-ga no$^n$-bthe tha bi do$^n$ a', bi$^n$ da, ṭsi ga,

98. U'-no$^n$ a bi -the ḳi-the mo$^n$-thi$^n$ ṭa bi a', wi-ço$^n$-ga, e'-ḳi-a, bi a, a bi$^n$ da, ṭsi ga.

12

99. Shi' wiⁿ thiⁿ-ge a-tha, wi-çoⁿ-ga, e-ḳi-a bi a', biⁿ da, ṭsi ga,

100. O'-ṭoⁿ-be tha-the ṭse a', wi-çoⁿ-ga, e'-ḳi-a bi a', a biⁿ da, ṭsi ga,

101. Ga' xtsi hi-tha i doⁿ a', a biⁿ da, ṭsi ga,

102. Dse' go-da ḳoⁿ-ha dsi xtsi a', a biⁿ da, ṭsi ga,

103. Do' thiⁿ-kshe noⁿ a', a biⁿ da, ṭsi ga,

104. E'-dsi xtsi hi noⁿ-zhiⁿ-e doⁿ a', a biⁿ da, ṭsi ga,

105. He'-dsi xtsi a-thiⁿ gi-e doⁿ a', a biⁿ da, ṭsi ga,

106. Ha'! wi-zhiⁿ-the, e' a-gthi noⁿ-zhiⁿ a', a biⁿ da, ṭsi ga,

107. The hoⁿ', wi-zhiⁿ-the, e' a-gthi noⁿ-zhiⁿ a', a biⁿ da, ṭsi ga,

108. Ha'! wi-çoⁿ-ga, e'-gi-a bi a', a biⁿ da, ṭsi ga,

109. She' e-shnoⁿ u-tha-dse tha-thiⁿ-she a', wi-çoⁿ-ga, e-gi-a bi a', a
     biⁿ da, ṭsi ga,

110. I'-ḳ'u-tse a-ṭsi-a-tha bi doⁿ a', a biⁿ da, ṭsi ga,

111. Ba'-çe-ni e-goⁿ tha-dsu-zhe gtha bi a', a biⁿ da, ṭsi ga,

112. Zhiⁿ'-ga noⁿ-bthe the moⁿ-thiⁿ ṭa biⁿ da', a biⁿ da, ṭsi ga,

113. Zhiⁿ'-ga noⁿ-bthe the moⁿ-thiⁿ bi doⁿ a', a biⁿ da, ṭsi ga,

114. U'-noⁿ a bi i-the ḳi-the moⁿ-thiⁿ ṭa biⁿ da', a biⁿ da, ṭsi ga,

115. A'-dsu-ṭa i-ga-çi-ge ḳi-the moⁿ-thiⁿ ṭa biⁿda, a biⁿ da, ṭsi ga.

## U'-NOⁿ WI'-GI-E

1

1. He'-dsi xtsi a', a biⁿ da, ṭsi ga,

2. Hoⁿ'-ga u-dse-the ᵖe-thoⁿ-ba ni-ḳa-shi-ga ba doⁿ a', a biⁿ da,
   ṭsi ga,

3. Zhu'-i-ga tha bi wa-thiⁿ-ga bi a tha, e'-ḳi-a bi a', a biⁿ da, ṭsi ga,

4. He'-dsi xtsi a', a biⁿ da, ṭsi ga,

5. Wa'-zhiⁿ-ga wa-tha-xthi thiⁿ-ge thiⁿ-kshe noⁿ a', a biⁿ da, ṭsi ga,

6. Ha! wi-ṭsi-go-e', e-gi-a bi a', a biⁿ da, ṭsi ga,

7. Zhiⁿ'-ga zhu-i-ga tha bi wa-thiⁿ-ga bi a-tha, e'-gi-a bi a, a biⁿ
   da, ṭsi ga,

8. He'-dsi xtsi a', a biⁿ da, ṭsi ga,

9. Wa'-zhiⁿ-ga wa-tha-xthi thiⁿ-ge thiⁿ-kshe noⁿ a', a biⁿ da, ṭsi ga,

10. Zhiⁿ'-ga zhu-i-ga oⁿ-tha bi doⁿ a', a biⁿ da, ṭsi ga,

11. U'-noⁿ a bi e-toⁿ-ha i-the ḳi-the moⁿ-thiⁿ ṭa bi a-tha, e'-ṭsi-the
    a', a biⁿ da, ṭsi ga,

12. Wa-zhiⁿ-ga wa-tha-xthi thiⁿ-ge thiⁿ-kshe noⁿ a, a biⁿ da, ṭsi ga,

13. Çi'-ᵖa-hi thi-çtu-the ga ṭse shki a', a biⁿ da, ṭsi ga,

14. U'-noⁿ a-gi-the a-thiⁿ-he a-tha, e'-ṭsi-the a', a biⁿ da, ṭsi ga,

15. Zhiⁿ'-ga u-noⁿ oⁿ-tha bi doⁿ a', a biⁿ da, ṭsi ga,

16. U'-noⁿ a bi e-ṭoⁿ-ha i-the ḳi-the moⁿ-thiⁿ ṭa i ṭse a-tha, e' ṭsi-the
    a', a biⁿ da, ṭsi ga.

17. No$^{n'}$-xpe-hi ba-ç'i$^n$-tha ga țse shki a', a bi$^n$ da, țsi ga,
18. U'-no$^n$ a-gi-the a-thi$^n$ he a-tha, e' țsi-the a', a bi$^n$ da, țsi ga,
19. Zhi$^{n'}$-ga u-no$^n$ o$^n$-tha bi do$^n$ a', a bi$^n$ da, țsi ga,
20. U'-no$^n$ a bi e-țo$^n$-ha i-the ķi-the mo$^n$-thi$^n$ ța i țse a-tha, e' țsi-the a', a bi$^n$ da, țsi ga.

21. Wa'-zhi$^n$-ga wa-tha-xthi thi$^n$-ge thi$^n$-kshe no$^n$ a', a bi$^n$ da, țsi ga,
22. Shi'-no$^n$-dse ba-ç'i$^n$-tha ga țse shki a', a bi$^n$ da, țsi ga,
23. U'-no$^n$ a-gi-the a-thi$^n$-he a tha, e'țsi-the a', a bi$^n$ da, țsi ga,
24. Zhi$^{n'}$-ga u-no$^n$ o$^n$-tha bi do$^n$ a', a bi$^n$ da, țsi ga,
25. U'-no$^n$ a bi e-țo$^n$-ha i-the ķi-the mo$^n$-thi$^n$ ța i țse a-tha, e'țsi-the a, a bi$^n$ da, țsi ga.

26. Țse'-wa-țse u-ga-wa ga thi$^n$-kshe shki a', a bi$^n$ da, țsi ga,
27. U'-no$^n$ a-gi-the a-thi$^n$-he a-tha, e'-țsi-the a', a bi$^n$ da, țsi ga,
28. Zhi$^{n'}$-ga u-no$^n$ o$^n$-tha bi do$^n$ a', a bi$^n$ da, țsi ga,
29. U'-no$^n$ a bi e-țo$^n$-ha i-the ķi-the mo$^n$-thi$^n$ ța i țse a-tha, e'țsi-the a', a bi$^n$ da, țsi ga.

30. Mo$^{n'}$-ge thi-çtu-the ga țse shki a', a bi$^n$ da, țsi ga,
31. U'-no$^n$ a-gi-the a-thi$^n$ he a-tha, e țsi-the a', a bi$^n$ da, țsi ga,
32. Zhi$^{n'}$-ga u-no$^n$ o$^n$-tha bi do$^n$ a', a bi$^n$ da, țsi ga,
33. U'-no$^n$ a bi e-țo$^n$-ha i-the ķi-the mo$^n$-thi$^n$ ța i țse a-tha, e'țsi-the a', a bi$^n$ da, țsi ga.

34. A'-zhu-ga-wa ga thi$^n$-kshe shki a', a bi$^n$ da, țsi ga,
35. U'-no$^n$ a-gi-the a-thi$^n$ he a-tha, e'țsi-the a', a bi$^n$ da, țsi ga,
36. Zhi$^{n'}$-ga u-no$^n$ o$^n$-tha bi do$^n$ a', a bi$^n$ da, țsi ga,
37. U'-no$^n$ a bi e-țo$^n$-ha i-the ķi-the mo$^n$-thi$^n$ ța i țse a-tha e țsi-the a, a bi$^n$ da, țsi ga.

38. A'-ba-ț'u-xa ga thi$^n$-kshe shki a', a bi$^n$ da, țsi ga,
39. U'-no$^n$ a-gi-the a-thi$^n$ he a-tha, e țsi-the a', a bi$^n$ da, țsi ga,
40. Zhi$^{n'}$-ga u-no$^n$ o$^n$-tha bi do$^n$ a', a bi$^n$ da, țsi ga,
41. A'-ba-ț'u-xa e-go$^n$ a bi i-the ķi-the mo$^n$-thi$^n$ ța i țse a-tha, e țsi-the a', a bi$^n$ da, țsi ga.

42. Du'-dse u-ga-wa ga thi$^n$-kshe shki a', a bi$^n$ da, țsi ga,
43. U'-no$^n$ a-gi-the a-thi$^n$-he a-tha, e'-țsi-the a', a bi$^n$ da, țsi ga,
44. Zhi$^{n'}$-ga u-no$^n$ o$^n$-tha bi do$^n$ a', a bi$^n$ da, țsi ga,
45. U'-no$^n$ a bi e-țo$^n$-ha ķi-the i-the mo$^n$-thi$^n$ ța i țse a-tha, e'țsi-the a', a bi$^n$ da, țsi ga.

46. I$^{n'}$-shta-the-dse bi-xo$^n$ ga thi$^n$-kshe shki a', a bi$^n$ da, țsi ga,
47. U'-no$^n$ a-gi-the a-thi$^n$-he a-tha, e țsi-the a', a bi$^n$ da, țsi ga,
48. Zhi$^{n'}$-ga u-no$^n$ o$^n$-tha bi do$^n$ a', a bi$^n$ da, țsi ga,
49. I$^{n'}$-shta-the-dse bi-xo$^n$ a bi i-the ķi-the mo$^n$-țhi$^n$ ta i țse e'țsi-the a', a bi$^n$ da, țsi ga.

50. I$^n$'-shta-ha bi-xo$^n$ ga ṭse a', a bi$^n$ da, ṭsi ga,

51. U'-no$^n$ a-gi-the a-thi$^n$-he a-tha, e'ṭsi-the a', a bi$^n$ da, ṭsi ga,

52. Zhi$^n$'-ga u-no$^n$ o$^n$-tha bi do$^n$ a', bi$^n$ da, ṭsi ga.

53. I$^n$'-shta-ha bi-xo$^n$ a bi i-the ḳi-the mo$^n$-thi$^n$ ṭa i ṭse a-tha, e ṭsi-the a', a bi$^n$ da, ṭsi ga.

54. Ṭa'-xpi hi$^n$ ça-dse ga thi$^n$-kshe shki a', a bi$^n$ da, ṭsi ga,

55. U'-no$^n$ a-gi-the a-thi$^n$ he a-tha, e ṭsi-the a', a bi$^n$ da, ṭsi ga,

56. Zhi$^n$'-ga zhu-i-ga o$^n$-tha bi do$^n$ a', a bi$^n$ da, ṭsi ga,

57. Ṭa-xpi hi$^n$ ça-dse a bi i-the ḳi-the mo$^n$-thi$^n$ ṭa i ṭse a-tha, e ṭsi-the a, a bi$^n$ da, ṭsi ga.

## WA-ZHO'-I-GA-THE WI'-GI-E

### 1

1. Zhi$^n$'-ga zhu-i-ga-the thi$^n$-ge a-tha, wi-ço$^n$-ga, e-ḳi-e a-ka', a bi$^n$ da, ṭsi ga,

2. Ho'-ṭo$^n$-be ga-xa ba thi$^n$-ha, wi-ço$^n$-ga, e-ḳi-e a-ka', a bi$^n$ da, ṭsi ga,

3. Ka' ha-ge ṭo$^n$ a', a bi$^n$ da, ṭsi ga,

4. Zhi$^n$'-ga zhu-i-ga the thi$^n$-ge a-tha, wi-ço$^n$-ga, e-gi-e a-ka', a bi$^n$ da, ṭsi ga,

5. Ga' xtsi hi-tha i do$^n$ a', a bi$^n$ da, ṭsi ga,

6. Wa'-ḳo$^n$-da ho$^n$-ba do$^n$ thi$^n$-kshe a', a bi$^n$ da, ṭsi ga,

7. Wi'-ṭsi-go-e', e-gi-e a-ka', a bi$^n$ da, ṭsi ga,

8. Ha'! wi-tsu-shpa e', a bi$^n$ da, ṭsi ga,

9. Zhi$^n$'-ga zhu-i-ga-the thi$^n$-ge a-tha, wi-ṭsi-go-e', e-gi-e a-ka', a bi$^n$ da, ṭsi ga,

10. Zhi$^n$'-ga zhu-i-ga tha ba tho$^n$ ṭa ni-ḳa-shi-ga mi-kshi$^n$ da, a bi$^n$ da, ṭsi ga,

11. Wa'-ḳo$^n$-da ts'e wa-ṭse-xi wi-no$^n$ bthi$^n$ da', a bi$^n$ da, ṭsi ga,

12. Zhi$^n$'-ga zhu-i-ga o$^n$-tha bi do$^n$ a', a bi$^n$ da, ṭsi ga,

13. Ṭs'e' wa-ṭse-xi mo$^n$-thi$^n$ ṭa i tsi$^n$ da, a bi$^n$ da', ṭsi ga,

14. Wa'-ḳo$^n$-da e'-shki do$^n$ a', a bi$^n$ da, ṭsi ga,

15. Be'u-zho$^n$-ge o$^n$-tho$^n$ kshi-tha mo$^n$-zhi a-thi$^n$ he i$^n$ da', a bi$^n$ da, ṭsi ga,

16. Zhi$^n$'-ga zhu-i-ga o$^n$-tha bi do$^n$ a', a bi$^n$ da, ṭsi ga,

17. Wa'-ḳo$^n$-da e-shki do$^n$ a', a bi$^n$ da, ṭsi ga,

18. U'-zho$^n$-ge be i-kshi-tha ba zhi mo$^n$-thi$^n$ ṭa i tsi$^n$ da', a bi$^n$ da, ṭsi ga.

### 2

19. Ha'! wi-ço$^n$-ga, e-ḳi-e a-ka', a bi$^n$ da, ṭsi ga,

20. Ho'-ṭo$^n$-be ga-xa ba thi$^n$ ha', wi-ço$^n$-ga, e'-ḳi-e a-ka', a bi$^n$ da, ṭsi ga,

21. Zhi$^n$'-ga zhu-i-ga the thi$^n$-ge a-tha, wi-ço$^n$-ga, e'-ḳi-e a-ka', a bi$^n$ da, ṭsi ga,

22. Ka' ha-ge ṭo$^n$ a', a bi$^n$ da, ṭsi ga,
23. Wi'-ço$^n$-ga, e-gi-e a-ka', a bi$^n$ da, ṭsi ga,
24. Zhi$^{n\prime}$-ga zhu-i-ga the thi$^n$-ge a tha, wi-ço$^n$-ga, e'-gi-e a-ka', a bi$^n$ da, ṭsi ga,
25. Ho'-ṭo$^n$-be ga-xa thi$^n$ ha, wi-ço$^n$-ga, e-gi-e a-ka', a bi$^n$ da, ṭsi ga,
26. Ga'xtsi hi-tha i do$^n$ a', a bi$^n$ da, ṭsi ga,
27. Wa'-ḳo$^n$-da ho$^n$ do$^n$ thi$^n$-kshe a', a bi$^n$ da, ṭsi ga,
28. I'-ḳo-e, e-gi-e a-ka', a bi$^n$ da, ṭsi ga,
29. Ha'! wi-tsu-shpa tho$^n$, e', a bi$^n$ da, ṭsi ga,
30. Zhi$^{n\prime}$-ga zhu-i-ga the thi$^n$-ge a-tha, e-gi-e a-ka', a bi$^n$ da, ṭsi ga,
31. Zhi$^{n\prime}$-ga zhu-i-ga tha ba tho$^n$ ṭa ni-ḳa-shi-ga mi-kshi$^n$ da', a bi$^n$ da, ṭsi ga,
32. Wa'-ḳo$^n$-da ṭs'e wa-ṭse-xi bthi$^n$ da', a bi$^n$ da, ṭsi ga,
33. Zhi$^{n\prime}$-ga zhu-i-ga o$^n$-tha bi do$^n$ a', a bi$^n$ da, ṭsi ga,
34. Ṭs'e' wa-ṭse-xi mo$^n$-thi$^n$ ṭa i tsi$^n$ da', a bi$^n$ da, ṭsi ga,
35. Wa'-ḳo$^n$-da e-'shki do$^n$ a', a bi$^n$ da, ṭsi ga,
36. U'-zho$^n$-ge be o$^n$-tho$^n$-kshi-tha mo$^n$-zhi a-thi$^n$ he i$^n$ da', a bi$^n$ da, ṭsi ga,
37. Zhi$^{n\prime}$-ga zhu-i-ga o$^n$-tha bi do$^n$ a', a bi$^n$ da, ṭsi ga,
38. Wa'-ḳo$^n$-da e-shki do$^n$ a', a bi$^n$ da, ṭsi ga,
39. U'-zho$^n$-ge be i-kshi-tha ba zhi mo$^n$-thi$^n$ ṭa i tsi$^n$ da', a bi$^n$ da, ṭsi ga,
40. Wa'-ḳo$^n$-da e-shki do$^n$ a', a bi$^n$ da, ṭsi ga,
41. U'-zho$^n$-ge be o$^n$-wo$^n$-no$^n$-zhi$^n$ mo$^n$-zhi z-thi$^n$ he i$^n$ da', a bi$^n$ da, ṭsi ga,
42. Zhi$^{n\prime}$-ga zhu-i-ga o$^n$-tha bi do$^n$ a', a bi$^n$ da, ṭsi ga,
43. Wa'-ḳo$^n$-da e'-shki do$^n$ a', a bi$^n$ da, ṭsi ga,
44. U'-zho$^n$-ge be u-no$^n$-zhi$^n$ ba zhi ḳi-the mo$^n$-thi$^n$ ṭa i tsi$^n$ da', a bi$^n$ da, ṭsi ga,
45. U'-no$^n$ a bi shki u-hi a-ḳi-the a-thin he i$^n$ da', a bi$^n$ da, ṭsi ga,
46. Zhi$^{n\prime}$-ga zhu-i-ga o$^n$-tha bi do$^n$ a', a bi$^n$ da, ṭsi ga,
47. U'-no$^n$ a bi shki u-hi ḳi-the mo$^n$-thi$^n$ ṭa i tsi$^n$ da', a bi$^n$ da, ṭsi ga
48. Ho$^{n\prime}$-ba tha-gthi$^n$ shki u-hi a-ḳi-the a thi$^n$ he i$^n$ da', a bi$^n$ da, ṭsi ga,
49. Zhi$^{n\prime}$-ga zhu-i-ga o$^n$-tha bi do$^n$ a', a bi$^n$ da, ṭsi ga,
50. Ho$^{n\prime}$-ba tha-gthi$^n$ shki u-hi ḳi-the mo$^n$-thi$^n$ ṭa i tsi$^n$ da', a bin da, ṭsi ga.

3

51. Zhi$^{n\prime}$-ga zhu-i-ga the thi$^n$-ge a-tha, wi-ço$^n$-ga, e'-ḳi-e a-ka', a bi$^n$ da, ṭsi ga,
52. U'-to$^n$-be ga-xa ba thi$^n$ ha', a bi$^n$ da, ṭsi ga,
53. Ka' ha-ge ṭo$^n$ a', a bi$^n$ da, ṭsi ga,
54. Wi'-ço$^n$-ga, e-gi-e a-ka', a bi$^n$ da, ṭsi ga,

55. Zhi$^n$'-ga zhu-i-ga the thi$^n$-ge a-tha, e'-gi-e a-ka', a bi$^n$ da, ṭsi ga,

56. U'-ṭo$^n$-be ga-xa thi$^n$ ha, wi-ços$^n$-ga, e-gi-e a-ka', a bi$^n$ da, ṭsi ga.

57. Ga' xtsi hi-tha i do$^n$ a', a bi$^n$ da, ṭsi ga,

58. Wa'-ṭse do-ga thi$^n$-kshe a', a bi$^n$ da, ṭsi ga,

59. Wi'-ṭsi-go-e, e-gi-e a-ka', a bi$^n$ da, ṭsi ga,

60. Ha'! wi-tsu-shpa, e', a bi$^n$ da, ṭsi ga,

61. Zhi$^n$'-ga zhu-i-ga the thi$^n$-ge a-tha, wi-ṭsi-go-e', e-gi-e a-ka', a bi$^n$ da, ṭsi ga,

62. Zhi$^n$-ga zhu-i-ga tha ba tho$^n$ ṭa ni-ḵa-shi-ga mi-kshi$^n$ da', a bi$^n$ da, ṭsi ga,

63. Wa-ḵo$^n$-da ts'e wa-ṭse-xi wi-no$^n$ bthi$^n$ i$^n$ da, a bi$^n$ da, ṭsi ga,

64. Zhi$^n$'-ga zhu-i-ga o$^n$-tha bi do$^n$ a', a bi$^n$ da, ṭsi ga,

65. Ṭs'e' wa-ṭse-xi mo$^n$-thi$^n$ ṭa i ṭsi$^n$ da', a bi$^n$ da, ṭsi ga,

66. Wa'-ḵo$^n$-da e-shki do$^n$ a', a bi$^n$ da, ṭsi ga,

67. U'-zho$^n$-ge be o$^n$-tho$^n$-kshi-tha mo$^n$-zhi a-thi$^n$ he i$^n$ da', a bi$^n$ da, ṭsi ga.

68. Zhi$^n$'-ga zhu-i-ga o$^n$-tha bi do$^n$ a', a bi$^n$ da, ṭsi ga,

69. Wa'-ḵo$^n$-da e'-shki do$^n$ a', a bi$^n$ da, ṭsi ga,

70. U'-zho$^n$-ge be i-kshi-tha ba zhi mo$^n$-thi$^n$ ṭa i tsi$^n$ da', a bi$^n$ da, ṭsi ga,

71. Wa'-ḵo$^n$-da e-shki do$^n$ a', a bi$^n$ da, ṭsi ga,

72. U'-zho$^n$-ge be o$^n$-wo$^n$-no$^n$-zhi$^n$ mo$^n$-zhi a-thi$^n$ he i$^n$ da', a bi$^n$ da, ṭsi ga,

73. Zhi$^n$'-ga zhu-i-ga o$^n$-tha bi do$^n$ a', a bi$^n$ da, ṭsi ga,

74. Wa'-ḵo$^n$-da e-shki do$^n$ a', a bi$^n$ da, ṭsi ga,

75. U'-zho$^n$-ge be u-no$^n$-zhi$^n$ ba zhi mo$^n$-thi$^n$ ṭa i tsi$^n$ da', a bi$^n$ da, ṭsi ga,

76. U'-no$^n$ a bi shki u-hi a-ḵi-the a-thi$^n$ he i$^n$ da, a bi$^n$ da, ṭsi ga,

77. Zhi$^n$'-ga zhu-i-ga o$^n$-tha bi do$^n$ a', a bi$^n$ da, ṭsi ga,

78. U'-no$^n$ a bi shki i-the ḵi-the mo$^n$-thi$^n$ ṭa i tsi$^n$ da', a bi$^n$ da, ṭsi ga,

79. Ho$^n$'-ba tha-gthi$^n$ shki i-the a-ḵi-the a-thi$^n$ he i$^n$ da', a bi$^n$ da, ṭsi ga,

80. Zhi$^n$'-ga zhu-i-ga o$^n$-tha bi do$^n$ a', a bi$^n$ da, ṭsi ga,

81. Ho$^n$'-ba tha-gthi$^n$ shki u-hi ḵi-the mo$^n$-thi$^n$ ṭa i tsi$^n$ da', a bi$^n$ da, ṭsi ga.

4

82. Ha'! wi-ço$^n$-ga, e-ḵi-e a-ka', a bi$^n$ da, ṭsi ga,

83. Zhi$^n$'-ga zhu-i-ga the thi$^n$-ge a-tha, wi-ço$^n$-ga, e-ḵi-e a-ka', a bi$^n$ da, ṭsi ga,

84. Ho'-ṭo$^n$-be ga-xa ba thi$^n$ ha, wi-ço$^n$-ga, e-ḵi-e, a-ka', a bi$^n$ da, ṭsi ga,

85. Ka' ha-ge ṭo$^n$ a', a bi$^n$ da, ṭsi ga,

86. Wi'-ço$^n$-ga, e-gi-e a-ka', a bi$^n$ da, ṭsi ga,

87. Zhi$^n$'-ga zhu-i-ga the thi$^n$-ge a-tha, wi-ço$^n$-ga, e'-gi-e a-ka', a
    bi$^n$ da, ṭsi ga,
88. O'-ṭo$^n$-be ga-xa thi$^n$ ha, e'-gi-e a-ka', a bi$^n$ da, ṭsi ga,
89. Ga' xtsi hi-tha i-do$^n$ a', a bi$^n$ da, ṭsi ga,
90. Wa'-ṭse mi-ga thi$^n$-kshe a', a bi$^n$ da, ṭsi ga,
91. I'-ḳo-e, e-gi-e a-ka', a bi$^n$ da, ṭsi ga,
92. Ha'! wi-tsu-shpa, e', a bi$^n$ da, ṭsi ga,
93. Zhi$^n$'-ga shu-i-ga the thi$^n$-ge a-tha, i-ḳo-e, e-gi-e a-ka', a bi$^n$ da,
    ṭsi ga,
94. Zhi$^n$-ga zhu-i-ga o$^n$-tha ba tho$^n$ ṭa ni-ḳa-shi-ga mi-kshi$^n$ da, a
    bi$^n$ da, ṭsi ga,
95. Wa'-ḳo$^n$-da ts'e wa-ṭse-xi wi-no$^n$ bthi$^n$ da', a bi$^n$ da, ṭsi ga,
96. Zhi$^n$'-ga zhu-i-ga o$^n$-tha bi do$^n$ a', a bi$^n$ da, ṭsi ga,
97. Ṭs'e wa'-ṭse-xi ḳi-the mo$^n$-thi$^n$ ṭa i tsi$^n$ da', a bi$^n$ da, ṭsi ga,
98. Wa-ḳo$^n$'-da e-shki do$^n$ a', a bi$^n$ da, ṭsi ga,
99. U'-zho$^n$-ge be o$^n$-wo$^n$-no$^n$-zhi$^n$ mo$^n$-zhi a-thi$^n$ he i$^n$ da,' a bi$^n$
    da, ṭsi ga,
100. Zhi$^n$'-ga zhu-i-ga o$^n$-tha bi do$^n$ a', a bi$^n$ da, ṭsi ga,
101. Wa'-ḳo$^n$-da e-shki do$^n$ a', a bi$^n$ da, ṭsi ga,
102. U-zho$^n$-ge be u-no$^n$-zhi$^n$ ba zhi mo$^n$-thi$^n$ ṭa i tsi$^n$ da', a bi$^n$ da,
    ṭsi ga,
103. U'-no$^n$ a bi shki u-hi a-ḳi-the a-thi$^n$ he i$^n$ da', a bi$^n$ da, ṭsi ga,
104. Zhi$^n$'-ga zhu-i-ga o$^n$-tha bi do$^n$ a', a bi$^n$ da, ṭsi ga,
105. U'-no$^n$ a bi shki u-hi ḳi-the mo$^n$-thi$^n$ ṭa i tsi$^n$ da', a bi$^n$ da, ṭsi
    ga,
106. Ho$^n$'-ba tha-gthi$^n$ shki u-hi a-ḳi-the a-thi$^n$ hi$^n$ da, a bi$^n$ da
    ṭsi ga,
107. Zhi$^n$'-ga zhu-i-ga o$^n$-tha bi do$^n$ a', a bi$^n$ da, ṭsi ga,
108. Ho$^n$'-ba tha-gthi$^n$ skhi u-hi ḳi-the mo$^n$-thi$^n$ ṭa i tsi$^n$ da', a bi$^n$
    da, ṭsi ga.

5

109. Ha'! wi-ço$^n$-ga, e-ḳi-e a-ka', bi$^n$ da, ṭsi ga,
110. Zhi$^n$'-ga zhu-i-ga the thi$^n$-ge a-tha, wi-ço$^n$-ga, e' ḳi-e a-ka', a bi$^n$
    da, ṭsi ga,
111. Ka' ha-ge to$^n$ a', a bi$^n$ da, ṭsi ga,
112. Wi'-ço$^n$-ga, e-gi-e a-ka', a bi$^n$ da, ṭsi ga,
113. O'-ṭo$^n$-be ga-xa thi$^n$ ha, wi-ço$^n$-ga, e'gi-e a-ka', a bi$^n$ da, ṭsi ga,
114. Ga'xtsi hi-tha i do$^n$ a', a bi$^n$ da, ṭsi ga,
115. Wa'-ba-ha ṭo$^n$ no$^n$ a', a bi$^n$ da, ṭsi ga,
116. Wi'-ṭsi-go-e', e-gi-e a-ka', a bi$^n$ da, ṭsi ga,
117. Zhi$^n$'-ga zhu-i-ga the thi$^n$-ge a-tha, wi-ṭsi-go-e, e-gi-e a-ka', a
    bi$^n$ da, ṭsi ga,
118. Zhi$^n$'-ga zhu-i-ga tha ba tho$^n$ ṭa ni-ḳa-shi-ga mi-kshi$^n$ da, a bi$^n$
    da, ṭsi ga,
119. ·Wa'-ḳo$^n$-da ṭs'e wa-ṭse-xi bthi$^n$ da', a bi$^n$ da, ṭsi ga,

120. Zhi$^n$'-ga zhu-i-ga o$^n$-tha bi do$^n$ a', a bi$^n$ da, ṭsi ga,

121. Ṭs'e' wa-ṭse-xi mo$^n$-thi$^n$ ṭa i tsi$^n$ da', a bi$^n$ da, ṭsi ga,

122. Wa'-ḳo$^n$-da e-shki do$^n$ a', a bi$^n$ da, ṭsi ga,

123. U'-zho$^n$-ge be o$^n$-tho$^n$-kshi-tha mo$^n$-zhi a-thi$^n$ he i$^n$ da', a bi$^n$ da, ṭsi ga,

124. Zhi$^n$'-ga zhu-i-ga o$^n$-tha bi do$^n$ a', a bi$^n$ da, ṭsi ga,

125. Wa'-ḳo$^n$-da e-shki do$^n$ a', a bi$^n$ da, ṭsi ga,

126. U'-sho$^n$-ge be i-kshi-tha ba zhi mo$^n$-thi$^n$ ṭa i tsi$^n$ da', a bi$^n$ da, ṭsi ga,

127. Wa'-ḳo$^n$ da e-shki do$^n$ a', a bi$^n$ da, ṭsi ga,

128. U'-zho$^n$-ge be o$^n$-wo$^n$-no$^n$-zhi$^n$ mo$^n$-zhi a-thi$^n$ he i$^n$ da', a bi$^n$ da, ṭsi ga,

129. Zhi$^n$'-ga zhu-i-ga o$^n$-tha bi do$^n$ a', a bi$^n$ da, ṭsi ga,

130. Wa'-ḳo$^n$-da e-shki do$^n$ a', a bi$^n$ da, ṭsi ga,

131. U'-zho$^n$-ge be u-no$^n$-zhi$^n$ ba zhi mo$^n$-thi$^n$ ṭa i tsi$^n$ da', a bi$^n$ da, ṭsi ga

132. U'-no$^n$ a bi shki i-the a-ḳi-the a-thi$^n$ he i$^n$ da', a bi$^n$ da, ṭsi ga,

133. Zhi$^n$'-ga zhu-i-ga o$^n$-tha bi do$^n$ a', a bi$^n$ da, ṭsi ga,

134. U'-no$^n$ a bi shki i-the ḳi-the mo$^n$-thi$^n$ ṭa i tsi$^n$ da', a bi$^n$ da, ṭsi ga,

135. Ho$^n$'-ba tha-gthi$^n$ shki u-hi a -ḳi-the a-thi$^n$ he i$^n$ da, a bi$^n$ da, ṭsi ga.

136. Zhi$^n$'-ga zhu-i-ga o$^n$-tha bi do$^n$ a', a bi$^n$ da, ṭsi ga,

137. Ho$^n$'-ba tha-gthi$^n$ shki u-hi ḳi-the mo$^n$-thi$^n$ ṭa i tsi$^n$ da', a bi$^n$ da, ṭsi ga.

6

138. Zhi$^n$'-ga zhu-i-ga the thi$^n$-ge a-tha, wi-ço$^n$-ga, e-ḳi-e a-ka', a bi$^n$ da, ṭsi ga,

139. Ho'-ṭo$^n$-be ga-xa ba thi$^n$ ha, wi-ço$^n$-ga, e-ḳi-e a-ka, a bi$^n$ da, ṭsi ga,

140. Ka'ha-ge ṭo$^n$ a', a bi$^n$ da, ṭsi ga,

141. Wi'-ço$^n$-ga, e-gi-e a-ka', a bi$^n$ da, ṭsi ga,

142. Zhi$^n$'-ga zhu-i-ga the thi$^n$-ge a-tha, wi-ço$^n$-ga, e'-gi-e a-ka', a bi$^n$ da, ṭsi ga,

143. Ga'xtsi hi-tha i do$^n$ a', a bi$^n$ da, ṭsi ga,

144. Ṭa'-pa thi$^n$-kshe no$^n$ a', a bi$^n$ da, ṭsi ga.

145. I'-ḳo-e', e-gi-e a-ka', a bi$^n$ da, ṭsi ga,

146. Ha'! wi-tsu-shpa tho$^n$, e', a bi$^n$ da, ṭsi ga,

147. Zhi$^n$'-ga zhu-i-ga the thi$^n$-ge a-tha, e'-gi-e a-ka', a bi$^n$ da, ṭsi ga,

148. Zhi$^n$'-ga zhu-i-ga tha ba tho$^n$ ṭa ni-ḳa-shi-ga mi-kshi$^n$ da', a bi$^n$ da, ṭsi ga,

149. Wa'-ḳo$^n$-da ṭs'e wa-ṭse-xi bthi$^n$ da', ṭsi ga,

150. Zhi$^n$'-ga zhu-i-ga o$^n$-tha bi do$^n$ a', a bi$^n$ da, ṭsi ga,

151. Ṭs'e' wa-ṭse-xi ḳi-the mo$^n$-thi$^n$ ṭa i ṭsi$^n$ da', a bi$^n$ da, ṭsi ga.

152. Wa'-ḳo$^n$ da e-shki do$^n$ a', a bi$^n$ da, ṭsi ga,

153. U'-zho$^n$-ge be o$^n$-tho$^n$-kshi-tha mo$^n$-zhi a-thi$^n$ he i$^n$ da, a bi$^n$ da, ṭṡi ga,

154. Zhi$^n$'-ga zhu-i-ga o$^n$-tha bi do$^n$ a', a bi$^n$ da, ṭsi ga,

155. Wa'-ḳo$^n$-da e-shki do$^n$ a', a bi$^n$ da, ṭsi ga,

156. U'-zho$^n$-ge be i-kshi-tha be zhi mo$^n$-thi$^n$ ṭa i tsi$^n$ da', a bi$^n$ da, ṭsi ga.

157. Wa'-ḳo$^n$-da e-shki do$^n$ a', a bi$^n$ da, ṭsi ga,

158. U'-zho$^n$-ge be o$^n$-wo$^n$-no$^n$-zhi$^n$ mo$^n$-zhi a-thi$^n$ he i$^n$ da', a bi$^n$ da, ṭsi ga,

159. Zhi$^n$'-ga zhu-i-ga o$^n$-tha bi do$^n$ a', a bi$^n$ da, ṭsi ga,

160. Wa'-ḳo$^n$-da e-shki do$^n$ a', a bi$^n$ da, si ṭga,

161. U'-zho$^n$-ge be u-no$^n$-zhi$^n$ ba zhi mo$^n$-thi$^n$ ṭa i tsi$^n$ da', a bi$^n$ da, ṭsi ga,

162. U'-no$^n$ a bi shki i-the a-ḳi-the a-thi$^n$ he i$^n$ da', a bi$^n$ da, ṭsi ga,

163. Zhi$^n$'-ga zhu-i-ga o$^n$-tha bi do$^n$ a', a bi$^n$ da, ṭsi ga,

164. U'-no$^n$ a bi shki i-the ḳi-the mo$^n$-thi$^n$ ṭa i tsi$^n$ da', a bi$^n$ da, ṭsi ga,

165. Ho$^n$'-ba tha-gthi$^n$ shki u-hi a-ḳi-the a-thi$^n$ he i$^n$ da', a bi$^n$ da, ṭsi ga,

166. Zhi$^n$'-ga zhu-i-ga o$^n$-tha bi do$^n$ a', a bi$^n$ da, ṭsi ga,

167. Ho$^n$'-ba tha-gthi$^n$ shki u-hi ḳi-the mo$^n$-thi$^n$ ṭa i tsi$^n$ da', a bi$^n$ da, ṭsi ga.

### 7

168. Zhi$^n$'-ga zhu-i-ga the thi$^n$-ge a-tha, wi-ço$^n$-ga, e'-ḳi-e a-ka', a bi$^n$ da, ṭsi ga,

169. O'-ṭo$^n$-be ga-xa ba thi$^n$ ha, wi-ço$^n$-ga, e-ḳi-e, a-ka', a bi$^n$ da, ṭsi ga,

170. Ka' ha-ge ṭo$^n$ a', a bi$^n$ da, ṭsi ga,

171. Wi'-ço$^n$-ga, e-gi-e a-ka', a bi$^n$ da, ṭsi ga,

172. Zhi$^n$'-ga zhu-i-ga the thi$^n$-ge a-tha, wi-ço$^n$-ga, e'-gi-e a-ka', a bi$^n$ da, ṭsi ga,

173. O'-ṭo$^n$-be ga-xa thi$^n$ ha, e-gi-e a-ka', a bi$^n$ da, ṭsi ga,

174. Ga' xtsi hi-tha i do$^n$ a', a bi$^n$ da, ṭsi ga,

175. Ṭa' tha-bthi$^n$ ṭo$^n$ no$^n$ a', a bi$^n$ da, ṭsi ga,

176. Wi'-ṭsi-go-e', e-gi-e a-ka', a bi$^n$ da, ṭsi ga,

177. Zhi$^n$'-ga zhu-i-ga the thi$^n$-ge a-tha, wi-ṭsi-go-e, e-gi-e a-ka', a bi$^n$ da, ṭsi ga,

178. Zhi$^n$'-ga zhu-i-ga tha ba tho$^n$ ṭa ni-ḳa-shi-ga mi-kshi$^n$ da', a bi$^n$ da, ṭsi ga,

179. Wa'-ḳo$^n$-da ṭs'e wa-ṭse-xi bhi$^n$ da', a bi$^n$ da, ṭsi ga,

180. Zhi$^n$'-ga zhu-i-ga o$^n$-tha bi do$^n$ a', a bi$^n$ da, ṭsi ga,

181. Ṭs'e' wa-ṭse-xi mo$^n$-thi$^n$ ṭa i tsi$^n$ da', a bi$^n$ da, ṭsi ga,

182. Wa'-ḳo$^n$-da e-shki do$^n$ a', a bi$^n$ da, ṭsi ga,

183. U'-zho$^n$-ge be o$^n$-tho$^n$-kshi-tha mo$^n$-zhi a thi$^n$ he i$^n$ da', a bi$^n$ da, ṭsi ga,

184. Zhi$^n$'-ga zhu-i-ga o$^n$-tha bi do$^n$ a', a bi$^n$ da, ṭsi ga,

185. Wa'-ḳo$^n$-da e-shki do$^n$ a', a bi$^n$ da, ṭsi ga,

186. U'-zho$^n$-ga be i-kshi tha ba zhi mo$^n$-thi$^n$ ṭa i tsi$^n$ da', a bi$^n$ da, ṭsi ga,

187. Wa'-ḳo$^n$-da e-shki do$^n$ a', a bi$^n$ da, ṭsi ga,

188. U'-zho$^n$-ge be u-wo$^n$-no$^n$-zhi$^n$ mo$^n$-zhi a-thi$^n$ he i$^n$ da', a bi$^n$ da, ṭsi ga,

189. Zhi$^n$'-ga zhu-i-ga o$^n$-tha bi do$^n$ a', a bi$^n$ da, ṭsi ga,

190. Wa'-ḳo$^n$-da e-shki do$^n$ a', a bi$^n$ da, ṭsi ga,

191. U'-zho$^n$-ge be u-no$^n$-zhi$^n$ ba zhi ḳi-the mo$^n$-thi$^n$ ṭa i tsi$^n$ da' a bi$^n$ da, ṭsi ga,

192. U'-no$^n$ a bi shki u-hi a-ḳi-the a-thi$^n$ he i$^n$ da', a bi$^n$ da, ṭsi ga,

193. Zhi$^n$'-ga zhu-i-ga o$^n$-tha bi do$^n$ a', a bi$^n$ da, ṭsi ga,

194. U'-no$^n$ a bi shki u-hi ḳi-the mo$^n$-thi$^n$ ṭa i tsi$^n$ da', a bi$^n$ da, ṭsi ga,

195. Ho$^n$'-ba tha-gthi$^n$ shki u-hi a-ḳi-the a-thi$^n$ he i$^n$ da', a bi$^n$ da, ṭsi ga,

196. Zhi$^n$'-ga zhu-i-ga o$^n$-tha bi do$^n$ a', a bi$^n$ da, ṭsi ga,

197. Ho$^n$'-ba tha-gthi$^n$ shki u-hi ḳi-the mo$^n$-thi$^n$ ṭa i tsi$^n$ da', a bi$^n$ da, ṭsi ga.

8

198. Zhi$^n$'-ga zhu-i-ga the thi$^n$-ge a-tha, wi-ço$^n$-ga, e-ḳi-e a-ka', a bi$^n$ da, ṭsi ga,

199. O'-ṭo$^n$-be ga-xa thi$^n$ ha', a bi$^n$ da, ṭsi ga,

200. Ka' ha-ge ṭo$^n$ a', a bi$^n$ da, ṭsi ga,

201. Wi'-ço$^n$-ga, e-gi-e a-ka', a bi$^n$ da, ṭsi ga,

202. Zhi$^n$'-ga zhu-i-ga the thi$^n$-ge a-tha, wi-ço$^n$-ga, e'-gi-e a-ka', a bi$^n$ da, ṭsi ga,

203. O'-ṭo$^n$-be ga-xa thi$^n$ ha', a bi$^n$ da, ṭsi ga,

204. Ga' xtsi hi-tha i do$^n$ a', a bi$^n$ da, ṭsi ga,

205. Mi'-ḳa-ḳ'e u-ḳi-tha-ç'i$^n$ thi$^n$-kshe no$^n$ a', a bi$^n$ da, ṭsi ga,

206. I'-ḳo-e, e-gi-e a-ka', a bi$^n$ da, ṭsi ga,

207. Zhi$^n$'-ga zhu-i-ga the thi$^n$-ge a-tha, e'-gi-e a-ka', a bi$^n$ da, ṭsi ga,

208. Zhi$^n$'-ga zhu-i-ga tha ba tho$^n$ ṭa ni-ḳa-shi-ga mi-kshi$^n$ da', a bi$^n$ da, ṭsi ga,

209. Wa'-ḳo$^n$-da ṭs'e wa-ṭse-xi bthi$^n$ da', a bi$^n$ da, ṭsi ga,

210. Zhi$^n$'-ga zhu-i-ga o$^n$-tha bi do$^n$ a', a bi$^n$ da, ṭsi ga,

211. Ṭs'e' wa-ṭse-xi mo$^n$-thi$^n$ ṭa i tsi$^n$ da', a bi$^n$ da, ṭsi ga,

212. Wa'-ḳo$^n$-da e-shki do$^n$ a', a bi$^n$ da, ṭsi ga,

213. U'-zho$^n$-ge be o$^n$-tho$^n$-kshi-tha mo$^n$-zhi a-thi$^n$ he i$^n$ da', a bi$^n$ da, ṭsi ga,

214. Zhi$^n$'-ga zhu-i-ga o$^n$-tha bi do$^n$ a', a bi$^n$ da, ṭsi ga,

215. Wa'-ḳo$^n$-da e-shki do$^n$ a', a bi$^n$ da, ṭsi ga,

216. U'-zho$^n$-ge be i-kshi-tha ba zhi mo$^n$-thi$^n$ ṭa i tsi$^n$ da', a bi$^n$ da, ṭsi ga,

217. Wa'-ḳo$^n$-da e-shki do$^n$ a', a bi$^n$ da, ṭsi ga,
218. U'-zho$^n$-ge be o$^n$-wo$^n$-no$^n$-zhi$^n$ mo$^n$-zhi a-thi$^n$ he i$^n$ da', a bi$^n$
     da, ṭsi ga,
219. Zhi$^{n\prime}$-ga zhu-i-ga o$^n$-tha bi do$^n$ a', a bi$^n$ da, ṭsi ga,
220. Wa'-ḳo$^n$-da e-shki do$^n$ a', a bi$^n$ da, ṭsi ga,
221. U'-zho$^n$-ge be u-no$^n$-zhi$^n$ ba zhi mo$^n$-thi$^n$ ṭa i tsi$^n$ da', a bi$^n$
     da, ṭsi ga,
222. U'-no$^n$ a bi shki u-hi a-ḳi-the a-thi$^n$ he i$^n$ da', a bi$^n$ da, ṭsi ga,
223. Zhi$^{n\prime}$-ga zhu-i-ga o$^n$-tha bi do$^n$ a', a bi$^n$ da, ṭsi ga,
224. U'-no$^n$ a bi shki u-hi ḳi-the mo$^n$-thi$^n$ ṭa i tsi$^n$ da', a bi$^n$ da, ṭsi
     ga
225. Ho$^{n\prime}$-ba tha-gthi$^n$ shki u-hi a-ḳi-the a-thi$^n$ he i$^n$ da', a bi$^n$ da,
     ṭsi ga,
226. Zhi$^{n\prime}$-ga zhu-i-ga o$^n$-tha bi do$^n$ a', a bi$^n$ da, ṭsi ga,
227. Ho$^{n\prime}$-ba tha-gthi$^n$ shki u-hi ḳi-the mo$^n$-thi$^n$ ṭa i tsi$^n$ da', a
     bi$^n$ da, ṭsi ga.

## ZHA'-ZHE ḲI-ṬO$^N$ WI'-GI-E

### 1

1. Ha! wi-ço$^n$-ge- e'-ḳi-e a-ka'-a bi$^n$ da, ṭsi ga,
2. Zhi$^{n\prime}$-ga zhu-i-ga the thi$^n$-ge a-tha, wi-ço$^n$-ga, e'-ḳi-e a-ka',
   a bi$^n$ da, ṭsi ga,
3. O'-ṭo$^n$-be ga-xa ba thi$^n$ ha', wi-ço$^n$-ga, e'-ḳi-e a-ka', a bi$^n$ da,
   ṭsi ga,
4. Ka' ha-ge ṭo$^n$ a', a bi$^n$ da, ṭsi ga,
5. Wi'-ço$^n$-ga, e-gi-e a-ka', a bi$^n$ da, ṭsi ga,
6. Zhi$^{n\prime}$-ga zhu-i-ga the thi$^n$-ge a-tha, wi-ço$^n$-ga, e-gi-e a-ka', a
   bi$^n$ da, ṭsi ga,
7. O'-ṭo$^n$-be ga-xa thi$^n$ ha', wi-ço$^n$-ga, e'-gi-e a-ka', a bi$^n$ da, ṭsi ga,
8. Ga' xtsi hi-tha i do$^n$ a', a bi$^n$ da, ṭsi ga,
9. Mo$^{n\prime}$-xe u-ça-ḳi-ba wi$^n$ a', a bi$^n$ da, tsi ga,
10. E'-dsi xtsi hi no$^n$-zhi$^n$ ṭo$^n$ a', a bi$^n$ da, ṭsi ga,
11. Zhi$^{n\prime}$-ga ni-ḳa-shi-ga zhi a-ka i$^n$ da', a bi$^n$ da, ṭsi ga,

### 2

12. Ha'!wi-ço$^n$-ga, e-ḳi-e a-ka', a bi$^n$ da, ṭsi ga,
13. Zhi$^{n\prime}$-ga zhu-i-ga the thi$^n$-ge a-tha, wi-ço$^n$-ga, e'-ḳi-e a-ka', a
    bi$^n$ da, ṭsi ga,
14. O'-ṭo$^n$-be ga-xa ba thi$^n$ ha', wi-ço$^n$-ga, e-'ḳi-e a-ka', a bi$^n$ da,
    ṭsi ga,
15. Ka' ha-ge ṭo$^n$ a', a bi$^n$ da, ṭsi ga,
16. Wi'-ço$^n$-ga, e-gi-e a-ka', a bi$^n$ da, ṭsi ga,
17. O'-ṭo$^n$-ba ga-xa thi$^n$ ha, wi-ço$^n$-ga- e-gi-e a-ka', a bi$^n$ da, ṭsi ga,
18. Mo$^{n\prime}$-xe u-ca-ḳi-ba we-tho$^n$-ba kshe a', a bi$^n$ da, ṭsi ga,

19. E'-dsi xtsi a', a bi$^n$ da, ṭsi ga,
20. He' go$^n$ tho$^n$-ta zhi i$^n$ da', a bi$^n$ da, ṭsi ga,
21. Zhi$^{n\prime}$-ga ni-ḳi-shi-ga zhi a-ka i$^n$ da', a bi$^n$ da, ṭsi ga,

### 3

22. Ha! wi-ço$^n$-ga, e-ḳi-e a-ka, a bi$^n$ da, ṭsi ga,
23. Zhi$^{n\prime}$-ga zhu-i-ga the thi$^n$-ge a-tha, wi-ço$^n$-ga, e-ḳi-e a-ka', a bi$^n$ da, ṭsi ga,
24. O'-ṭo$^n$-be ga-xa ba thi$^n$ ha', a bi$^n$ da, ṭsi ga,
25. Ḳa' ha-ge ṭo$^n$ a', a bi$^n$ da, ṭsi ga,
26. Wi'-ço$^n$-ga, e'-gi-e a-ka', a bi$^n$ da, ṭsi ga,
27. Zhi$^{n\prime}$-ga zhu-i-ga the thi$^n$-ge a-tha, wi-ço$^n$-ga, e'-gi-e a-ka', a bi$^n$ da, ṭsi ga,
28. O'-ṭo$^n$-be ga-xa thi$^n$ ha, wi-ço$^n$-ga, e-gi-e a-ka', a bi$^n$ da, ṭsi ga,
29. Ga' xtsi hi-tha i do$^n$ a', a bi$^n$ da, ṭsi ga,
30. Mo$^{n\prime}$-xe u-ça-ḳi-ba we-tha-bthi$^n$ kshe a', a bi$^n$ da, ṭsi ga,
31. Zhi$^{n\prime}$-ga ni-ḳa-shi-ga zhi a-ka i$^n$ da', a bi$^n$ da, ṭsi ga.

### 4

32. He'-dsi xtsi a', a bi$^n$ da, ṭsi ga,
33. Zhi$^{n\prime}$-ga zhu-i-ga the thi$^n$-ge a-tha, wi-ço$^n$-ga, e'-ḳi-e, a-ka', a bi$^n$ da, ṭsi ga,
34. O'-ṭo$^n$-be ga-xa thi$^n$ ha', a bi$^n$ da, ṭsi ga,
35. Ḳa'-e ha-ge ṭo$^n$ a', a bi$^n$ da, ṭsi ga,
36. Wi'-ço$^n$-ga, e-gi-e a-ka', a bi$^n$ da, ṭsi ga,
37. Zhi$^{n\prime}$-ga zhu-i-ga the thi$^n$-ge a-tha, wi-ço$^n$-ga, e'-gi-e a-ka', a bi$^n$ da, ṭsi ga,
38. O'-ṭo$^n$-be ga-xa thi$^n$ ha, wi-ço$^n$-ga, e'-gi-e a-ka', a bi$^n$ da, ṭsi ga,
39. Ga' xtsi hi-tha i do$^n$ a', a bi$^n$ da, ṭsi ga,
40. Mo$^{n\prime}$-xe u-ça-ḳi-ba we-do-ba kshe a', a bi$^n$ da, ṭsi ga,
41. Wa'-zhi$^n$-ga wa-tha-xthi thi$^n$-ge kshe no$^n$ a', a bi$^n$ da, ṭsi ga,
42. Ṭsi'-he u-gi-zho$^n$ xtsi ni-ḳa-shi-ga kshe a', a bi$^n$ da, ṭsi ga,
43. Mo$^n$-zho$^n$ u-ṭo$^n$-ga xtsi thi$^n$-kshe dsi a', a bi$^n$ da, ṭsi ga,
44. Ni'-ḳa-shi-ga ṭo$^n$ i$^n$ da', a bi$^n$ da, ṭsi ga,
45. Mo$^{n\prime}$-zho$^n$ shki zha-zhe o$^n$-ḳi-ṭo$^n$ ṭa i tsi$^n$ da', a bi$^n$ da, ṭsi ga,
46. Mo$^{n\prime}$-zho$^n$ ga-sho$^n$ xtsi ni-ḳa-shi-ga ṭo$^n$ i$^n$ da', a bi$^n$ da, tsi ga,
47. Mo$^{n\prime}$-zho$^n$ ga-sho$^n$ shki zha-zhe o$^n$-ḳi-ṭo$^n$ ṭa i tsi$^n$ da,' a bi$^n$ da, ṭsi ga,
48. Mo$^{n\prime}$-zho$^n$ u-çko$^n$-çka xtsi ni-ḳa-shi-ga ṭo$^n$ i$^n$ da', a bi$^n$ da, ṭsi ga,
49. Mo$^{n\prime}$-zho$^n$ u-çko$^n$-çka shki zha-zhe o$^n$-ḳi-ṭo$^n$ ṭa i tsi$^n$ da,' a bi$^n$ da, ṭsi ga,
50. Zhi$^{n\prime}$-ga ni-ḳa-shi-ga bi$^n$ da', a bi$^n$ da, ṭsi ga,
51. Xi-tha-da wi$^n$ shki zha-zhe o$^n$-ḳi-ṭo$^n$ ṭa i tsi$^n$ da, a bi$^n$ da, ṭsi ga,
52. Hi$^{n\prime}$-i-ḳi$^n$-da-bi shki zha-zhe o$^n$-ḳi-ṭo$^n$ ṭa i tsi$^n$ da', a bi$^n$ da, ṭsi ga,

53. Hi$^n$'-ga-mo$^n$-ge shki zha-zhe o$^n$-ḳi-ṭo$^n$ ṭa i tsi$^n$ da', a bi$^n$ da, ṭsi ga,

54. No$^n$'-be-çi shki zha-zhe o$^n$-ḳi-ṭo$^n$ ṭa i tsi$^n$ da', a bi$^n$ da, ṭsi ga,

55. Wa'-zhi$^n$-ga-hi$^n$ shki zha-zhe o$^n$-ḳi-ṭo$^n$ ṭa i tsi$^n$ da', a bi$^n$ da, ṭsi ga.

5

56. He'-dsi xtsi a', a bi$^n$ da, ṭsi ga,

57. Çi'-pa-hi xthu-k'a ga ṭse a', a bi$^n$ da, ṭsi ga,

58. U'-no$^n$ pa-xe i$^n$ da', a bi$^n$ da, ṭsi ga,

59. Zhi$^n$'-ga zhu-i-ga o$^n$-tha bi do$^n$ a', a bi$^n$ da, ṭsi ga,

60. Çi'-pa-hi xthu-k'a a bi shki i-the ḳi-the mo$^n$-thi$^n$ ṭa i tsi$^n$ da', a bi$^n$ da, ṭsi ga.

61. No$^n$'-xpe-hi ha ba-ç'i$^n$-tha ga ge shki a', a bi$^n$ da, ṭsi ga,

62. U'-no$^n$ pa-xe i$^n$ da', a bi$^n$ da, ṭsi ga,

63. Zhi$^n$'-ga zhu-i-ga o$^n$-tha bi do$^n$ a', a bi$^n$ da, ṭsi ga,

64. No$^n$'-xpe-hi ha ba-ç'i$^n$-tha a bi shki i-the ḳi-the mo$^n$-thi$^n$ ṭa i tsi$^n$ da, a bi$^n$ da, ṭsi ga.

65. Shi'-tho$^n$-dse ba-xo$^n$ ga ṭse a', a bi$^n$ da, ṭsi ga,

66. U'-no$^n$ pa-xe i$^n$ da', a bi$^n$ da, ṭsi ga,

67. Zhi$^n$'-ga zhu-i-ga o$^n$-tha bi do$^n$ a', a bi$^n$ da, ṭsi ga,

68. Shi'-tho$^n$-dse ba-xo$^n$ a bi shki i-the ḳi-the mo$^n$-thi$^n$ ṭa i tsi$^n$ da', a bi$^n$ da, ṭsi ga.

69. I'-ṭsi-hi$^n$ ga-gthe-çe ga ge a', a bi$^n$ da, ṭsi ga,

70. U'-no$^n$ pa-xe i$^n$ da', a bi$^n$ da, ṭsi ga,

71. Zhi$^n$'-ga zhu-i-ga o$^n$-tha bi do$^n$ a', a bi$^n$ da, ṭsi ga,

72. I'-ṭsi-ga-gthe-çe a bi shki i-the ḳi the mo$^n$-thi$^n$ ṭa i tsi$^n$ da', a bi$^n$ da, ṭsi ga.

73. Mo$^n$'-ge hi$^n$ ga-gthe-çe ga ge shki a', a bi$^n$ da, ṭsi ga,

74. U'-no$^n$ pa-xe i$^n$ da', a bi$^n$ da, ṭsi ga,

75. Zhi$^n$'-ga zhu-i-ga o$^n$-tha bi do$^n$ a', bi$^n$ da, ṭsi ga,

76. Mo$^n$'-ge ga-gthe-çe a bi shki i-the ḳi-the mo$^n$-thi$^n$ ṭa i tsi$^n$ da', a bin da, ṭsi ga.

77. I'-the-dse hi$^n$ ga-gthe-çe ga ge a', a bi$^n$ da, ṭsi ga,

78. U'-no$^n$ pa-xe i$^n$ da', a bi$^n$ da, ṭsi ga,

79. Zhi$^n$'-ga zhu-i-ga o$^n$-tha bi do$^n$ a', a bi$^n$ da, ṭsi ga,

80. I'-the-dse ga-gthe-çe a bi shki i-the ḳi-the mo$^n$-thi$^n$ ṭa i tsi$^n$ da', a bi$^n$ da, ṭsi ga.

81. Pe' hi$^n$ ga-gthe-çe ga ge a', bi$^n$ da, ṭsi ga,

82. U'-no$^n$ pa-xe i$^n$ da', a bi$^n$ da, ṭsi ga,

83. Zhi$^n$'-ga zhu-i-ga o$^n$-tha bi do$^n$ a', a bi$^n$ da, ṭsi ga,

84. Pe' ga-gthe-çe a bi shki i-the ḳi-the mo$^n$-thi$^n$ ṭa i tsi$^n$ da', a bi$^n$ da, ṭsi ga.

85. I$^n$'-shta-ha bi-xo$^n$ ga ge a', a bi$^n$ da, ṭsi ga,
86. U'-no$^n$ pa-xe i$^n$ da', a bi$^n$ da, ṭsi ga,
87. Zhi$^n$'-ga zhu-i-ga o$^n$-tha bi do$^n$ a', a bi$^n$ da, ṭsi ga,
88. I$^n$'-shta-ha bi-xo$^n$ a bi shki i-the ḳi-the mo$^n$-thi$^n$ ṭa i tsi$^n$ da', a bi$^n$ da, ṭsi ga.

89. U'-no$^n$ a bi shki u-hi a-ḳi-the a-thi$^n$ he i$^n$ da, a bi$^n$ da', ṭsi ga,
90. Zhi$^n$-ga zhu-i-ga o$^n$-tha bi do$^n$ a', a bi$^n$ da, ṭsi ga,
91. U'-no$^n$ a bi shki i-the ḳi-the mo$^n$-thi$^n$ ṭa i tsi$^n$ da', a bi$^n$ da, ṭsi ga.

92. Ho$^n$'-ba tha-gthi$^n$ shki u-hi a-ḳi-the a-thi$^n$ he i$^n$ da', a bi$^n$ da, ṭsi ga,
93. Zhi$^n$'-ga zhu-i-ga o$^n$-tha bi do$^n$ a', a bi$^n$ da, ṭsi ga,
94. Ho$^n$'-ba tha-gthi$^n$ shki u-hi ḳi-the mo$^n$-thi$^n$ ṭa i tsi$^n$ da', a bi$^n$ da, ṭsi ga.

## WA-ZHO'-I-GA-THE WI'-GI-E

### 1

1. He'-dsi xtsi a', a bi$^n$ da, ṭsi ga,
2. Ṭsi'-shu u-dse-the pe-tho$^n$-ba ni-ḳa-shi-ga ba do$^n$ a', a bi$^n$ da, ṭsi ga,
3. Wi'-ço$^n$-ga, e'-ḳi-a bi a', a bi$^n$ da, ṭsi ga,
4. Zhi$^n$'-ga zho-i-ga-the thi$^n$-ge i$^n$ da, e'-ḳi-e a-ka', a bi$^n$ da, ṭsi ga,
5. He'-dsi xtsi a', a bi$^n$ da, ṭsi ga,
6. Sho'-ḳa wa-ba-xi ṭo$^n$ a', a bi$^n$ da, ṭsi ga,
7. Wi'-ço$^n$-ga, e'-gi-a bi a', a bi$^n$ da, ṭsi ga,
8. Zhi$^n$'-ga zho-i-ga-the thi$^n$-ge i$^n$ da, e'-gi-a bi a', a bi$^n$ da, ṭsi ga,
9. O'-ṭo$^n$-be ga-xa thi$^n$ ha, e'-gi-e a-ka', a bi$^n$ da, ṭsi ga,
10. He'-dsi xtsi a', a bi$^n$ da, ṭsi ga,
11. Sho'-ḳa wa-ba-xi ṭo$^n$ a', a bi$^n$ da, ṭsi ga,
12. Thu-e' xtsi the-e do$^n$ a', a bi$^n$ da, ṭsi ga,
13. Wa'-ḳo$^n$-da Ho$^n$-ba do$^n$ thi$^n$-kshe a', bin da, ṭsi ga,
14. Zho'-gthe gi-e do$^n$ a', a bi$^n$ da, ṭsi ga,
15. Wi'-ṭsi-go-e, e-gi-e a-ka', a bi$^n$ da, ṭsi ga,
16. Zhi$^n$'-ga zho-i-ga the thi$^n$-ge a-tha, e'-gi-e a-ka',a bi$^n$ da, ṭsi ga,
17. He'-dsi xtsi a', a bi$^n$ da, ṭsi ga,
18. She' sho$^n$ e tho, e-ṭsi-the a', a bi$^n$ da, ṭsi ga,
19. Wa'-ḳo$^n$-da ho-wa-ḳi-pa-ṭse a', a bi$^n$ da, ṭsi ga,
20. Wi'no$^n$ wa-ḳo$^n$-da bthi$^n$ i$^n$ da', a bi$^n$ da, ṭsi ga,
21. Zhi$^n$'-ga zho-i-ga o$^n$-the ṭa i tsi$^n$ da', a bi$^n$ da, ṭsi ga,
22. Wa'-ḳo$^n$-da e-shki do$^n$ a', a bi$^n$ da, ṭsi ga,
23. O'-zho$^n$-ge be o$^n$-tho$^n$-kshi tha mo$^n$-zhi a-thi$^n$ he no$^n$ a-tha', a bi$^n$ da, ṭsi ga,
24. Zhi$^n$'-ga zho-i-ga o$^n$-tha bi do$^n$ a', a bi$^n$ da, ṭsi ga,
25. Wa'-ḳo$^n$-da e-shki do$^n$ a', a bi$^n$ da, ṭsi ga,

26. O'-zho$^n$-ge be i-kshi-tha ba zhi ḳi-the ṭa i tsi$^n$ da e' ṭsi-the a', a bi$^n$
　　da, ṭsi ga,
27. Wa'-ḳo$^n$-da e'-shki do$^n$ a', a bi$^n$ da, ṭsi ga,
28. O'-zho$^n$-ge be o$^n$-gi-thi-ṭa mo$^n$-zhi a-thi$^n$ he no$^n$ i$^n$ da', a bi$^n$ da,
　　ṭsi ga,
29. Zhi$^{n'}$-ga zho-i-ga o$^n$-tha bi do$^n$ a', a bi$^n$ da, ṭsi ga,
30. Wa'-ḳo$^n$-da e-shki do$^n$ a', a bi$^n$ da, ṭsi ga,
31. O'-zho$^n$-ge be a-gi-thi-ṭa ba zhi ḳi-the mo$^n$-thi$^n$ ṭa i tsi$^n$ da, e'
　　ṭsi-the a', a bi$^n$ da, ṭsi ga,
32. Wa'-ḳo$^n$-da e-shki do$^n$ a', a bi$^n$ da, ṭsi ga,
33. O'-zho$^n$-ge be o$^n$-wo$^n$-no$^n$-zhi$^n$ ṭse a, hi$^n$ a', a bi$^n$ da, ṭsi ga,
34. Zhi$^{n'}$-ga zho-i-ga o$^n$-tha bi do$^n$ a', a bi$^n$ da, ṭsi ga,
35. Wa'-ḳo$^n$-da e-shki do$^n$ a', a bi$^n$ da, ṭsi ga,
36. O'-zho$^n$-ge be o-no$^n$-zhi$^n$ ba zhi ḳi-the ṭa i tsi$^n$ da, e' ṭsi-the a',
　　a bi$^n$ da, ṭsi ga,
37. Wa'-ḳo$^n$-da wi'no$^n$ bthi$^n$ mo$^n$-zhi i$^n$ da', a bi$^n$ da, ṭsi ga,
38. O'-ṭo$^n$-be ga-xa ba thi$^n$ ha, e ṭsi-the a', a bi$^n$ da, ṭsi ga,

2

39. He'-dsi xtsi a', a bi$^n$ da, ṭsi ga,
40. Sho'-ḳa wa-ba-xi ṭo$^n$ a', a bi$^n$ da, ṭsi a,
41. Thu-e' xtsi the-e do$^n$ a', a bi$^n$ da, ṭsi ga,
42. Wa'-ḳo$^n$-da Ho$^n$ do$^n$ thi$^n$-kshe a', a bi$^n$ da, ṭsi ga,
43. Zho'-gthe gi-e do$^n$ a', a bi$^n$ da, ṭsi ga,
44. I'-ḳo-e e-gi-e a-ka', a bi$^n$ da, ṭsi ga,
45. Zhi$^{n'}$-ga zho-i-ga the thi$^n$-ge a-tha, e'-gi-e a-ka', a bi$^n$ da, ṭsi ga,
46. E'-dsi xtsi a', a bi$^n$ da, ṭsi ga,
47. She' sho$^n$ e tho, e ṭsi-the a', a bi$^n$ da, ṭsi ga,
48. Wa'-ḳo$^n$-da ho-wa-ḳi-pa-ṭse a', a bi$^n$ da, ṭsi ga,
49. Wi'-no$^n$ wa-ḳo$^n$-da bthi$^n$ i$^n$ da', a bi$^n$ da, ṭsi ga,
50. Wa'-ḳo$^n$-da e-shki do$^n$ a', a bi$^n$ da, ṭsi ga,
51. O'-zho$^n$-ge be o$^n$-tho$^n$-kshi-tha mo$^n$-zhi a-thi$^n$ he no$^n$ i$^n$ da', a
　　bi$^n$ da, ṭsi ga,
52. Zhi$^{n'}$-ga zho-i-ga o$^n$-tha bi do$^n$ a', a bi$^n$ da, ṭsi ga,
53. Wa'-ḳo$^n$-da e-shki do$^n$ a', a bi$^n$ da, ṭsi ga,
54. O'-zho$^n$-ge be i-kshi-tha ba zhi ḳi-the ṭa i tsi$^n$ da, e' ṭsi-the a', a
　　bi$^n$ da, ṭsi ga,
55. Wa'-ḳo$^n$-da e-shki do$^n$ a', a bi$^n$ da, ṭsi ga,
56. O'-zho$^n$-ge be o$^n$-gi-thi-ṭa mo$^n$-zhi a-thi$^n$ he no$^n$ i$^n$ da', a bi$^n$
　　da, ṭsi ga,
57. Zhi$^{n'}$-ga zho-i-ga o$^n$-tha bi do$^n$ a', a bi$^n$ da, ṭsi ga,
58. Wa'-ḳo$^n$-da e-shki do$^n$ a', a bi$^n$ da, ṭsi ga,
59. O'-zho$^n$-ge be a-gi-thi-ṭa ba zhi ḳi-the ṭa i tsi$^n$ da, e' ṭsi-the a',
　　a bi$^n$ da, ṭsi ga.
60. Wa'-ḳo$^n$-da e'-shki do$^n$ a', a bi$^n$ da, ṭsi ga,

61. O'-zho$^n$-ge be o$^n$-wo$^n$-no$^n$-zhi$^n$ ṭse a, hi$^n$ a', a bi$^n$ da, ṭsi ga,
62. Zhi$^{n\prime}$-ga zho-i-ga o$^n$-tha bi do$^n$ a', a bi$^n$ da, ṭsi ga,
63. Wa'-ḳo$^n$-da e-shki do$^n$ a', a bi$^n$ da, ṭsi ga,
64. O'-zho$^n$-ge be o-no$^n$-zhi$^n$ ba zhi ḳi-the ṭa i tsi$^n$ da, e' ṭsi-the a',
    a bi$^n$ da, ṭsi ga,
65. Wa'-ḳo$^n$-da wi no$^n$ bthi$^n$ mo$^n$-zhi i$^n$ da', a bi$^n$ da, ṭsi ga,
66. O'-ṭo$^n$-be ga-xa thi$^n$ ha, e' ṭsi-the a', a bi$^n$ da, ṭsi ga,

3

67. E'-dsi xtsi a', a bi$^n$ da, ṭsi ga,
68. Sho'-ḳa wa-ba-xi ṭo$^n$ a', a bi$^n$ da, ṭsi ga,
69. Thu-e' xtsi the-e do$^n$ a', a bi$^n$ da, ṭsi ga,
70. Mi'-ḳa-ḳ'e Ho$^n$-ba do$^n$ thi$^n$-kshe a', a bi$^n$ da, ṭsi ga,
71. Zho-'gthe gi-e do$^n$ a', a bi$^n$ da, ṭsi ga,
72. Wi'-ṭsi-go-e, e-gi-e a-ka', a bi$^n$ da, ṭsi ga,
73. Zhi$^{n\prime}$-ga zho-i-ga the thi$^n$-ge a-tha, e'-gi-e a-ka', a bi$^n$ da, ṭsi ga,
74. He'-dsi xtsi a', a bi$^n$ da, ṭsi ga,
75. She' sho$^n$ e tho e' ṭsi-the a', a bi$^n$ da, ṭsi ga,
76. Zhi$^{n\prime}$-ga zho-i-ga o$^n$-the ṭa i tsi$^n$ da, e' ṭsi-the a', a bi$^n$ da, ṭsi ga,
77. Wa'-ḳo$^n$-da ho-wa-ḳi-pa-ṭse a', a bi$^n$ da, ṭsi ga,
78. Wi'no$^n$ wa-ḳo$^n$-da bthi$^n$ i$^n$ da', a bi$^n$ da, ṭsi ga,
79. Zhi$^{n\prime}$-ga zho i-ga o$^n$-the ṭa i tsi$^n$ da, e ṭsi-the a', a bi$^n$ da, ṭsi ga',
80. Wa'-ḳo$^n$-da e'-shki do$^n$ a', a bi$^n$ da, ṭsi ga,
81. O'-zho$^n$-ge be o$^n$-tho$^n$-kshi-tha mo$^n$-zhi a thi$^n$ he no$^n$ da', a
    bi$^n$ da, ṭsi ga,
82. Zhi$^{n\prime}$-ga zho-i-ga o$^n$-tha bi do$^n$ a', a bi$^n$ da, ṭsi ga,
83. Wa'-ḳo$^n$-da e-shki do$^n$ a', a bi$^n$ da, ṭsi ga,
84. O'-zho$^n$-ge be i-kshi-tha ba zhi ḳi-the ṭa i tsi$^n$ da, e'ṭsi-the a',
    a bi$^n$ da, ṭsi ga.
85. Wa'-ḳo$^n$-da e-shki do$^n$ a', a bi$^n$ da, ṭsi ga,
86. O'-zho$^n$-ge be o$^n$-gi-thi-ṭa mo$^n$-zhi a-thi$^n$ he no$^n$ i$^n$ da', a bi$^n$
    da, ṭsi ga,
87. Zhi$^{n\prime}$-ga zho-i-ga o$^n$-tha bi do$^n$ a', a bi$^n$ da, ṭsi ga,
88. Wa'-ḳo$^n$-da e-shki do$^n$ a', a bi$^n$ da, ṭsi ga,
89. O'-zho$^n$-ge be a gi-thi-ṭa ba zhi ḳi-the ṭa i tsi$^n$ da, e' ṭsi-the a',
    a bi$^n$ da, ṭsi ga,
90. Wa'-ḳo$^n$-da e'-shki do$^n$ a', a bi$^n$ da, ṭsi ga,
91. O'-zho$^n$-ge be o$^n$-wo$^n$-no$^n$-zhi$^n$ ṭse a, hi$^n$ a', bi$^n$ da, ṭsi ga,
92. Zhi$^{n\prime}$-ga zho-i-ga o$^n$-tha bi do$^n$ a', a bi$^n$ da, ṭsi ga,
93. Wa'-ḳo$^n$-da e'-shki do$^n$ a', bi$^n$ da, ṭsi ga,
94. O'-zho$^n$-ge be o-no$^n$-zhi$^n$ ba zhi ḳi-the ṭa i tsi$^n$ da, e' ṭsi-the a',
    a bi$^n$ da, ṭsi ga,
95. Wa'-ḳo$^n$-da wi no$^n$ bthi$^n$ mo$^n$-zhi i$^n$ da', a bi$^n$ da, ṭsi ga,
96. Ho'-ṭo$^n$-be ga-xa thi$^n$ ha, e' ṭsi-the a', a bi$^n$ da, ṭsi ga,

4

97. Sho'-ḳa wa-ba-xi ṭo$^n$ a', a bi$^n$ da, ṭsi ga,
98. Thu-e' xtsi the-e do$^n$ a', e bi$^n$ da, ṭsi ga,
99. Mi'-ḳa-ḳ'e Ho$^n$ do$^n$ thi$^n$-kshe no$^n$ a', a bi$^n$ da, ṭsi ga,
100. Zho'-gthe gi-e do$^n$ a', a bi$^n$ da, ṭsi ga,
101. I'-ḳo-e, e-gi-e a-ka', a bi$^n$ da, ṭsi ga,
102. Zhi$^n$'-ga zho-i-ga the thi$^n$-ge a-tha, e'-gi-e a-ka', a bi$^n$ da, ṭsi ga,
103. He'-dsi xtsi a', a bi$^n$ da, ṭsi ga,
104. She' sho$^n$ e no$^n$, e'ṭsi-the a', a bi$^n$ da, ṭsi ga,
105. Wa'-ḳo$^n$-da ho-wa-ḳi-pa-ṭse a', a bi$^n$ da, ṭsi ga,
106. Wi' no$^n$ wa-ḳo$^n$-da bthi$^n$ i$^n$ da', a bi$^n$ da, ṭsi ga,
107. Zhi$^n$'-ga zho-i-ga o$^n$-tha bi do$^n$ a', a bi$^n$ da, ṭsi ga,
108. Wa'-ḳo$^n$-da e'-shki do$^n$ a', a bi$^n$ da, ṭsi ga,
109. Ho'-zho$^n$-ge be i-kshi-tha ba zhi ḳi-the mo$^n$-thi$^n$ ṭa i tsi$^n$ da', e ṭsi-the a', a bi$^n$ da, ṭsi ga,
110. Wa'-ḳo$^n$-da e-shki do$^n$ a', a bi$^n$ da, ṭsi ga,
111. Ho'-zho$^n$-ge be o$^n$-gi-thi-ta mo$^n$-zhi a-thi$^n$ he no$^n$ i$^n$ da', a bi$^n$ da, ṭsi ga,
112. Zhi$^n$'-ga zho-i-ga o$^n$-tha bi do$^n$ a', a bi$^n$ da, ṭsi ga,
113. Wa'-ḳo$^n$-da e'-shki do$^n$ a', a bi$^n$ da, ṭsi ga,
114. Ho'-zho$^n$-ge be a-gi-thi-ta ba zhi ḳi-the mo$^n$-thi$^n$ ṭa i tsi$^n$ da', e' ṭsi-the-the a', a bi$^n$ da, ṭsi ga,
115. Wa'-ḳo$^n$-da e'-shki do$^n$ a', a bi$^n$ da, ṭsi ga,
116. Ho'-zho$^n$-ge be o$^n$-wo$^n$-no$^n$-zhi$^n$ ṭse a, hi$^n$ a', a bi$^n$ da, ṭsi ga,
117. Zhi$^n$'-ga zho-i-ga o$^n$-tha bi do$^n$ a', a bi$^n$ da, ṭsi ga,
118. Wa'-ḳo$^n$-da e'-shki do$^n$ a', a bi$^n$ da, ṭsi ga,
119. O'-zho$^n$-ge be o-no$^n$-zhi$^n$ ba zhi ḳi-the ṭa i tsi$^n$ da, e' ṭsi-the a', a bi$^n$ da, ṭsi ga.
120. Wa'-ḳo$^n$-da wi no$^n$ bthi$^n$ mo$^n$-zhi i$^n$ da', a bi$^n$ da, ṭsi ga,
121. O'-ṭo$^n$-be ga-xa ba thi$^n$ ha, e' ṭsi-the a', a bi$^n$ da, ṭsi ga.

5

122. He'-dsi xtsi a', a bi$^n$ da, ṭsi ga,
123. Sho'-ḳa wa-ba-xi ṭo$^n$ a', a bi$^n$ da, ṭsi ga,
124. Thu-c' xtsi the-e do$^n$ a', a bi$^n$ da, ṭsi ga,
125. Wa'-ba-ha ṭo$^n$ a', a bi$^n$ da, ṭsi ga,
126. Zho'-gthe gi-e do$^n$ a', a bi$^n$ da, ṭsi ga,
127. Wi'-ṭsi-go-e', e-gi-a bi a', a bi$^n$ da, ṭsi ga,
128. Zhi$^n$'-ga zho-i-ga the thi$^n$-ge a-tha, e'-gi-e a-ka', a bi$^n$ da, tsi ga,
129. He'-dsi xtsi a', a bi$^n$ da, ṭsi ga,
130. She' sho$^n$ e tho, e'tsi-the a', a bi$^n$ da, ṭsi ga,
131. Wa'-ḳo$^n$-da ho-wa-ḳi-pa-ṭse a', a bi$^n$ da, ṭsi ga,
132. Wi'no$^n$ wa-ḳo$^n$-da bthi$^n$ i$^n$ da', a bi$^n$ da, ṭsi ga,
133. Zhi$^n$'-ga zho-i-ga o$^n$-the ṭa i tsi$^n$ da, e'tsi-the a', a bi$^n$ da, ṭsi ga,

134. Wa'-ḳo$^n$-da e-shki do$^n$ a', a bi$^n$ da, ṭsi ga,
135. O'-zho$^n$-ge be o$^n$-tho$^n$-kshi-tha mo$^n$-zhi a-thi$^n$ he no$^n$ i$^n$ da', a bi$^n$ da, ṭsi ga,
136. Zhi$^{n'}$-ga zho-i-ga o$^n$-tha bi do$^n$ a', a bi$^n$ da, ṭsi ga,
137. Wa'-ḳo$^n$-da e-shki do$^n$ a', a bi$^n$ da, ṭsi ga,
138. O'-zho$^n$-ge be i-kshi-tha ba zhi ḳi-the mo$^n$-thi$^n$ ṭa i tsi$^n$ da, e' ṭsi-the a', a bi$^n$ da, ṭsi ga,
139. Wa'-ḳo$^n$-da e-shki do$^n$ a', a bi$^n$ da, ṭsi ga,
140. O'-zho$^n$-ge be o$^n$-gi-thi-ṭa mo$^n$-zhi a-thi$^n$ he no$^n$ i$^n$ da', a bi$^n$ da, ṭsi ga,
141. Zhi$^{n'}$-ga zho-i-ga o$^n$-tha bi do$^n$ a', a bi$^n$ da, ṭsi ga,
142. Wa'-ḳo$^n$-da e-shki do$^n$ a', a bi$^n$ da, ṭsi ga,
143. O'-zho$^n$-ge be a-gi-thi-ta ba zhi ḳi-the ṭa i tsi$^n$ da, e' ṭsi-the a', a bi$^n$ da, ṭsi ga,
144. Wa'-ḳo$^n$-da e-shki do$^n$ a', a bi$^n$ da, ṭsi ga,
145. O'-zho$^n$-ge be o$^n$-wo$^n$-no$^n$-zhi$^n$ ṭse a, hi$^n$ a', a bi$^n$ da, ṭsi ga,
146. Zhi$^{n'}$-ga zho-i-ga o$^n$-tha bi do$^n$ a', a bi$^n$ da, ṭsi ga,
147. Wa'-ḳo$^n$-da e-shki do$^n$ a', a bi$^n$ da, ṭsi ga,
148. O'-zho$^n$-ge be o-no$^n$-zhi$^n$ ba zhi ḳi-the ṭa i tsi$^n$ da, e' ṭsi-the a', a bi$^n$ da, ṭsi ga,
149. Wa'-ḳo$^n$-da wi'no$^n$ bthi$^n$ mo$^n$-zhi i$^n$ da', a bi$^n$ da, ṭsi ga,
150. O'-ṭo$^n$-be ga-xa ba thi$^n$ ha, e'-ṭsi-the a', a bi$^n$ da, ṭsi ga.

### 6

151. He'-dsi xtsi a', a bi$^n$ da, ṭsi ga,
152. Sho'-ḳa wa-ba-xi ṭo$^n$ a', a bi$^n$ da, ṭsi ga,
153. Thu-e' xtsi the-e do$^n$ a', a bi$^n$ da, ṭsi ga,
154. Ṭa'-pa ṭo$^n$ no$^n$ a', a bi$^n$ da, ṭsi ga,
155. Zho'-gthe gi-e do$^n$ a', a bi$^n$ da, ṭsi ga,
156. I'-ḳo-e, e-gi-e a-ka', a bi$^n$ da, ṭsi ga,
157. Zhi$^{n'}$-ga zho-i-ga the thi$^n$-ge a-tha, e'-gi-e a-ka', a bi$^n$ da, ṭsi ga,
158. He'-dsi xtsi a', a bi$^n$ da, ṭsi ga,
159. She' sho$^n$ e the, e' ṭsi-the a', a bi$^n$ da, ṭsi ga,
160. Wa'-ḳo$^n$-da ho-wa-ḳi-pa-ṭse a', a bi$^n$ da, ṭsi ga,
161. Wi'no$^n$ wa-ḳo$^n$-da bthi$^n$ i$^n$ da', a bi$^n$ da, ṭsi ga,
162. Wa'-ḳo$^n$-da e-shki do$^n$ a', a bi$^n$ da, ṭsi ga,
163. O'-zho$^n$-ge be o$^n$-tho$^n$-kshi-tha mo$^n$-zhi a-thi$^n$ he no$^n$ i$^n$ da', a bi$^n$ da, ṭsi ga,
164. Zhi$^{n'}$-ga zho-i-ga o$^n$-tha bi do$^n$ a', a bi$^n$ da, ṭsi ga,
165. Wa'-ḳo$^n$-da e'-shki do$^n$ a', a bi$^n$ da, ṭsi ga,
166. O'-zho$^n$-ge be i-kshi-tha ba zhi ḳi-the ṭa i tsi$^n$ da, e' ṭsi-the a', a bi$^n$ da, ṭsi ga,
167. Wa'-ḳo$^n$-da e'-shki do$^n$ a', a bi$^n$ da, ṭsi ga,
168. O'-zho$^n$-ge be o$^n$-gi-thi-ṭa mo$^n$-zhi a-thi$^n$ he no$^n$ i$^n$ da', a bi$^n$ da, ṭsi ga,
169. Zhi$^{n'}$-ga zho-i-ga o$^n$-tha bi do$^n$ a', a bi$^n$ da, ṭsi ga,

170. Wa'-ko$^n$-da e-shki do$^n$ a', a bi$^n$ da, ṭsi ga,
171. O'-zho$^n$-ge be a-gi-thi-ṭa ba zhi ḳi-the ṭa i ṭsi$^n$ da, e' ṭsi-the a', a bi$^n$ da, ṭsi ga,
172. Wa'-ko$^n$-da e-shki do$^n$ a', a bi$^n$ da, ṭsi ga,
173. O'-zho$^n$-ge be o$^n$-wo$^n$-no$^n$-zhi$^n$ ṭse a, hi$^n$ a', a bi$^n$ da, ṭsi ga,
174. Zhi$^{n'}$-ga zho-i-ga o$^n$-tha bi do$^n$ a', a bi$^n$ da, ṭsi ga,
175. Wa'-ko$^n$-da e'-shki do$^n$ a', a bi$^n$ da, ṭsi ga,
176. O'-zho$^n$-ge be o$^n$-no$^n$-zhi$^n$ ba zhi ḳi-the ṭa i tsi$^n$ da, e' ṭsi-the a', a bi$^n$ da, ṭsi ga,
177. Wa'-ko$^n$-da wi no$^n$ bthi$^n$ mo$^n$-zhi i$^n$ da', a bi$^n$ da, ṭsi ga,
178. O'-ṭo$^n$-be ga-xa thi$^n$ ha, e'-ṭsi-the a', a bi$^n$ da, ṭsi ga.

### 7

179. He-dsi xtsi a, a bi$^n$ da, ṭsi ga,
180. Sho'-ḳa wa-ba-xi to$^n$ a', a bi$^n$ da, ṭsi ga,
181. Thu-e' xtsi the-e do$^n$ a', a bi$^n$ da, ṭsi ga,
182. Ṭa' Tha-bthi$^n$ thi$^n$-kshe no$^n$ a', a bi$^n$ da, ṭsi ga,
183. Zho'-gthe gi-e do$^n$ a', a bi$^n$ da, ṭsi ga,
184. Wi'-ṭsi-go-e', e-gi-e a-ka', a bi$^n$ da, ṭsi ga,
185. Zhi$^{n'}$-ga zho-i-ga the thi$^n$-ge a-tha, e'-gi-e a-ka', a bi$^n$ da, ṭsi ga,
186. He'-dsi xtsi a', a bi$^n$ da, ṭsi ga,
187. Wa'-ko$^n$-da ho-wa-ḳi-pa-ṭse a', a bi$^n$ da, ṭsi ga,
188. Wi no$^n$ wa-ko$^n$-da bthi$^n$ i$^n$ da, a bi$^n$ da, ṭsi ga,
189. Zhi$^{n'}$-ga zho-i-ga o$^n$-the ṭa i tsi$^n$ da, e' ṭsi-the a', a bi$^n$ da, ṭsi ga,
190. Wa'-ko$^n$-da e-shki do$^n$ a', a bi$^n$ da, ṭsi ga,
191. O'-zho$^n$-ge be o$^n$-tho$^n$-kshi-tha mo$^n$-zhi a-thi$^n$ he no$^n$ i$^n$ da', a bi$^n$ da, ṭsi ga,
192. Zhi$^{n'}$-ga zho-i-ga o$^n$-tha bi do$^n$ a', a bi$^n$ da, ṭsi ga,
193. Wa'-ko$^n$-da e'-shki do$^n$ a', a bi$^n$ da, ṭsi ga,
194. O'-zho$^n$-ge be i-kshi-tha ba zhi ḳi-the ṭa i tsi$^n$ da, e' ṭsi-the a', a bi$^n$ da, ṭsi ga,
195. Wa'-ko$^n$-da e'-shki do$^n$ a', a bi$^n$ da. ṭsi ga,
196. O'-zho$^n$-ge be o$^n$-gi-thi-ṭa mo$^n$-zhi a-thi$^n$ he no$^n$ i$^n$ da', a bi$^n$ da, ṭsi ga,
197. Zhi$^{n'}$-ga zho-i-ga o$^n$-tha bi do$^n$ a', a bi$^n$ da, ṭsi ga,
198. Wa'-ko$^u$-da e'-shki do$^u$ a', a bi$^n$ da, ṭsi ga,
199. O'-zho$^n$-ge be a-gi-thi-ṭa ba zhi ḳi-the ṭa i tsi$^n$ da, e'-ṭsi-the a', a bi$^n$ da, ṭsi ga.
200. Wa'-ko$^n$-da e'-shki do$^n$ a', a bi$^n$ da, ṭsi ga,
201. O'-zho$^n$-ge be o$^n$-wo$^n$-no$^n$-zhi$^n$ ṭse a, hi$^n$ a', a bi$^n$ da, ṭsi ga,
202. Zhi$^{n'}$-ga zho-i-ga o$^n$-tha bi do$^n$ a', a bi$^n$ da, ṭsi ga,
203. Wa'-ko$^n$-da e-shki do$^n$ a', a bi$^n$ da, ṭsi ga,
204. O'-zho$^n$-ge be o-no$^n$-zhi$^n$ ba zhi ḳi-the ṭa i tsi$^n$ da, e' ṭsi-the a', a bi$^n$ da, ṭsi ga,
205. Wa'-ko$^n$-da wi no$^n$ bthi$^n$ mo$^n$-zhi i$^n$ da', a bi$^n$ da, ṭsi ga,
206. O'-ṭo$^n$-be ga-xa thi$^n$ ha, e' ṭsi-the a', a bi$^n$ da, ṭsi ga.

8

207. He'-dsi xtsi a', a bi$^n$ da, ṭsi ga,
208. Sho'-ḳa wa-ba-xi ti$^n$ a', a bi$^n$ da, ṭsi ga,
209. Thu-e' xtsi the-e do$^n$ a', a bi$^n$ da, ṭsi ga,
210. Mi'-ḳa-ḳ'e u-ki-tha-ç'i$^n$ thi$^n$-kshe no$^n$ a', a bi$^n$ da, ṭsi ga,
211. Zho'-gthe gi-e do$^n$ a', a bi$^n$ da, ṭsi ga,
212. I-ḳo-e', e-gi-e a-ka', a bi$^n$ da, ṭsi ga,
213. Zhi$^n$'-ga zho-i-ga the thi$^n$-ge a-tha, e'-gi-e a-ka', a bi$^n$ da, ṭsi ga,
214. He'-dsi xtsi a', a bi$^n$ da, ṭsi ga,
215. She' sho$^n$ e the, e' ṭsi-the a', a bi$^n$ da, ṭsi ga,
216. Wa'-ḳo$^n$-da ho-wa-ḳi-pa-ṭse a', a bi$^n$ da, ṭsi ga,
217. Wi'no$^n$ wa-ḳo$^n$-da bthi$^n$ i$^n$ da', a bi$^n$ da, ṭsi ga,
218. Wa'-ḳo$^n$-da e'-shki do$^n$ a', a bi$^n$ da, ṭsi ga,
219. O'-zho$^n$-ge be o$^n$-tho$^n$-kshi-tha mo$^n$-zhi a-thi$^n$ he no$^n$ i$^n$ da', a bi$^n$ da, ṭsi ga,
220. Zhi$^n$'-ga zho-i-ga o$^n$-tha bi do$^n$ a', a bi$^n$ da, ṭsi ga,
221. Wa'-ḳo$^n$-da e'-shki do$^n$ a', a bi$^n$ da, ṭsi ga,
222. O'-zho$^n$-ge be i-kshi-tha ba zhi ḳi-the ṭa i tsi$^n$ da, e' ṭsi-the a', a bi$^n$ da, ṭsi ga,
223. Wa'-ḳo$^n$-da e'-shki do$^n$ a', a bi$^n$ da, ṭsi ga,
224. O'-zho$^n$-ge be o$^n$-gi-thi-ṭa mo$^n$-zhi a-thi$^n$ he no$^n$ i$^n$ da', a bi$^n$ da, ṭsi ga,
225. Zhi$^n$'-ga zho-i-ga o$^n$-tha bi do$^n$ a', a bi$^n$ da, ṭsi ga,
226. Wa'-ḳo$^n$-da e'-shki do$^n$ a', a bi$^n$ da, ṭsi ga,
227. O'-zho$^n$-ge be a$^n$-gi-thi-ṭa ba zhi ki-the ṭa i tsi$^n$ da, e' ṭsi-the a', a bi$^n$ da, ṭsi ga,
228. Wa'-ḳo$^n$-da e'-shki do$^n$ a', a bi$^n$ da, ṭsi ga,
229. O'-zho$^n$-ge be o$^n$-wo$^n$-no$^n$-zhi$^n$ ṭse a, hi$^n$ a', a bi$^n$ da, ṭsi ga,
230. Zhi$^n$'-ga zho-i-ga o$^n$-tha bi do$^n$ a', a bi$^n$ da, ṭsi ga,
231. Wa'-ḳo$^n$-da e'-shki do$^n$ a', a bi$^n$ da, ṭsi ga,
232. O'-zho$^n$-ge be o-no$^n$-zhi$^n$ ba zhi ḳi-the ṭa i tsi$^n$ da, e' ṭsi-the a', a bi$^n$ da, ṭsi ga,
233. Wa'- ḳo$^n$-da wi no$^n$ bthi$^n$ mo-$^n$zhi i$^n$ da', a bi$^n$ da, ṭsi ga,
234. O'-ṭo$^n$-be ga-xa ba thi$^n$ ha, e' ṭsi-the a', a bi$^n$ da, ṭsi ga.

9

235. He-'-dsi xtsi a', a bi$^n$ da, ṭsi ga,
236. Sho'-ḳa wa-ba xi ṭo$^n$ a', a bi$^n$ da, ṭsi ga,
237. Thu-e' xtsi the-e do$^n$ a', a bi$^n$ da, ṭsi ga,
238. Mi'-ḳa-ḳ'e zhu-dse thi$^n$-kshe no$^n$ a', a bi$^n$ da, ṭsi ga,
239. Zho'-gthe gi-e do$^n$ a', a bi$^n$ da, ṭsi ga,
240. Wi'-ṭsi-go-e', e-gi-e a-ka', a bi$^n$ da, ṭsi ga,
241. Zhi$^n$'-ga zho-i-ga the thi$^n$-ge a-tha, e'-gi-e a-ka', a bi$^n$ da, ṭsi ga,
242. She' sho$^n$ e tho, e' ṭsi-the a', a bi$^n$ da, ṭsi ga,
243. Wa'-ḳo$^n$-da ho-wa-ḳi-pa-ṭse a', a bi$^n$ da, ṭsi ga,

244. Wi'no$^n$ wa-ḳo$^n$-da bthi$^n$ i$^n$ da,' a bi$^n$ da, ṭsi ga,
245. Zhi$^{n'}$-ga zhu-i-ga o$^n$-the ṭa i tsi$^n$ da, e' ṭsi-the a', bi$^n$ da, ṭsi ga,
246. Wa'-ḳo$^n$-da e'-shki do$^n$ a', a bi$^n$ da, ṭsi ga,
247. O'-zho$^n$-ge be o$^n$-tho$^n$-kshi-tha mo$^n$-zhi a-thi$^n$ he no$^n$ i$^n$ da', a bi$^n$ da, ṭsi ga,
248. Zhi$^{n'}$-ga zho-i-ga o$^n$-tha bi do$^n$ a', a bi$^n$ da, ṭsi ga,
249. Wa'-ḳo$^n$-da e-shki do$^n$ a', a bi$^n$ da, ṭsi ga,
250. O'-zho$^n$-ge be i-kshi-tha ba zhi ḳi-the ṭa i tsi$^n$ da, e' ṭsi-the a', a bi$^n$ da, ṭsi ga,
251. Wa'-ḳo$^n$-da e-shki do$^n$ a', a bi$^n$ da, ṭsi ga,
252. O'-zho$^n$-ge be o$^n$-gi-thi-ṭa mo$^n$-zhi a-thi$^n$ he no$^n$ i$^n$ da', a bi$^n$ da, ṭsi ga,
253. Zhi$^{n'}$-ga zho-i-ga o$^n$-tha bi do$^n$ a', a bi$^n$ da, ṭsi ga,
254. Wa'-ḳo$^n$-da e'-shki do$^n$ a', a bi$^n$ da, ṭsi ga,
255. O'-zho$^n$-ge be a-gi-thi-ṭa ba zhi ḳi-the ṭa i tsi$^n$ da, e' ṭsi-the a', a bi$^n$ da, ṭsi ga,
256. Wa'-ḳo$^n$-da e'-shki do$^n$ a', a bi$^n$ da, ṭsi ga,
257. O'-zho$^n$-ge be o$^n$-wo$^n$-no$^n$-zhi$^n$ ṭse a, hi$^n$ a', a bi$^n$ da, ṭsi ga,
258. Zhi$^{n'}$-ga zho-i-ga o$^n$-tha bi do$^n$ a', a bi$^n$ da, ṭsi ga,
259. Wa'-ḳo$^n$-da e-shki do$^n$ a', a bi$^n$ da, ṭsi ga,
260. O'-zho$^n$-ge be o-no$^n$-zhi$^n$ ba zhi ḳi-the ṭa i tsi$^n$ da, e' ṭsi-the a', a bi$^n$ da, ṭsi ga,
261. Wa'-ḳo$^n$-da wi no$^n$ bthi$^n$ mo$^n$-zhi i$^n$ da', a bi$^n$ da, ṭsi ga,
262. O'-ṭo$^n$-be ga-xa ba thi$^n$ ha, e' ṭsi-the a', a bi$^n$ da, ṭsi ga.

10

263. He'-dsi xtsi a', a bi$^n$ da, ṭsi ga,
264. Sho'-ḳa wa-ba xi ṭo$^n$ a', a bi$^n$ da, ṭsi ga,
265. Thu-e' xtsi the-e do$^n$ a', a bi$^n$ da, ṭsi ga,
266. Mo$^{n'}$-xe a-tha-ḳ'a-be dsi a', a bi$^n$ da, ṭsi ga,
267. Sho$^{n'}$-ge a-ga-ḳ'e e'-go$^n$ kshe no$^n$ a', a bi$^n$ da, ṭsi ga,
268. He'-dsi xtsi zho-gthe gi-e do$^n$ a', a bi$^n$ da, ṭsi ga,
269. Wi'-ṭsi-go-e', e-gi-e a-ka', a bi$^n$ da, ṭsi ga,
270. Zhi$^{n'}$-ga zho-i-ga the thi$^n$-ge a-tha, e-gi-e a-ka', a bi$^n$ da, ṭsi ga,
271. He'-dsi xtsi a', a bi$^n$ da, ṭsi ga,
272. Zhi$^{n'}$-ga zho-i-ga o$^n$-the ṭa i tsi$^n$ da, e ṭsi-the a', a bi$^n$ da, ṭsi ga,
273. Çi'-pa-hi thi-çtu-be ga ṭse a', a bi$^n$ da, ṭsi ga,
274. Wa'-thi$^n$-e-çka she mo$^n$ mo$^n$-zhi i$^n$ da', a bi$^n$ da, ṭsi ga,
275. O'-no$^n$ pa-xe i$^n$ da', a bi$^n$ da, ṭsi ga,
276. Zhi$^{n'}$-ga zho-i-ga o$^n$-tha bi do$^n$ a', a bi$^n$ da, ṭsi ga,
277. Ni'-ḳa no$^n$ hi do$^n$ a', a bi$^n$ da, ṭsi ga,
278. Çi'-pa-hi thi-çtu-be e'no$^n$ bi no$^n$ a', a bi$^n$ da, ṭsi ga,
279. I'-the ḳi-the ṭa i tsi$^n$ da, e' ṭsi-the a', a bi$^n$ da, ṭsi ga.

280. Hi'-ko$^n$ ba-xo$^n$ ga ge a', a bi$^n$ da, ṭsi ga,
281. Wa'-thi$^n$-e-çka she-mo$^n$ mo$^n$-zhi i$^n$ da', a bi$^n$ da, ṭsi ga,
282. O'-no$^n$ pa-xe i$^n$ da', a bi$^n$ da, ṭsi ga,
283. Zhi$^{n'}$-ga zho-i-ga o$^n$-tha bi do$^n$ a', a bi$^n$ da, ṭsi ga,
284. Ni'-ḳa no$^n$ hi do$^n$ a', a bi$^n$ da, ṭsi ga,
285. Hi'-ko$^n$ ba xo$^n$ e' no$^n$ bi no$^n$ a', a bi$^n$ da, ṭsi ga,
286. I'-the ḳi-the ṭa i tsi$^n$ da, e' ṭsi-the a', a bi$^n$ da, ṭsi ga.

287. Ṭse'-wa-ṭse u-ga-wa ga thi$^n$-kshe a', a bi$^n$ da, ṭsi ga,
288. Wa'-thi$^n$-e-çka she-mo$^n$ mo$^n$-zhi i$^n$ da', a bi$^n$ da, ṭsi ga,
289. O'-no$^n$ pa-xe i$^n$ da', a bi$^n$ da, ṭsi ga,
290. Zhi$^{n'}$-ga zho-i-ga o$^n$-tha bi do$^n$ a', a bi$^n$ da, ṭsi ga,
291. Ni'-ḳa no$^n$ hi do$^n$ a', a bi$^n$ da, ṭsi ga,
292. Ṭse'-wa-ṭse u-ga-wa a bi i-the ḳi-the mo$^n$-thi$^n$ ṭa i tsi$^n$ da, e ṭsi
    the a', a bi$^n$ da, ṭsi ga.

293. I$^{n'}$-kshe-dse u-bi-ço$^n$-dse ga thi-kshe a', a bi$^n$ da, ṭsi ga,
294. Wa'-thi$^n$-e-çka she-mo$^n$ mo$^n$-zhi i$^n$ da', a bi$^n$ da, ṭsi ga,
295. O'-no$^n$ pa-xe i$^n$ da', a bi$^n$ da, ṭsi ga,
296. Zhi$^{n'}$-ga zho-i-ga o$^n$-tha bi do$^n$ a', a bi$^n$ da, ṭsi ga,
297. Ni'-ḳa no$^n$ hi do$^n$ a', a bi$^n$ da, ṭsi ga,
298. I$^{n'}$-kshe-dse u-bi-ço$^n$-dse a bi i-the ḳi-the mo$^n$-thi$^n$ ṭa i tsi$^n$ da,
    e ṭsi-the a, a bi$^n$ da, ṭsi ga.

299. Do'-dse u-ga-wa ga thi$^n$-kshe a', a bi$^n$ da, ṭsi ga,
300. Wa'-thi$^n$-e-çka she-mo$^n$ mo$^n$-zhi i$^n$ da', a bi$^n$ da, ṭsi ga,
301. O'-no$^n$ pa-xe i$^n$ da', a bi$^n$ da ṭsi ga,
302. Zhi$^{n'}$-ga zho-i-ga o$^n$-tha bi do$^n$ a', a bi$^n$ da, ṭsi ga,
303. Ni'-ḳa no$^n$ hi do$^n$ a', a bi$^n$ da, ṭsi ga,
304. Do'-dse u-ga-wa a bi i-the ḳi-the mo$^n$-thi$^n$ ṭa i tsi$^n$ da, e' ṭsi-the
    a', a bi$^n$ da, ṭsi ga.

305. I'-the-dse ba-ç'i$^n$-tha ga ṭse a', a bi$^n$ da, ṭsi ga,
306. Wa'-thi$^n$-e-çka she-mo$^n$ mo$^n$- zhi i$^n$ da', a bi$^n$ da, ṭsi ga,
307. O'-no$^n$ pa-xe i$^n$ da', a bi$^n$ da, ṭsi ga,
308. Zhi$^{n'}$ga zho-i-ga o$^n$-tha bi do$^n$ a', a bi$^n$ da, ṭsi ga,
309. Ni'-ḳa no$^n$ hi do$^n$ a', a bi$^n$ da, ṭsi ga,
310. I'-the-dse ba-ç'i$^n$-tha a bi i-the ḳi-the mo$^n$-thi$^n$ ṭa i tsi$^n$ da,
    e' ṭsi-the a', a bi$^n$ da, ṭsi ga.

311. I$^{n'}$-shta-the-dse-bi-xo$^n$ ga ṭse a', a bi$^n$ da, ṭsi ga,
312. Wa'-thi$^n$-e-çka she-mo$^n$ mo$^n$-zhi i$^n$ da', a bi$^n$ da, ṭsi ga,
313. O'-no$^n$ pa-xe i$^n$ da', a bi$^n$ da, ṭsi ga,
314. Zhi$^{n'}$-ga zho-i-ga o$^n$-tha bi do$^n$ a', a bi$^n$ da, ṭsi ga,
315. Ni'-ḳa no$^n$ hi do$^n$ a', a bi$^n$ da, ṭsi ga,
316. I$^{n'}$-shta-the-dse bi-xo$^n$ a bi i-the ḳi-the mo$^n$-thi$^n$ ṭa i tsi$^n$ da,
    e' ṭsi-the a', a bi$^n$ da, ṭsi ga.

317. Pa′pa-çi ga-ṭse a′, a bi$^n$ da, ṭsi ga,
318. Wa′-thi$^n$-e-çka she-mo$^n$ mo$^n$-zhi i$^n$ da′, a bi$^n$ da, ṭsi ga,
319. Wa′-ḳo$^n$-da i-ga-dsi-çe pa-xe i$^n$ da′, a bi$^n$ da, ṭsi ga,
320. Wa′-ḳo$^n$-da u-ṭsi-the thi$^n$-ge a-wa-kshi-the no$^n$ i$^n$ da′, a bi$^n$ da, ṭsi ga,
321. Zhi$^n$′-ga sho-i-ga o$^n$-tha bi do$^n$ a′, a bi$^n$ da, ṭsi ga,
322. Wa′-ḳo$^n$-da i-ba-çi a-thi$^n$ mo$^n$-thi$^n$ ṭa i tsi$^n$ da, e′ ṭsi-the a′, a bi$^n$ da, ṭsi ga.

323. Ṭa′-xpi hi$^n$ ga-ça-dse ga thi$^n$-kshe a′, a bi$^n$ da, ṭsi ga,
324. Wa′-thi$^n$-e-çka she-mo$^n$ mo$^n$-zhi$^n$ i$^n$ da′, a bi$^n$ da, ṭsi ga,
325. O′-no$^n$ pa-xe i$^n$ da′, a bi$^n$ da, ṭsi ga,
326. Zhi$^n$′-ga zho-i-ga o$^n$-tha bi do$^n$ a′, a bi$^n$ da, ṭsi ga,
327. Ni′-ḳa no$^n$ hi do$^n$ a′, a bi$^n$ da, ṭsi ga,
328. Pa′çka u-gtho$^n$ e-go$^n$ e′ no$^n$ bi no$^n$ a′, a bi$^n$ da, ṭsi ga,
329. I′-the ḳi-the mo$^n$-thi$^n$ ṭa i tsi$^n$ da,′ a bi$^n$ da, ṭsi ga.

330. Wo$^n$′shki do$^n$ a′, a bi$^n$ da, ṭsi ga,
331. Ho$^n$′-ba tha-gthi$^n$ wi$^n$ shki o$^n$-hi no$^n$ i$^n$ da′, a bi$^n$ da, ṭsi ga,
332. Zhi$^n$′-ga ho$^n$-ba tha-gthi$^n$ wi$^n$ shki i-the ḳi-the mo$^n$-thi$^n$ ṭa i tsi$^n$ da, e ṭsi-the a, a bi$^n$ da, ṭsi ga.

## NATIVE NAMES OF OSAGE FULL BLOODS (AS FAR AS COULD BE ASCERTAINED), USED BY EACH GENS OF THE TRIBE

### Names of the Gentes and Subgentes

The following are the names of the gentes and subgentes of the two great tribal divisions, in their fixed, sequential order, as given by Sho$^n$′-to$^n$-ça-be, Black-dog, to Miss Alice C. Fletcher, in 1896. The name Sho′-ḳa is the title of a subgens from which the principal gens chooses a man or woman to act as official messenger at the performance of a tribal rite. The official messenger also bears the title.

#### FIXED ORDER OF THE GENTES AND SUBGENTES

##### Gentes of the Ho$^N$′-ga Great Division

###### WA-ZHA′-ZHE SUBDIVISION

1. Wa-zha′-zhe-çka; White Wa-zha′-zhe. Refers to the life symbol of the gens, the fresh water mussel, with its shell. The Sun also is a life symbol of this gens.

      I$^n$-gtho$^n$′-ga Ni Mo$^n$-tse; Puma-in-the-Water. Sho′-ḳa.
2. Ḳe′-ḳ′i$^n$; Carrier-of-the-Turtle.

      Ba′-ḳ′a Zho-i-ga-the; Cotton-tree People. Sho′-ḳa.
3. Mi-ḳe′-the-stse-dse; Cat-tail (*Typha latifolia*).

      Ka′-xe-wa-hu-ça; Youngest brother. Sho′-ḳa.

4. Wa'-tse-tsi; Star-that-came-to-Earth.

   Xu-tha' Pa-çon Zho-i-ga-the; Bald Eagle People.  Sho'-ka.

5. O-çu'-ga-xe; They-who-make-the-way-Clear.

   Mon-sho-dse-mon-in; Travelers-in-the-Mist.  Sho'-ka.

6. Ṭa-tha'-xin; Deer's-Lungs, or Ṭa-çin'-dse-çka; White-tailed-Deer.

   Wa-dsu'-ṭa-zhin-ga; Small-Animals.  Sho'-ka.

7. Ho' I-ni-ka-shi-ga; Fish-People.

   E-non' Min-dse-ṭon; Sole-owner-of-the-Bow.  Refers to the office of the gens of making the ceremonial bow and arrows that symbolize night and day.

8. Hon'-ga U-ṭa-non-dsi; The-Isolated-Hon'-ga.  The Earth.

   Mon-hin-çi; Flint-Arrow-Point.  Sho'-ka.

### HONʹ-GA SUBDIVISION

1. Wa-ça'-be-ṭon; Owners-of-the-Black-Bear.

   Wa-ça'-be-çka; The-White-Bear.  Sho'-ka.

2. In-gthon'-ga; Puma.

   Hin-wa'-xa-ga; Thorny-hair, Porcupine.  Sho'-ka.

3. O'-pon; Elk.

   Ṭa He Sha-be; Dark-horned Deer.  Sho'-ka.

4. Mon'-in-ka-ga-xe; Maker-of-the-Earth.

5. Hon-ga Gthe-zhe; The-Mottled-Sacred-One (the immature golden eagle).

6. Xu-tha; Eagle (the adult golden eagle).

7. Hon'-ga Zhin-ga; The-Little-Sacred-One.

   I'-ba-tse Ṭa-dse; The-Gathering-of-the-Winds.  Sho'-ka.

### Gentes of the Ṭsi'-zhu Great Division

1. Ṭsi'-zhu Wa-non; Elder Ṭsi-zhu, or Wa-kon'-da Non-pa-bi; The-God-Who-is-Feared-by-All.  Refers to the life symbol of the gens, the Sun.

   Wa-ba'-xi; The-Awakeners.  Refers to the office of this sub-gens of urging the messengers to prompt action.  Sho'-ka.

2. Çin'-dse A-gthe; Wearers-of-Symbolic-Locks.

   Shon'-ge Zho-i-ga-the; Dog-People.  Refers to the life symbol of this subgens, the dog-star.  The name Shon'-ge includes coyotes, gray wolves, and all other kinds of dogs.  Sho'-ka.

3. Ṗe'-ṭon Ṭon-ga Zho-i-ga-the; Great-Crane-People.

   (Not sub-gens) Ṭsi'-zhu Wa-shta-ge; The-Gentle-Ṭsi-zhu.  Refers to the office of the gens of Peace-maker.

4. Ṭse-do'-ga In-dse; Buffalo-Bull-Face-People.  Closely related to the Ṭsi'-zhu Wa-non.

   Ṭse-a'-kon; corruption of Ṭse-thon-ka; Buffalo-back.  Sho'-ka.

5. Mi-ḳ'in' Wa-non; Elder Carriers-of-the-Sun-and-Moon.  Refers to the life symbols of the gens, all the heavenly bodies.

6. Ho{$^n$}' Zho-i-ga-the; Night-People.   Refers to the life symbol of the gens, the Night.

   Ṭa-pa' Zho-i-ga-the; Deer-head or Pleiades People.   Sho'-ḳa.
7. Ṭsi'-zhu U-thu-ha-ge; The-Last-Ṭsi'-zhu, or the last in the sequential order of the Ṭsi'-zhu gentes.

### The Ṭsi' Ha-shi (Those-Who-Were-Last-to-Come)

A. Ni'-ḳa Wa-ḳo{$^n$}-da-gi; Men of Mystery, or Thunder People.

   Xo{$^n$}'-dse Wa-ṭse.   Meaning uncertain; it is said that it probably refers to the office of keepers of all the Wa-ṭse, or war honors.   Sho'-ḳa.
B. Tho'-xe; Buffalo-bull (archaic name for the buffalo bull).   These two gentes are joint keepers of the Hawk War-symbols.

### Wa'-ṭse-ṭsi or Po{$^N$}'-ḳa Wa-shta-ge

Names ceremonially bestowed on each of the first three sons and on each of the first three daughters born to a Wa'-ṭse-ṭsi man and his wife.   As given by No{$^n$}'-xe-çka-zhi, a member of the gens:

#### BOYS

1. I{$^n$}-gtho{$^n$}' name, Wa-çi'-çta.   Meaning uncertain.
2. Ksho{$^n$}'-ga name, Wa'-ṭse-mo{$^n$}-i{$^n$}, Star-that-travels.
3. Ka'-zhi{$^n$}-ga name, Ni-ga'-ṭo-xe, Water-splasher.

#### GIRLS

1. Mi'-na name, Ho{$^n$}-be'-do-ḳa, Wet-moccasins.
2. Wi'-he name, Wa-ṭo{$^n$}-i-ça-e, meaning uncertain, or Mi'-ga-sho{$^n$}-e, Sun-that-travels.
3. A-çi{$^n$}'-ga name, Gia'-ço{$^n$}-ba, meaning uncertain.

#### OTHER NAMES

##### Male

Ga-çka', meaning uncertain.   Son of Xu-tha'-da-wi{$^n$}, Ṭsi'-zhu Wa-shta-ge and Po{$^n$}'-ḳa-zhi{$^n$}-ga, Po{$^n$}-ḳa Wa-shta-ge.

Ga-çka, meaning uncertain.   Son of Tho{$^n$}'-dse-ṭo{$^n$}-ga, Wa'-ṭse-ṭsi, and Xu-tha'-da-wi{$^n$}, Ṭsi'-zhu Wa-shta-ge.

Gi-thi-ḳo{$^n$}-bi, One-for-whom-they-make-way.   (In the Tha'-ṭa-da gens of the Omaha tribe.)   Husband of Mo{$^n$}'-çi-ṭse-xi, Ṭsi'-zhu Wa-shta-ge.

Gtha-i-gtho{$^n$}-thi{$^n$}-ge, meaning uncertain.   Son of Tho{$^n$}'-dse-ṭo{$^n$}-ga, Wa'-ṭse-ṭsi and Xu-tha'-da-wi{$^n$}, Ṭsi'-zhu Wa-shta-ge.

Gthe-do{$^n$}'-wa-ḳo{$^n$}-tha, Attacking-hawk.   (Tho'-xe name.)   Refers to the aggressive character of the bird.   Son of Ṭsi'-zhu-a-ḳi-pa and Ho{$^n$}-be'-do-ḳa, Ṭa' I-ni-ka-shi-ga.

Hi'-tho-ka-thi$^n$, Bare-legs. (In the Tha'-ta-da gens of the Omaha.) Also Ku-zhi'-wa-tse, Strikes-in-a-far-off-country. (In the I$^n$-shta'-çon-da gens of the Omaha.)

Hi'-tho-ka-thi$^n$ or Long-bow.

Ka-çi', meaning uncertain.

Ko'-zhi-çi-gthe, Tracks-far-away. Husband of Xu-tha-'da-wi$^n$, Tsi-'zhu Wa-shta-ge.

Ksho$^n$'-ga. Not name but a special kinship term for the second born son. Should have been named A'-be-zhi$^n$-ga, Slender-leaf, of the cat-tail.

Ku'-zhi-çi-gthe. Husband of Zho$^n$'-btha-çka-wi$^n$ of the Ho$^n$'-ga U-ta-no$^n$-dsi gens.

Mo$^n$-i$^{n}$'-ka-mo$^n$-i$^n$, Walks-on-the-earth. Husband of Xu-tha'-da-wi$^n$ of the Çi$^{n}$'-dse-a-gthe gens.

Mo$^n$-ko$^{n}$'-thi$^n$, Possessor-of-medicine. (Not a Ni'-ki-e name.)

Ni'-ka-çtu-e, Gathering-of-men. Son of Tho$^{n}$'-dse-to$^n$-ga and Xu-tha-da-wi$^n$.

Ni'-ka-wa-zhi$^n$-to$^n$-ga, Man-of-great-courage. Refers to the war-like character of this gens. Husband of Wa-xthe-'tho$^n$-ba of the Tsi'-zhu Wa-no$^n$ gens.

Po$^{n}$'-ka-wa-da-i$^n$-ga, Playful-Po$^n$-ka. Husband of Wa-xthe'-tho$^n$-ba of the Tsi'-zhu Wa-no$^n$ gens.

Tho$^{n}$'-dse-to$^n$-ga, Big-heart. Also Wa-zhi$^{n}$'-wa-xa, Greatest-in-courage. Refers to the warlike character of this gens. Husband of Xu'-tha-da-wi$^n$ of the Tsi'-zhu Wa-shta-ge gens.

Tsi'-zhu-a-ki-pa, He-who-met-the-Tsi'-zhu. Refers to the first meet-ing of the Tsi'-zhu and the Wa-zha'-zhe gentes. Husband of Ho$^n$-be'-do-ka of the Ta' I-ni-ka-shi-ga gens.

Tsi'-zhu-a-ki-pa (same as above). Husband of Wa-xthe'-tho$^n$-ba of the Tsi'-zhu Wa-no$^n$ gens.

U-dse'-ta-wa-xa, Winner-of-the-race-against-the-U-dse-ta. (Not a Ni'-ki-e name.) Refers to a race between two bands in which a member of the Wa'-tse-tsi gens won.

U-thu'-ga-e, meaning uncertain. (Not Ni'-ki-e.)

Wa-çi'-çta, meaning uncertain. Son of Po$^{n}$'-ka-wa-da-i$^n$-ga and Wa-xthe'-tho$^n$-ha, Tsi'-zhu Wa-no$^n$ gens.

Wa'-çi-çta, Son of Wa-shka'-dse and No$^n$-mi-tse-xi, Wa-ça'-be gens.

Wa-shka'-dse, meaning uncertain. Husband of No$^{n}$'-mi-tse-xi of the Wa-ça'-be gens.

Wa-stse'-e-do$^n$, Good-doctor. (Wa-xthi'-zhi thinks that the boy's right name is Wa'-tse-mo$^n$-i$^n$.) Son of Po$^{n}$'-ka-wa-da-i$^n$-ga and Wa-xthe-'tho$^n$-ba, Tsi'-zhu Wa-no$^n$ gens.

Wa'-tse-a-xe, Cries-for-a-star. Son of U-thu'-ga-e.

Wa'-tse-ga-hi-ge, Star-chief. Refers to the selection of the chief of the Ho$^n$'-ga Great Division, from the Wa'-tse-tsi gens.

Wa'-ṭse-moⁿ-iⁿ, The-traveling-star.    Husband of Wa'-ḳoⁿ-ça-moⁿ-in of the Ṭa' I-ni-ḳa-shi-ga gens.

Wa'-ṭse-moⁿ-in.    Son of Wa-k'o'-ga-hi-ge of the Ṭsi'-zhu Wa-shta-ge gens.

Wa'-ṭse-moⁿ-iⁿ.    Son of Ḳo'-zhi-çi-gthe and Xu-tha-'da-wiⁿ, Ṭsi'-zhu Wa-shta-ge gens.

Wa'-ṭse-moⁿ-iⁿ.    Son of Hi'-tho-ḳa-thiⁿ.    (Long-bow.)

Wa-ṭse-ṭoⁿ-ga, Big-star.

Wa-zhiⁿ'-wa-xa, Greatest-in-courage.    Refers to the warlike character of the Wa-zha'-zhe subdivision.    Husband of Moⁿ-zhoⁿ'-dsi-i-ṭa of the Ṭsi'-zhu Wa-shta-ge gens.

Wa-zhiⁿ'-wa-xa.    Son of Moⁿ-ḳoⁿ'-a-thiⁿ.

Xu-tha'-xtsi, Real-eagle.    (In the Tha'-ṭa-da gens of the Omaha tribe.)    Husband of Wa-ḳ'o'-ga-hi-ge of the Ṭsi'-zhu Wa-shta-ge gens.

Çoⁿ-çi'-gthe, Footprints-in-the-woods.    Refers to the deer.    Wife of Hoⁿ'-ba-hiu of the Ṭa' I-ni-ḳa-shi-ga gens.

Gia'-çoⁿ-ba, meaning uncertain.    Wife of U-hoⁿ'-ge-u-zhoⁿ of the Çiⁿ'-dse-a-gthe gens.

Gia'-çoⁿ-ba.    Wife of Ḳa'-wa-çi of the I'-ba-ṭse gens.

Gia-çoⁿ-ba.    Daughter of Ṭsi'-zhu-a-ḳi-pa and Wa-xthe'-thoⁿ-ba of the Ṭsi'-zhu Wa-noⁿ gens.

Gia-çoⁿ-ba.    Mother of Mi'-hoⁿ-ga, Xu-tha'-wa-ḳoⁿ-da and Sha'-ge-wa-biⁿ of the Ṭsi'-zhu Wa-noⁿ gens.

Gia'-çoⁿ-ba.    Daughter of Ḳo'-zhi-çi-gthe and Xu-tha'-da-wiⁿ of the Ṭsi'-zhu Wa-shta-ge gens.

Gia'-çoⁿ-ba.    Daughter of Wa-shka'-dse and Noⁿ'-mi-ṭse-xi.

Gia'-çoⁿ-ba.    Wife of Tho-xe-zhiⁿ-ga of the Tho'-xe gens.

Hoⁿ-be'-do-ka, Wet-moccasins.    Daughter of Wa-zhiⁿ'-wa-xa and Moⁿ-zhoⁿ'-dsiⁿ-i-ta of the Ṭsi'-zhu Wa-shta-ge gens.

Hoⁿ-be'-do-ka.    Daughter of U-thu'-ga-e.

Hoⁿ-be-'do-ka.    Daughter of Ṭsi'-zhu-a-ḳi-pa and Wa-xthe'-thoⁿ-be, of the Ṭsi'-zhu Wa-noⁿ gens.

Hoⁿ'-be-do-ka.    Mother of Xu-tha'-wa-ḳoⁿ-da, Gia'-çoⁿ-ba and Xu-tha'-da-wiⁿ of the Ṭsi'-zhu Wa-noⁿ gens.

Hoⁿ-be'-do-ka.    Daughter of Moⁿ-koⁿ'-a-thiⁿ.

Hoⁿ-be'-do-ka.    Wife of Moⁿ-zhoⁿ-a'-ḳi-da of the Ṭsi'-zhu Wa-shta-ge gens.

Hoⁿ-be'-do-ka.    Wife of Ha-xiⁿ-u'-mi-zhe of the Ṭsi'-zhu Wa-shta-ge gens.

Hoⁿ-be'-do-ka.    Daughter of Wa'-ṭse-a-xe and Pa'-moⁿ-shi-wa-gthoⁿ of the O'-poⁿ gens.

Hoⁿ-be'-do-ka.    Daughter of Ḳo'-zhi-çi-gthe and Xu-tha'-da-wiⁿ of the Ṭsi-'zhu Wa-shta-ge gens.

Ho$^n$-be'-do-ka.  Daughter of Wa-shka'-dse and No$^n$-'mi-ṭse-xi of the Wa'-ça'-be gens.

Mi'-ga-sho$^n$-i$^n$, Sun-that-travels.  (In the Tha'-ṭa-da gens of the Omaha tribe.)  Daughter of Po$^{n'}$-ḳa-wa-da-i$^n$-ga and Wa-xthe'-tho$^n$-ba of the Ṭsi'-zhu Wa-no$^n$ gens.   •

Mi'-ga-sho$^n$-i$^n$.  Wife of Mo$^{n'}$-zhi'-çka-ḳ'i$^n$-ga-xthi of the Wa-ça'-be gens.

Mi'-ga-sho$^n$-i$^n$.  Wife of Gthe-do$^{n'}$-çka of the Ni'-ḳa-wa-ḳo$^n$-da-gi gens.

Mi'-tha-gthi$^n$, Good-sun.  Daughter of Mo$^n$-i$^{n'}$-ḳa-mo$^n$-i$^n$ and Xu-tha'-da-wi$^n$ of the Çi$^{n'}$-dse-a-gthe gens.

Ṗo$^{n'}$-ḳa-wi$^n$, Ṗo$^{n'}$-ḳa-woman.  (This woman held the office of Wa-dse'-pa-i$^n$, Official Crier.)

Wa'-ḳo$^n$-ça-mo$^n$-i$^n$, meaning uncertain.  Daughter of U-thu'-ga-e.

Wa'-ḳo$^n$-ça-mo$^n$-i$^n$.  Mother of Tho'-ṭa-a-ça, Xo'-ṭa-wi$^n$ and Xo$^{n'}$-dse-mo$^n$-i$^n$ of the Ni'-ḳa-wa-ḳo$^n$-da-gi gens.

Wa'-ḳo$^n$-ça-mo$^n$-i$^n$.  Wife of Ṭse'-çe-ṭo$^n$-ga of the Tho'-xe gens.

Wa'-ḳo$^n$-ça-mo$^n$-i$^n$.  Daughter of Wa-ḳ'o'-ga-hi-ge of the Ṭsi'-zhu Wa-shta-ge gens.

Wa'-ḳo$^n$-ça-mo$^n$-i$^n$.  Wife of Mi'-she-tsi-e of the Ho$^{n'}$-ga gens.

Wa'-ḳo$^n$-ça-mo$^n$-i$^n$.  Wife of Wa-ni'-e-to$^n$ of the Ṭsi'-zhu Wa-shta-ge gens.

Wa'-ḳo$^n$-ça-mo$^n$-in.  Daughter of Wa'-ṭse-a-xe and Pa'-mo$^n$-shi-wa-gtho$^n$.

Wa'-ḳo$^n$-ça-mon-i$^n$.  Daughter of Ḳo'-zhi-çi-gthe and Xu-tha'-da-wi$^n$.

Wa'-ḳo$^n$-ça-mo$^n$-i$^n$.  Daughter of Tho$^{n'}$-dse-ṭo$^n$-ga and Xu-tha'-da-wi$^n$. ·

Wa'-ḳo$^n$-ça-mo$^n$-i$^n$.  Daughter of Wa-shka'-dse and No$^{n'}$-mi-ṭse-xi.

Wa-ṭo$^{n'}$-i-ça-e, meaning uncertain.  Wife of Mo$^{n'}$-ga-xe of the I$^n$-gtho$^{n'}$-ga gens.

Wa-ṭo$^{n'}$-i-ça-e.  Wife of O-pa'-sho-e of the Ṭsi'-zhu Wa-shta-ge gens.

Wa-ṭo$^{n'}$-i-ça-e.  Wife of I'-ṭo$^n$-mo$^n$-i$^n$ of the Mi-ḳ'i$^{n'}$ gens.

Wa-ṭo$^{n'}$-i-ça-e.  Daughter of Ṗo$^{n'}$-ḳa-wa-da-i$^n$-ga and Wa-xthe'-ṭho$^n$-ba.

Wa-ṭo$^{n'}$-i-ça-e.  Wife of No$^{n'}$-po-e of the Ho$^{n'}$-ga U-ṭa-no$^n$-dsi gens.

Wa-ṭo$^{n'}$-i-ça-e.  Daughter of Wa'-ṭse-ga-hi-ge.

Wa-ṭo$^{n'}$-i-ça-e.  Wife of Ḳa'-wa-xo-dse of the I'-ba-ṭse gens.

Wa-ṭo$^{n'}$-i-ça-e.  Daughter of Wa-shka'-dse and No$^{n'}$-mi-ṭse-xi.

Wi'-he.  Not name but a special kinship term for the second daughter in a family.  Daughter of Wa'-ṭse-ga-hi-ge.

Xu-tha'-da-wi$^n$ Good-eagle-woman.  Daughter of Ṭsi'-zhu-a-ḳi-pa and Ho$^{n'}$-be-do-ḳa of the Ṭa' I-ni-ḳa-shi-ga gens.

## ṬA' I-NI-ḲA-SHI-GA

Special kinship terms and names of the first three sons and the first three daughters in a family of the Ṭa' I-ni-ḳa-shi-ga, or Deer gens, as given by Ṭsi-zhe'-wa-the, a member of the gens.

### BOYS

1. In-gthon' name, Wa-zha'-zhe-hon-ga, Sacred Wa-zha'-zhe.
2. Kshon-ga, Ṭo'-ho-ho-e, Blue-fish.
3. Ḳa-zhin-ga, Ho-ḳi-gthi-çi, Wriggling-fish.

### GIRLS

1. Mi'-na name, Wa-zha'-zhe-mi-ṭse-xi, Wa-zha'-zhe-sacred-sun.
2. Wi-he' name, Hon'-be-do-ḳa, Wet-moccasins.
3. Çi'-ge name, Zhon-çi'-gthe, Footprints-in-the-woods.

### OTHER NAMES

#### MALE

A'-ḳi-da-zhin-ga, Little-soldier. The title of a subordinate officer chosen from this gens to enforce the orders of the two hereditary chiefs. Husband of Xu-tha'-da-win of the Ṭsi'-zhu Wa-shta-ge gens.

Chi-zhe-wa-the, meaning uncertain. Husband of Ni'-ḳa-shi-ṭsi-e of the Hon' I-ni-ḳa-shi-ga gens.

Çon-dse'-ḳon-ha, Edge-of-the-forest. Refers to the habit of the deer in feeding along the edge of the forest. Husband of Xu-tha'-da-win of the Ṭsi'-zhu Wa-shta-ge gens.

E-non'-min-dse-ṭon, Sole-owner-of-the-bow. Name of the gens from whom a member is selected to make the bow and arrows symbolic of night and day, to be used at a tribal ceremony. Son of Ṭo'-ho-ho-e.

E-non'-min-dse-ṭon. Son of Ho'-ḳi-e-çi and Mi'-ṭse-xi of the Hon'ga gens.

E-non'-min-dse-ṭon. Son of Ṭa-he'-ga-xe and Wa-hiu'-çon-e of the I'-ba-ṭse gens.

Ga-hi'-ge-non-zhin, Standing-chief. Refers to the permanency of the position of the chief chosen to represent the Hon'-ga great division. Husband of Xu-tha'-da-win of the Ṭsi'-zhu Wa-shta-ge gens.

Ga-hi'-ge-tha-gthin, Good-chief. Refers to the duty of the chief to promote peace among men. Son of Mi'-ṭse-xi of the Hon' I-ni-ḳa-shi-ga gens.

Ga-hi'-ge-zhin-ga, Young-chief. (The name appears in the In-ke'-ça-be gens of the Omaha tribe.)

Ho-çon', White-fish. Son of A'-ḳ'a-win of the I'-ba-ṭse gens.

Ho'-ḳi-a-çi, Wriggling-fish. Son of Ṭo'-ho-ho-e.

Ho'-ķi-a-çi, Wriggling-fish. Son of Ţa-he'-ga-xe and Wa-hiu'-ço$^n$-e of the I'-ba-ţse gens.

Ho'-ķi-a-çi, also Ķo'-zhi-mo$^n$-i$^n$, Wanders-far-away. Husband of Mi'-ţse-xi of the Ho$^{n'}$-ga gens.

Ho-xo', Fish-scales. Son of Mi'-ţse-xi of the Ho$^{n'}$-ga gens.

Ho-xo'-e, Fish-scales. Son of Ţo'-ho-ho-e.

Mo$^n$-kchi'-xa-bi, For-whom-arrows-are-made. Refers to the arrows used in the ceremony of opening the deer-hunting season. Son of Ga-hi'-ge-no$^n$-zhi$^n$ and Xu-tha'-da-wi$^n$ of the Ţsi'-zhu Wa-shta-ge gens.

No$^n$-zhi$^{n'}$-wa-the, Causes-them-to-stand. Father of Wa-zha'-zhe-mi-ţse-xi.

O-ho$^{n'}$-bi, One-who-is-cooked. Refers to the use of the deer for food. Son of Do$^{n'}$-ba-bi of the Ho$^{n'}$-ga U-ţa-no$^n$-dsi gens.

Ţa-çi$^{n'}$-e, Deer's tail.

Ţa-he'-ga-xe, Deer-with-branching-horns. (The name appears in the I$^n$-shta'-ço$^n$-de gens of the Omaha tribe.) Husband of Wa-hiu-ço$^n$-e of the I'-ba-ţse gens.

Ţa-zhe'-ga, Deer's-leg.

Thi-hi'-bi, Scared-up. Refers to the flight of the deer from the hunter. Husband of Mi'-ţse-xi of the Ho$^{n'}$ I-ni-ķa-shi-ga gens.

Ţo'-ho-ho-e, Blue-fish.

Ţo'-ho-ho-e. Son of Ho'-ki-e-çi and Mi'-ţse-xi of the Ho$^{n'}$-ga gens.

Ţse-do'-ha, Buffalo-hide (a Tho'-xe name); also Wa-zha'-no$^n$-pa-i$^n$, meaning uncertain.

Wa-ķ'o$^{n'}$-ţsi-e, One-who-triumphs. Refers to the warlike character of the Wa-zha'-zhe subdivision. Husband of Hi$^{n'}$-i-ķi-a-bi of the Ţsi'-zhu Wa-shta-ge gens.

Wa-zha'-e-no$^n$-pa-i$^n$, meaning uncertain. Son of Ţa-zhe'-ga.

Wa-zha'-e-no$^n$-pa-i$^n$. Son of Mi'-ţse-xi of the Ho$^{n'}$-ga gens.

Wa-zha'-ho$^n$-ga, Sacred-Wa-zha-zhe. Son of Ţo'-ho-ho-e.

Wa-zha'-ho$^n$-ga. Husband of Mi'-gthe-do$^n$-wi$^n$.

Wa-zha'-ho$^n$-ga. Son of Wa-zha'-ho$^n$-ga and Mi'-gthe-do$^n$-wi$^n$.

Wa-zha-zhe, meaning uncertain. Name of the tribal subdivision representing the water portion of the earth. Son of Mi'-ţse-xi of the Ho$^{n'}$-ga gens.

FEMALE

Çon-çi'-gthe, Footprints-in-the-woods. Refers to the footprints of deer in the woods. Wife of Ţo$^{n'}$-wo$^n$-ga-xe of the Ţsi'-zhu Wa-shta-ge gens.

Ço$^n$-çi'-gthe. Wife of Ţse-wa'-hiu of the Ţsi'-zhu Wa-no$^n$ gens.

Ço$^n$-çi'-gthe. Daughter of Chi-zhe-wa-the and Ni'-ķa-shi-ţsi-e of the Ho$^{n'}$ I-ni-ķa-shi-ga gens.

Gthe-do$^{n'}$-wi$^n$-zhi$^n$-ga, Young-hawk-woman. Wife of Gi-wa'-xthi-zhe of the Ho$^{n'}$-ga U-ţa-no$^n$-dsi gens.

Ho$^n$-be'-do-ka, Wet-moccasins. Wife of Tsi'-zhu-a-ki-pa of the Po$^n$-ka Wa-shta-ge gens.

Ho$^n$-be'-do-ka. Wife of I$^n$-gtho$^n$'-ga-zhi$^n$-ga of the Wa-ça'-be gens.

Ho$^n$-be'-do-ka. Wife of We-to$^n$'-ha-i$^n$-ge of the Ni'-ka-wa-ko$^n$-da-gi gens.

Ho$^n$-be'-do-ka. Daughter of Ga-hi'-ge-no$^n$-zhi$^n$ and Xu-tha'-da-wi$^n$ of the Tsi'-zhu Wa-shta-ge gens.

Ho$^n$-be'-do-ka. Wife of Ho$^n$'-ba-hiu of the Ho$^n$' I-ni-ka-shi-ga gens.

Ho$^n$-be'-do-ka. Daughter of To'-ho-ho-e.

Ni'-a-bi, Permitted-to-live. Refers to the fawn the hunter allows to escape.

Ni'-do$^n$-be, Sees-water. Daughter of To'-ho-ho-e.

Pa-hiu'-gthe-çe, Spotted-hair. Mother of Andrew O-pah of the O'-po$^n$ gens.

Pa'-xpi-ço$^n$-dse, Stunted-oaks. Refers to the habit of the deer in frequenting stunted oak bushes.

Pa'-xpi-ço$^n$-dse. Wife of Xu-tha'-to$^n$-ga of the Ho$^n$'-ga gens.

Pa'-xpi-ço$^n$-dse. Wife of Tse-çi$^n$-dse of the Tho'-xe gens.

Pa'-xpi-ço$^n$-dse. Wife of To'-thi-xthi-xtho-dse of the Tsi'-zhu Wa-shta-ge gens.

Wa-ko$^n$'-ça-mo$^n$-i$^n$, meaning uncertain. Wife of Wa'-tse-mo$^n$-i$^n$ of the Po$^n$-ka Wa-shta-ge gens.

Wa-to$^n$'-i-ça-e, meaning uncertain. Wife of Mo$^n$-ga'-shu-e of the Tho'-xe gens.

Wa-zha'-zhe-mi-tse-xi, Wa-zha'-zhe-sacred-sun. Daughter of No$^n$-zhi$^n$'-wa -the.

Wa-zha'-zhe-mi-tse-xi. Wife of Pa-çi'-do-ba of the Tho'-xe gens.

Wa-zha'-zhe-mi-tse-xi. Wife of Ba'-çiu-to$^n$-ga, a Kaw Indian.

Wa-zha'-zhe-mi-tse-xi. Wife of No$^n$-be'-çi of the Tsi'-zhu Wa-shta-ge gens.

Wa-zha'-zhe-mi-tse-xi. Daughter of Wa-k'o$^n$'-tsi-e and Hi$^n$'-i-ki$^n$-da-bi of the Tsi'-zhu Wa-shta-ge gens.

Wa-zha-zhe-mi-tse-xi. Daughter of Chi-zhe'-wa-the and Ni'-ka-shi-tsi-e of the Ho$^n$' I-ni-ka-shi-ga gens.

Wa-zha'-zhe-mi-tse-xi. Daughter of Ga-hi'-ge-no$^n$-zhi$^n$ and Xu-tha'-da-wi$^n$ of the Tsi'-zhu Wa-shta-ge gens.

Wa-zha'-zhe-mi-tse-xi. Daughter of Mi'-tse-xi of the Ho$^n$'-ga gens.

## HO' I-NI-KA-SHI-GA (FISH PEOPLE)

Special kinship terms and names of the first three sons and daughters in a Ho' I-ni-ka-shi-ga family.

### SONS

1. I$^n$-gtho$^n$'. Name, Wa-zha'-ho$^n$-ga, Sacred Wa-zha'-zhe.
2. Ksho$^n$'-ga. Name, To'-ho-ho, Blue-fish.
3. Ka'-zhi$^n$-ga. Name, Ho-xo'-e, Fish scales.

### DAUGHTERS

1. Mi'-na.   Name, Wa-zha'-zhe-mi-ṭse-xi, Wa-zha'-zhe Sacred-sun.
2. Wi'-he.   Name, Hon-be'-do-ḳa, Wet-moccasins.
3. Çi'-ge.   Name, Wa-zha'-mi-ṭse-xi, Wa-zha'-zhe Sacred-sun.

### OTHER NAMES

#### MALE

Chi-zhe'-wa-the, Rustles-the-leaves.  Refers to the rustling of the leaves by a deer as he feeds in the woods.

E-non'-min-dse-ṭon, Sole-owner-of-the-bow.  Refers to the office of this gens of making the ceremonial bow for use in a tribal ceremony.

Ga-hi'-ge-non-zhin, Standing-chief.

Ga-hi'-ge-tha-gthin, Handsome-chief.

Ga-hi'-ge-ṭon-ga, Big-chief.

Ga-hi'-ge-zhin-ga, Little-chief.  (In the In-ḳe'-ça-be gens of the Omaha tribe.)

Ga-hi-'ge-xtsi, Real-chief.  (In the In-ḳe'-ça-be gens of the Omaha tribe.)

He'-çka-mon-in, White-horn-walks.  Refers to the buck deer with white horns.

Ho-btha'-çka-zhin-ga, Little-flat-fish.

Ho-çka', White-fish.

Ho-çon', Braided-fish.  Refers to the braidlike appearance of the scales of a fish.

Ho-ga'-xa, fish-fins.

Ho'-ki-e-çi, Splashing-fish.  Refers to the splashing of the water by a fish as he plays.

Ho-pa', Fish-head.

Ho-wa'-hi, Fish-bone.

Ho-xin'-ha, Fish-skin.

In-shta'-pe-dse, Fire-eyes.  (In the In-ḳe'-ça-be gens of the Omaha tribe.)

Ḳo'-zhi-mon-in, Travels-in-distant-lands.

Mi-ḳa'-xa-ge, Crying-raccoon.  (In the Ṭa-pa' gens of the Omaha tribe.)

Min'-dse-ni-e, Fences-with-the-bow.

Ni'-u-ba-shu-dse, Muddies-the-water.  Refers to the mud stirred up by the fish as they move about in the bottom of a stream.

Ṭa-he'-ga-xe, Antlered-deer.  (In the In-shta'-çon-da gens of the Omaha tribe.)

Ṭa-he'-xa-ga, Rough-horned-deer.

Ṭse-do'-ha, Buffalo-skin.  (A name belonging to the Tho'-xe gens.)

FEMALE

Ço$^n$-çi'-gthe, Here-are-the-footprints.   Refers to the footprints of the deer.

Mi'-gthe-do$^n$-wi$^n$, Hawk-woman.

No$^n$'-ḳa-çka, White-back.   Refers to the whitish color of the deer at certain seasons.

No$^n$-ṭa'-çka, White-ears.   Refers to the white hair on the ears of the deer.

Ṗa-hiu'-gthe-zhe, Spotted-hair.   Refers to the spots on the fawn.

Ṗa'-xpe-ço$^n$-dse, Frequenter-of-bushes.

Wa-ḳo$^n$'-çi, Small animal.

Wa-xthe'-tho$^n$-ba.   (Meaning uncertain.)

### Ho$^N$'-GA U-ṬA-NO$^N$-DSI

Names of the first three sons and the first three daughters.

#### SONS

I$^n$-gtho$^n$'.   Ṭa-dse'-k'u-e, Soughing-of-the-wind.

Ksho$^n$'-ga.   Ṭa-dse'-to$^n$, Owner-of-the-wind.   (In the I$^n$-ḳe'-ça-be gens of the Omaha tribe.)
    Ho$^n$'-ga U-ṭa-no$^n$-dsi, The-solitary-Ho$^n$'-ga.

Ḳa'-zhi$^n$-ga.   Ho$^n$'-ga-ṭsi-no$^n$-zhi$^n$, Standing-house-of-the-Ho$^n$'-ga.
    Ho$^n$'-ga-ṭo$^n$-ga, Great-Ho$^n$'-ga.
    Ṭsi'-wa-ḳo$^n$-da-gi, Mystery-house.
    Ṭsi'-wa-the-she, Tears-down-the-house.   Refers to the tearing down of the house of mystery after a ceremony.

#### DAUGHTERS

Mi'-na.   Mi'-ṭse-xi, Mi'-na-the-favored.

Wi-he'.   Xiu-tha'-do$^n$-wi$^n$, Sees-the-eagle.

Çi'-ge.   Mi'-ṭse-xi-Ho$^n$-ga, Mi'-na-ho$^n$-ga-the-favored.

#### OTHER NAMES

##### MALE

Gi-wa'-xthi-zhi, Not-stingy.   Husband of Gthe-do$^n$'-wi$^n$-zhin-ga of the Ṭa' I-ni-ḳa-shi-ga gens.

Ho$^n$-ga-ṭo$^n$-ga, Great-Ho$^n$'-ga.   Also Ho$^n$'-mo$^n$-da-ḳo$^n$, Light-on-the-earth-at-night.   Husband of Ṗa'-zhi-hi of the Ho$^n$'-ga gens.

Ḳo$^n$'-çe-ho$^n$-ga, Resembling-the-Ho$^n$'-ga.   (In the Mo$^n$'-thi$^n$-ḳa-ga-xe gens of the Omaha.)   Husband of Bo$^n$-giu'-da of the Tho'-xe gens.

Mo$^n$'-xe-a-gthe, Reaches-the-sky.   Refers to the wind.   Husband of Wa-ḳo$^n$'da-hi-tho$^n$-be of the Ṭsi'-zhu Wa-no$^n$ gens.

No$^n$-po'-e, Flames-at-every-step. Refers to the white spot on the throat of the black bear that is a symbol of fire. Husband of Wa-ṭo$^{n\prime}$-i-ça-e of the Ṗo$^{n\prime}$-ḳa Wa-shta-ge gens.

Ṭa-dse'-k'o-e, Soughing-of-the-wind. Refers to the wind, the life symbol of the gens.

Ṭa-dse'-ṭo$^n$, Owner-of-the-wind. (In the I$^n$-ḳe'-ça-be gens of the Omaha tribe.) Son of Ḳo$^{n\prime}$-çe-ho$^n$-ga and Bo$^n$-giu'-da.

Ho$^n$-'ga-wa-da-i$^n$-ga, Playful-Ho$^{n\prime}$-ga.

I'-hu-tha-bi, From-whom-permission-is-obtained. Refers to the authority vested in this gens to give the order to go to the buffalo chase. (Also used by the Omaha.)

Mo$^{n\prime}$-hi$^n$-çi, Fire. Refers to the fire drawn from the stone. Or Arrow-head.

U-pa'-shi-e, Counsellor.

Wa-no$^{n\prime}$-pa-zhi, Not-afraid. (Also used by the Omaha.)

Wa-zhi$^n$-u-ṭsi, Courageous.

FEMALE

A'-hiu-do-ba, Four-wings.

Do$^{n\prime}$-ba-bi, Seen-by-all. Daughter of Ḳo$^{n\prime}$-çe-ho$^n$-ga and Bo$^n$-giu'-da of the Tho'-xe gens.

Do$^n$-do$^n$-ba, Seen-from-time-to-time. Daughter of Ho$^{n\prime}$-ga-ṭo$^n$-ga and Ṗa'-zhi-hi of the Ho$^{n\prime}$-ga gens.

Do$^{n\prime}$-do$^n$-ba, Mother of O-ho$^{n\prime}$-bi of the Ṭa' I-ni-ḳa-shi-ga gens.

Mi'-ṭse-xi, Mi'-na-the-favorite. Daughter of Ho$^{n\prime}$-ga-ṭo$^n$-ga and Ṗa'-zhi-hi.

Mi'-ṭse-xi-ho$^n$-ga, Mi'-na-the-sacred-one. Daughter of Ḳo$^{n\prime}$-çe-ho$^n$-ga and Bo$^n$-giu'-da.

Mi'-ṭse-xi-ho$^n$-ga, Mi'-na-the-sacred-one. Wife of O'-ḳi-ça of the Ṭsi'-zhu Wa-shta-ge gens.

Wa'-ṭse-wi$^n$, Star-woman. Daughter of Ho$^{n\prime}$-ga-ṭo$^n$-ga and Ṗa'-zhi-hi.

Zho$^{n\prime}$-btha-$^n$çka-wi$^n$, Flat-wood-woman. Wife of I$^n$-shta'-gthe-çe of the Wa-ça'-be gens.

Zho$^{n\prime}$-btha-çka-wi$^n$, Daughter of Ho$^{n\prime}$-ga-ṭo$^n$-ga and Ṗa'-zhi-hi.

## HO$^{N\prime}$-GA SUBDIVISION

### WA-ÇA'-BE

Special kinship terms and names of the first three sons and the first three daughters in a family of the Wa-ça'-be or Black Bear gens as given by Wa-ṭse'-mo$^n$-i$^n$.

SONS

1. I$^n$-gtho$^{n\prime}$. Zhi$^n$-ga'-ga-hi-ge, Little-chief. (In the Ṭa-pa' gens of the Omaha tribe.)

2. Ksho$^{n\prime}$-ga. Gthe-do$^{n\prime}$-xo-dse, Gray-hawk. (In the Tha'-ṭa-da gens of the Omaha tribe.)

3. Ka-ge'. Mo$^{n}$'-hi$^{n}$-wa-ko$^{n}$-da, Mysterious-knife. Refers to the scalping-knife in the keeping of the Black Bear gens.

## DAUGHTERS

1. Mi'-na. Mi'-tse-xi, Mi'-na-the-favorite.
2. Wi'-he. Mi'-ho$^{n}$-i$^{n}$.
3. Çi'-ge or A-çi$^{n}$'-ga. Go$^{n}$'-ba-kshe, Flashing-eyes. Refers to the flashing eyes of the black bear.

## OTHER NAMES

### MALE

I'-ba-zhu-ɒse, Red-handle. Refers to the red-handled knife that is in the keeping of this gens for ceremonial use.

I$^{n}$-gtho$^{n}$'-ga-zhi$^{n}$-ga, Little-puma. Husband of Ho$^{n}$-be'-do-ka of the Ṭa' I-ni-ka-shi-ga gens.

I$^{n}$-shta'-mo$^{n}$-çe, Flashing-eyes. Refers to the flashing eyes of the black bear. Husband of Xu-tha'-da-wi$^{n}$ of the Mi-k'i$^{n}$ gens.

Mo$^{n}$'-hi$^{n}$-zhu-dse, Red-knife. Refers to the red-handled ceremonial knife. Son of Mo$^{n}$-zhi-çka-k'i$^{n}$-ga-xthi and Mi'-ga-sho$^{n}$-i$^{n}$.

Mo$^{n}$'-thiu-xe, Ground-cleared-of-grass. Refers to the bare ground around the house of the bear. Son of Wa-tse'-mo$^{n}$-i$^{n}$ and Mo$^{n}$-ço$^{n}$-ho$^{n}$-i$^{n}$.

Mo$^{n}$'-zhi-çka-k'i$^{n}$-ga-xthi, Slayer-of-the-warrior-with-white-quiver (war name). Husband of Mi'-ga-sho$^{n}$-i$^{n}$ of the Ṗo$^{n}$'-ka Wa-shta-ge gens.

Mo$^{n}$-zho$^{n}$'-dsi-çi-gthe, Tracks-on-the-prairies. Refers to the bear tracks seen on the prairies.

Ni'-ka-wa-da-i$^{n}$-ga, Playful-man. Also Mo$^{n}$'-hi$^{n}$-wa-ko$^{n}$-da, Mysterious-knife. Refers to the ceremonial knife in the keeping of this gens.

Wa'-tse-ga-wa, Radiant-star. Son of Wa-tse'-mo$^{n}$-i$^{n}$ and Mo$^{n}$'-ço$^{n}$-ho$^{n}$-i$^{n}$.

Wa-tse'-mo$^{n}$-i$^{n}$, He-who-wins-war-honors (war name). Also Wa-shi$^{n}$'-ha. Refers to the fat on the skin of the bear. Husband of Mi'-ço$^{n}$-ho$^{n}$-i$^{n}$ of the O'-po$^{n}$ gens.

Zhi$^{n}$-ga'-ga-hi-ge, Young-chief. Son of I'-ba-zhu-dse.

### FEMALE

Go$^{n}$'-ba-kshe, The-light. Refers to the light in the eyes of the bear.

Go$^{n}$'-ba-kshe. Daughter of Wa-tse'-mo$^{n}$-i$^{n}$ and Mi'-ço$^{n}$-ho$^{n}$-i$^{n}$.

Mi'-ço$^{n}$-e', White-sun. Wife of Wa-ṭo$^{n}$'-i$^{n}$-ki-the of the Tho'-xe gens.

Mi'-ho$^{n}$-i$^{n}$ (meaning uncertain). Daughter of I$^{n}$-gtho$^{n}$'-ga-zhi$^{n}$-ga and Ho$^{n}$-be'-do-ka.

Mi'-ho$^{n}$-i$^{n}$. Daughter of Ni'-ka-wa-da-i$^{n}$-ga.

Mi'-ho$^n$-i$^n$.  Daughter of Wa-tse'-mo$^n$-i$^n$ and Mi'-ço$^n$-ho$^n$-i$^n$.

Mi'-tse-xi, Mi'-na-the-favorite.  Daughter of Mo$^{n\prime}$-zhi-çka-ḳ'i$^n$-ga-xthi and Mi'-ga-sho$^n$-i$^n$.

No$^{n\prime}$-mi-tse-xi, Mi'-na-the-favorite.  Daughter of Ni'-ḳa-wa-da-i$^n$-ga.

Wa-ça'-be-wa-k'o, Black-bear-woman.  Daughter of I$^n$-gtho$^{n\prime}$-ga-zhi$^n$-ga.

## I$^N$-GTHO$^{N\prime}$-GA

Names of the first three sons and first three daughters.

### SONS

1. I$^n$-gtho$^{n\prime}$.  Mi'-wa-ga-xe, Child-of-the-sun.
2. Ksho$^{n\prime}$-ga.  I'-e-çka-wa-the, Giver-of-speech.
3. Ḳa'-zhi$^n$-ga.  Mo$^{n\prime}$-ga-xe, Arrow-maker.

### DAUGHTERS

1. Mi'-no$^n$.  Mo$^{n\prime}$-çi-tse-xi, Sacred-arrow-shaft.
2. Wi'-he.  Mo$^{n\prime}$-zho$^n$-op-she-wi$^n$, Woman - who - travels - over - the-earth.
3. Çi'-ge.  No$^{n\prime}$-mi-tse-xi, Beloved-child-of-the-sun.

### OTHER NAMES

#### MALE

I$^n$-shta'-sha-be, Dark-eyes.  In the Tse-çi$^{n\prime}$-dse gens of the Omaha tribe.

Mi-wa'-ga-xe, Child-of-the-sun.  Also, Hi$^n$-wa'-xa-ga, Rough-hair.  Husband of Mi-'tse-xi of the Ho$^{n\prime}$-ga gens.

Mo$^{n\prime}$-ga-xe, Arrow-maker.  Husband of Wa-ṭo$^n$-i'-ça-e of the Ṗo$^{n\prime}$-ḳa Wa-shta-ge gens.  (Also Ṗa'-xe-ga, Brown-nose.  Refers to the brown nose of the black bear.)

Mo$^{n\prime}$-ga-xe.  Son of Wa-xthi'-zhi and Xu-tha'-da-wi$^n$.

Mo$^{n\prime}$-hi$^n$-wa-ḳo$^n$-da, Mysterious-knife.  Son of Wa-thu'-ṭs'a-ga-zhi and Mi'-tse-xi.

No$^n$-be'-wa-ḳo$^n$-da, Mysterious hand.  Mythical name, refers to the use of the index finger for killing animals before weapons were known.  Also refers to the ceremony performed by a member of the Wa-ça'-be gens when blessing a newborn child with the rays of the sun.  Son of Wa-thu'-ṭs'a-ga-zhi and Mi'-tse-xi.

Ṭo$^{n\prime}$-dse-a-shi$^n$ (meaning obscure).

Wa-thu'-ṭs'a-ga-zhi, Never-fails (war name).  The grandfather of the man who last bore this name never failed in his war exploits so the people gave him the name.  Husband of Mi'-tse-xi of the Ho$^{n\prime}$-ga gens.

Wa-xthi'-zhi, Generous (war name). A man of this gens was given the name because he always shared with the people the spoils he took in his war exploits. Husband of Xu-tha'-da-wi$^n$ of the Tsi'-zhu Wa-shta-ge gens.

### FEMALE

Mi'-ho$^n$-i$^n$. (Meaning obscure.) Mother of Xo'-ka of the Ni'-ka-wa-wa-ko$^n$-da-gi gens.

Mo$^n$'-çi-tse-xi, Sacred-arrowshaft. Daughter of Wa-xthi'-zhi and Xu-tha'-da-wi$^n$.

Mo$^n$'-çi-tse-xi. Mother of I$^{'n}$-sho$^n$-ba of the Ni'-ka-wa-ko$^n$-da-gi gens.

No$^n$'-mi-tse-xi, Only-sacred-sun. Refers to the sun, a life symbol of this gens. Daughter of Wa-xthi'-zhi and Xu-tha'-da-wi$^n$.

No$^n$'-mi-tse-xi. Wife of Wa-shka'-dse of the Po$^n$'-ka Wa-shta-ge gens.

Wa'-tse-wi$^n$, Star-woman. Wife of Xi-tha-u'-ga-sho$^n$ of the Ho$^n$'-ga gens.

### Ho$^{N'}$-GA GTHE-ZHE

Special kinship terms and names of the first three sons and the first three daughters in a family of the Ho$^n$'-ga Gthe-zhe, Mottled eagle, gens, as given by Mi'-she-tsi-the

#### SONS

1. I$^n$-gtho$^n$'. Mi-she-tsi-the, Yonder-the-sun-passes. Also Ho$^n$'-ga-a-shi$^n$, same as Ho$^n$'-ga-u-ga-sho$^n$, The Ho$^n$'-ga Messenger.
2. Ksho$^n$'-ga. Ho$^n$'-ga-a-gthi$^n$, Good-eagle. Refers to the eagle that is friendly to the people.
3. Ka'-zhi$^n$-ga. A'-hiu-çka, White-wings.

#### DAUGHTERS

1. Mi'-na. Mi'-tse-xi, Mi'-na-the-favorite.
2. Wi'-he. Mi'-ço$^n$-i$^n$, White-sun.
3. A-çi$^{n'}$-ga. Xu-tha'-mi-tse-xi, Eagle-sacred-sun. Also Xu-tha'-dsi-wi$^n$, Eagle-woman.

#### OTHER NAMES
##### MALE

A'-hiu-çka, White-wings.

A'-hiu-çka. Husband of I'-ni-a-bi of the Tsi'-zhu Wa-shta-ge gens.

A'-hiu-k'u-we, Holes-in-the-wings. Son of Wa-no$^n$'-she-zhi$^n$-ga and Mo$^n$'-çi-tse-xi.

Ho$^n$'-ga-a-shi$^n$, The-Ho$^n$'-ga-messenger.

Ho$^n$'-ga-a-shi$^n$. Eugene Blaine.

Ho$^n$'-ga-a-shi$^n$. Also Ta-shka'-wa.

Ho$^{n\prime}$-ga-tha-gthi$^n$, Good-eagle.

Ho$^{n\prime}$-ga-tha-gthi$^n$, Son of Wa-no$^{n\prime}$-she-zhi$^n$-ga and Ho$^{n\prime}$-ga-mi-ṭse-xi.

Ho$^{n\prime}$-ga-tha-gthi$^n$.  Son of Xu-tha$^\prime$-pa and Ṭse$^\prime$-mi-ṭse-xi.

Ho$^{n\prime}$-ga-zhi$^n$-ga, Young-Ho$^{n\prime}$-ga.  Son of Wa-no$^{n\prime}$-she-zhi$^n$-ga and Ho$^{n\prime}$-ga-mi-ṭse-xi.

Kshi$^\prime$-zhi, Never-reached-home.  Husband of Ni$^\prime$-ḳa of the Mi-ḳ$^\prime$i$^{n\prime}$ gens.

Lookout, John.  Husband of I$^\prime$-ga-mo$^n$-ge of the Ṭsi$^\prime$-zhu Wa-shta-ge gens.

Lookout, William.  Son of John Lookout and I$^\prime$-ga-mo$^n$-ge.

Mi$^\prime$-she-ṭsi-the.  Son of Mo$^{n\prime}$-çi-ṭse-xi of the Ṭsi$^\prime$-zhu Wa-shta-ge gens.

Mi$^\prime$-she-ṭsi-the.  Also No$^n$-xu$^\prime$-dse-thi$^n$-ge, No-ears.  Husband of Wa$^\prime$-ḳo$^n$-ça-mo$^n$-i$^n$ of the Po$^{n\prime}$-ka Wa-shta-ge gens.

Mi$^\prime$-she-ṭsi-the.  Husband of Wa-zha$^\prime$-xa-i$^n$ of the Ṭsi$^\prime$-zhu Wa-shta-ge gens.

Mo$^n$-shi$^\prime$-ṭa-mo$^n$-i$^n$, One-who-travels-above.  Refers to the eagle. Husband of Mo$^{n\prime}$-çi-ṭse-xi of the Ṭsi$^\prime$-zhu Wa-shta-ge gens.

O-ba$^\prime$-ho$^n$-mo$^n$-i$^n$, Walking-within.  Husband of Pa$^\prime$-zhi-hi of the Ho$^{n\prime}$-ga gens.

Sha$^\prime$-ge-çka, White-talons.  (In the Tha$^\prime$-ṭa-da gens of the Omaha tribe.)

Sha$^\prime$-ge-pa-hi, Sharp-talons.  Son of Xu-tha$^\prime$-pa and Ṭse$^\prime$-mi-ṭse-xi.

Tha$^\prime$-bthi$^n$-wa-xthi, Slayer-of-three    (War name.)

Ṭse-hi$^{n\prime}$-tha-ge, Wearer-of-buffalo-hair-head-band.  (Not gentile name.)

Wa-go$^{n\prime}$-tha, meaning obscure.  Also Wa-ṭse$^\prime$-gi-do$^n$-a-bi, One-whose-trophies-are-seen (war name).  Son of Wa-no$^{n\prime}$-she-zhi$^n$-ga and Mo$^{n\prime}$-çi-ṭse-xi.

Wa-ḳo$^{n\prime}$-tha-ṭo$^n$-ga, Great-attacker.  Husband of Mi$^\prime$-ṭse-xi of the O$^\prime$-po$^n$ gens.

Wa-no$^{n\prime}$-she-zhi$^n$-ga, Little-soldier.  (In the I$^n$-shta$^\prime$-ço$^n$-da gens of the Omaha tribe.)  Husband of Mo$^{n\prime}$-çi-ṭse-xi of the Wa-ça$^\prime$-be gens.

Wa-no$^{n\prime}$-she-zhi$^n$-ga.  Husband of Ho$^{n\prime}$-ga-mi-ṭse-xi of the I$^\prime$-ba-ṭse gens.

Wa-sho$^\prime$-she, Valorous.  Husband of Mo$^{n\prime}$-çi-ṭse-xi of the Ṭsi$^\prime$-zhu Wa-shta-ge gens.

Wa-sho$^\prime$-she.  Judge Lawrence.

Wa-xo$^{n\prime}$-xo$^n$, Twinkles.  Refers to the spaces in the wings of the eagle through which the sunlight twinkles as the bird flies.  Son of Wa-no$^{n\prime}$-she-zhi$^n$-ga and Mo$^{n\prime}$-çi-ṭse-xi.

Wa-xo$^{n\prime}$-xo$^n$.  James Blaine, jr.

Wa-zhi$^{n\prime}$-pa, Bird-head.  Son of Xu-tha$^\prime$-ṭo$^n$-ga and Pa$^\prime$-xpi-ço$^n$-dse.

Wa-zhi$^{n\prime}$-pa.  Son of Wa-no$^{n\prime}$-she-zhi$^n$-ga and Ho$^{n\prime}$-ga-mi-ṭse-xi.

Xu-tha'-p̣a, Eagle-head.   Husband of Ṭse'-mi-ṭse-xi of the Ṭse-tho$^n$-ka gens.

Xu-tha'-ṭo$^n$-ga, Big-eagle.   Husband of P̣a'-xpi-ço$^n$-dse of the Ṭa' I-ni-ḳa-shi-ga gens.

Xi-tha-u'-ga-sho$^n$, Eagle-that-travels.   Husband of Wa'-ṭse-wi$^n$ of the I$^n$-gtho$^{n\prime}$-ga gens.

Zhi$^n$-ga-'wa-ça.   (Meaning obscure.)   Also Ço$^{n\prime}$-ṭo$^n$-ça-be, Black-dog.   Husband of Gthe-do$^{n\prime}$-mi-ṭse-xi of the Ni'-ḳa-wa-ḳo$^n$-da-gi gens.

FEMALE

Lookout, Nora.   Daughter of Wa-no$^{n\prime}$-she-zhi$^n$-ga and Mo$^{n\prime}$-çi-ṭse-xi.

Mi'-çe-wi$^n$.   (Meaning obscure.)   Wife of Naranjo, a Pueblo Indian of Santa Clara, N. Mex.

Mi'-ço$^n$-e, White-sun.   Wife of P̣a-çi'-do-ba of the Tho'-xe gens.

Mi'-ço$^n$-i$^n$, White-sun.

Mi'-ço$^n$-i$^n$.   Wife of Ḳi-xi'-tha-ba-zhi of the Ni'-ḳa-wa-ḳo$^n$-da-gi gens.

Mi'-ṭse-xi, Sacred-sun.   (In the I$^n$-ḳe-ça-be gens of the Omaha tribe.)   Daughter of Mi'-she-ṭsi-the.

Mi'-ṭse-xi.   (Daughter of Zhi$^n$-ga'-wa-ça.)   Wife of Hi$^n$-wa'-xa-ga of the I$^n$-gtho$^{n\prime}$-ga gens.

Mi'-ṭse-xi.   Daughter of Wa-no$^{n\prime}$-she-zhi$^n$-ga and Ho$^{n\prime}$-ga mi-ṭse-xi.

Mi'-ṭse-xi.   Daughter of Xu-tha'-p̣a and Ṭse'-mi-ṭse-xi.

Mi'-ṭse-xi.   Wife of Ho'-ḳi-e-çi of the Ṭa' I-ni-ḳa-shi-ga gens.

Mi'-ṭse-xi.   Mother of Wa-zha'-zhe-mi-ṭse-xi, Ho-xo' and Wa-zha'-zhe of the Ṭa' I-ni-ḳa-shi-ga gens.

Mi'-ṭse-xi.   Mother of Wa-zha'-no$^n$-pa-i$^n$ of the Ṭa' I-ni-ḳa-shi-ga gens.

Mi'-ṭse-xi.   Daughter of Wa-no$^{n\prime}$-she-zhi-ga and Mo$^{n\prime}$-çi-ṭse-xi.

Mi'-ṭse-xi.   Wife of Wa-thu'-ṭs'a-ga-zhi of the I$^n$-ghto$^{n\prime}$-ga gens.

No$^{n\prime}$-k'on-çe-wi$^n$.   (Meaning obscure.)   Kate Whitehorn.

P̣a'-zhi-hi.   Reddish-head.   Refers to the reddish color of the head of the eagle.   Mary Cox.

P̣a'-zhi-hi.   Grace Entokah.

.P̣a'-zhi-hi.   Prudie Martin.

P̣a'-zhi-hi.   Daughter of Mi'-she-ṭsi-e and Wa'-ḳo$^n$-ça-mo$^n$-i$^n$.

P̣a'-zhi-hi.   Wife of O-ba'-ho$^n$-mo$^n$-i$^n$ (Ni-ḳa'-ça-e).

P̣a'-zhi-hi.   Daughter of Xu-tha'-ṭo$^n$-ga and P̣a'-xpi-ço$^n$-dse.

P̣a'-zhi-hi.   Wife of Ho$^{n\prime}$-mo$^n$-da-ḳo$^n$ of the Ho$^{n\prime}$-ga U-ṭa-no$^n$-dsi gens.

Xu'-tha-dsi-wi$^n$, Eagle-woman.   Wife of Ṭsi-zhu-zhi$^n$-ga of the Ṭsi'-zhu Wa-shta-ge gens.

Xu-tha'-mi-ṭse-xi, Eagle-sacred-sun.   Daughter of Mi'-she-ṭsi-the.

Xu-tha'-mi-ṭse-xi.   Daughter of Wa-sho'-she and Mo$^{n\prime}$-çi-ṭse-xi.

Xu-tha'-mi-ṭse-xi.   Wife of No$^n$-ba'-mo$^n$-thi$^n$ of the Tho'-xe gens.

Xu-tha$'$-mi-ṭse-xi. Wife of Wa$'$-thu-xa-ge of the Ṭsi$'$-zhu Wa-shta-ge.

Xu-tha$'$-wi$^n$, Eagle-woman. Daughter of Mi$'$-she-ṭsi-e and Wa$'$-ḳo$^n$-ça-mo$^n$-i$^n$.

Xu$'$-tha-wi$^n$. Wife of Xo$^n'$-dse-u-mo$^n$-i$^n$ of the Ho$^{n'}$ I-ni-ḳa-shi-ga gens.

### Ho$^{N'}$-GA U-THU-HA-GE

Special kinship terms and names of the first three sons and the first three daughters in a family of the Ho$^n$-ga U-thu-ha-ge (Last in the Ho$^n$-ga order) gens as given by Wa$'$-no$^n$-she-zhi$^n$-ga.

#### SONS

I$^n$gtho$^{n'}$. Xu-tha$'$-ha-hi-ge, Eagle-chief.

Ksho$^{n'}$-ga. Ṭse$'$-ga-mo$^n$-i$^n$, Goes-in-new-plumage. Refers to the young eagle.

Ḳa$'$-zhi$^n$-ga. I$^{n'}$-be-çka, White-tail. Refers to the tail of the mature golden eagle whose white tail feathers are tipped with black.

#### DAUGHTERS

Mi$'$-na. Mi-ṭse-xi, Mi$'$-na-the-favorite.

Wi$'$-he. Mi$'$-ço$^n$-e, White-sun.

Çi$'$-ge. Mi$'$-ṭse-xi-o$^n$-ba. (Meaning obscure.)

#### OTHER NAMES

##### MALE

A-hi$^{n'}$-u-ḳ$'$u-dse, Holes-in-the-wings. Refers to the spaces in the wings of the eagle.

Çka$'$-gthe, White-plumes. Refers to the three downy feathers taken from under the tail of the eagle and worn as life symbols by priests.

He-ba$'$-ḳu-ge, Blunt-horns. Name given in compliment to this gens by the Tho$'$-xe gens.

Hiu$'$-ça-da-zhi$^n$-ga, Young-hiu$'$-ça-da. Refers to the eagle's leg attached to the hanging strap of the wa-xo$'$-be or shrine.

Ho$^n$-ga, The-consecrated-one. Name of the gens.

Ho$^n'$-ga-gthe-zhe, Mottled-eagle. Refers to the immature golden eagle that is dark in plumage. This bird is regarded as sacred by many of the Indian tribes.

Ho$^n'$-ga-ṭo$^n$-ga, Great-eagle.

Ho$^n'$-ga-ṭsi-e-da, House-of-the-Ho$^n'$-ga. Refers to the House of Mystery that is in the keeping of the Ho$^n'$-ga gens.

Kshi$'$-zhi-wa-ga-xe, Causes them to fail to reach home. Refers to the attack of the eagle on its prey.

Mo$^n$'-çe, Metal. Wa-no$^n$-she-zhi$^n$-ga could not explain the meaning of this name.

Mo$^n$'-da-i-he. (Meaning obscure.)

Mo$^n$-i$^n$'-zhi, Does-not-walk. Refers to the eagle.

Mo$^n$'-shi-ha-mo$^n$-i$^n$, One-who-moves-above. Refers to the eagle. (In the I$^n$-shta'-ço$^n$-da gens of the Omaha tribe.)

Mo$^n$-shi'-ţa-mo$^n$-i$^n$, Moves-on-high. Refers to the eagle.

Mo$^n$'-sho$^n$-ho$^n$-ga, Sacred-plume. Refers to the eagle plumes worn by priests.

No$^n$-be'-çi, Yellow-hands. Refers to the yellow feet of the eagle.

Ṗa-hiu'-ga-zho$^n$, Hairy-head. Name given by the Tho'-xe gens to the Ho$^n$'-ga U-thu-ha-ge gens.

Sha'-ge-çka, White-talons. (In the Tha'-ţa-da gens of the Omaha tribe.)

Sha'-ge-ṗa-hi, Sharp-talons. Refers to the sharp talons of the eagle.

Sho$^n$'-ţo$^n$-ça-be, Black-dog. Thu-ts'a'-ga-bi.

Thu-ţs'a'-ga-bi, Hard-to-catch. Refers to the wariness of the eagle.

Ṭsi-do'-ba, Four-lodges. A valor name. A war party attacked four lodges and killed all the inhabitants. The commander was given the name by the people.

U-ga'-çi$^n$-dse, Breeze. Refers to the wind stirred by the eagle when flying.

U-ga'-sho$^n$, The wanderer. Refers to the office of messenger of this gens.

U-thi$^n$'-ge-no$^n$-zhi$^n$, Stands-holding. Refers to the hold of the eagle on its prey.

U-thi'-sho$^n$-mo$^n$-i$^n$, Moves-in-a-circle. Refers to the soaring of the eagle. (In the I$^n$-ķe'-ça-be gens of the Omaha tribe.)

Wa-ķo$^n$'-tha-ţo$^n$-ga, Great-attacker. Refers to the attack of the eagle on its prey.

Wa-sho'-she, Brave. (In the I$^n$-ķe'-ça-be gens of the Omaha tribe.)

Wa-xo$^n$'-xo$^n$, The-shining-one. Refers to the shining of the wings of the eagle.

Wa-zhi$^n$'-i-çi-wa-the, Hated-bird. Refers to the fear of the eagle by other birds.

Wa-zhi$^n$'-pa, Bird-head. Refers to the head of the eagle.

Wa-zhi$^n$'-zhi-e, Red-bird. (Red eagle.)

Xi-tha-u'-ga-sho$^n$, The-traveling-eagle. Refers to the tireless soaring of the eagle.

Xo$^n$-xo$^n$'-mo$^n$-i$^n$, Shines-as-he-moves. Refers to the reflection of the sun on the outspread wings of the eagle.

Xu-tha'-ni-ķa, Eagle-man. (In the Ṭa'-ṗa gens of the Omaha tribe.)

Xu-tha'-ṗa, Eagle-head.

Xu-tha'-sha-be, Dark-colored-eagle.

Xu-tha'-ṭoⁿ-ga, Big-eagle.

Xu-tha'-ṭs'a-ge, Aged-eagle. The eagle is a symbol of old age. (In the Tha'-ṭa-da gens of the Omaha tribe.)

Xu-tha'-wa-shu-she, Brave-eagle.

Zhiⁿ-ga'-wa-ça. (Meaning obscure.)

Zhoⁿ'-noⁿ-çu-ge, Bends-the-tree-top. Refers to the bending of the treetop by the weight of the eagle as he alights.

### FEMALE

Hiⁿ'-ga-moⁿ-ge, Feathers-blown-by-the-wind. Refers to the dropping of the downy feathers as the eagle rises to fly.

Mi'-çoⁿ-e, White-sun.

Noⁿ'-ḳoⁿ-çe-wiⁿ. (Meaning obscure.)

Pa'-çi-hi, Brown-head. Refers to the brown head of the eagle.

Xu-tha'-mi, Eagle-woman.

Xu-tha'-mi-ṭse-xi, Sacred-eagle-woman.

Xu-tha-ṭsa-wiⁿ, Eagle-woman.

## O'-POⁿ (ELK) GENS

### MALE

He'-çoⁿ-hoⁿ, White-horns. Son of Moⁿ'-ge-ça-be and Xu-tha'-da-wiⁿ.

Hoⁿ'-moⁿ-ça. (Meaning obscure.)

Hoⁿ'-moⁿ-ça. Son of Ḳi'-moⁿ-hoⁿ and Tho'-ṭa-a-ça.

Hoⁿ'-moⁿ-ça, also Mi-xo'-zhiⁿ-ga. (Not Ni'-ḳi-e.) Husband of Moⁿ'-çi-ṭse-xi of the Ṭsi'-zhu Wa-shta-ge gens.

Hoⁿ'-moⁿ-ça. Son of Hoⁿ'-moⁿ-ça and Moⁿ'-çi-ṭse-xi.

I'-e-çka-wa-the, Giver-of-speech. (A name of the Iⁿ-gthoⁿ'-ga gens.)

Ḳi'-moⁿ-hoⁿ, Against-the-wind. Refers to the habit of the elk of facing the wind when feeding. (In the We'-zhiⁿ-shte gens of the Omaha tribe.) Husband of Tho'-ṭa-a-ça of the Ni'-ḳa-wa-ḳoⁿ-da-gi gens.

Moⁿ'-ge-ça-be, Black-breast. Refers to the black hair on the breast of the elk. (In the We'-zhiⁿ-shte gens of the Omaha tribe.) Husband of Xu-tha'-da-wiⁿ of the Mi-ḳ'iⁿ' gens.

Moⁿ-iⁿ'-ḳa-zhiⁿ-ga, Little-clay. Refers to the four different colored clays given by the crawfish to the people for ceremonial use. (See section 25 of the Ni'-ḳi-e ritual, 36th Ann. Rept. Bur. Amer. Ethn.) Son of Ḳi-moⁿ-hoⁿ and Tho'-ṭa-a-ça.

Moⁿ-zhoⁿ'-ga-xe, Earth-maker. From the mythical story of the elk separating the waters from the earth, making it habitable for the people. (See pp. 165 to 169, 36th Ann. Rept. Bur. Amer. Ethn.) Son of Ḳi'-moⁿ-hoⁿ and Tho'-ṭa-a-ça.

O-pa', Andrew. Son of Pa-hiu'-gthe-zhe of the Ṭa' I-ni-ḳa-shi-ga gens.

FEMALE

Gtho$^n$-zho$^{n\prime}$-ba. (Meaning obscure.) Wife of Xo'-ḳa of the Ni'-ḳa-wa-ḳo$^n$-da-gi gens.

Ho$^{n\prime}$-ga-wi$^n$, Eagle-woman.

Ho$^{n\prime}$-ga-wi$^n$. Daughter of Mo$^{n\prime}$-ge-ça-be and Xu-tha'-da-wi$^n$.

Ho$^{n\prime}$-ga-wi$^n$. Daughter of Ḳi'-mo$^n$-ho$^n$ and Tho'-ṭa-a-ça.

Ho$^{n\prime}$-ga-wi$^n$. Wife of No$^{n\prime}$-pe-wa-the of the Ni'-ḳa-wa-ḳo$^n$-da-gi gens.

Ho$^{n\prime}$-'ga-wi$^n$. Wife of Mo$^{n\prime}$-çe-no$^n$-p'i$^n$ of the Ṭsi'-zhu Wa-shta-ge gens.

Mo$^{n\prime}$-ço$^n$-ho$^n$-i$^n$. (Meaning obscure.) Daughter of Ho$^{n\prime}$-mo$^n$-ça and Mo$^{n\prime}$-çi-ṭse-xi.

Mo$^{n\prime}$-ço$^n$-ho$^n$-i$^n$. Wife of Wa-ṭse-'mo$^n$-i$^n$ of the Wa-ça'-be gens.

Mo$^{n\prime}$-ça-ho$^n$-e. (Meaning obscure.) Wife of Edward Bigheart of the Ṗo$^{n\prime}$-ḳa Wa-shta-ge gens.

Mi'-ṭse-xi, Mi'-na-the-favorite. Wife of Wa-ḳo$^{n\prime}$-tha-ṭo$^n$-ga.

Ṗa'-mo$^n$-shi-wa-gtho$^n$. (Meaning obscure.) Wife of Wa'-ṭse-a-xe of the Ṗo$^{n\prime}$-ḳa Wa-shta-ge gens.

Tho'-ha-wa. (Meaning obscure.) Wife of Ṗi'-zhi-ṭo$^n$-ga of the Tho'-xe gens.

### I'-BA-ṬSE (WIND) GENS

MALE

A'-ḳ'a, South-wind. Refers to the wind, the life symbol of the gens. Son of Ḳa'-wa-xo-dse and Wa-ṭo$^{n\prime}$-i-ça-e.

A'-ḳ'a-hiu-e, Wind-is-from-the-south. Son of Ḳa'-wa-çi and Gia'-ço$^n$-ba.

Ga-hi'-gtho$^n$-i$^n$-ge. (Meaning obscure.) Son of Ho$^{n\prime}$-ga.

Hi$^n$-sha'-a-xthi, Slayer-of-a-Caddo. Also Zhi$^n$-ga'-ga-hi-ge, Young-chief. This name may be used by permission to honor a child. Husband of Xu-tha'-da-wi$^n$ of the Ṭsi'-zhu Wa-no$^n$.

Ho$^{n\prime}$-ga, The-sacred-one. A special name for the dark-plumaged immature golden eagle, the life symbol of this gens. Ho$^{n\prime}$-ga is also the name of the subdivision of the tribe representing the dry land of the earth. Son of Ḳa'-wa-çi.

Ho$^{n\prime}$-ga. Son of Ho$^{n\prime}$-ga.

Ho$^{n\prime}$-ga. (Alfred McKinley.)

I'-bi-ço$^n$-dse. (Meaning obscure.)

Ḳa'-wa-çi, Yellow-horse. (Not Ni'-ḳi-e.) Husband of Gia'-ço$^n$-ba of the Ṗo$^{n\prime}$-ḳa Wa-shta-ge gens.

Ḳa'-wa-xo-dse, Roan-horse. (Not Ni'-ḳi-e.) Also Çe'-çe-mo$^n$-i$^n$, Trots-as-he-travels. Refers to the restless movements of the elk. The I'-ba-ṭse is a subgens of the Elk and has the right to take names relating to that animal. Husband of Wa-ṭo$^n$-i'-ça-e of the Ṗc$^{n\prime}$-ḳa Wa-shta-ge gens.

Sho$^{n\prime}$-ge-ṭsi-e, Dog-passing-by.

Ṭa'-dse-hiu-e, The-coming-wind. Son of Ḳa'-wa-xo-dse and Wa-ṭoⁿ-i'-ça-e.

Tha-çiu'-e, Whistle. Refers to the whistle which this gens was permitted to consecrate and use as a wa-xo'-be in honor of a member who had won an important victory in battle. The name is not classed as Ni'-ḳi-e, that is, it was not one that was accepted as a gentile name by common consent of the Noⁿ'-hoⁿ-zhiⁿ-ga. The whistle wa-xo'-be is now in the United States National Museum (No. 276133). Husband of Mi'-ṭse-xi of the Hoⁿ' I-ni-ḳa-shi-ga gens.

Tha-çiu'-e. Son of Ḳa'-wa-xo-dse and Wa-ṭoⁿ'-i-ça-e of the Poⁿ'-ḳa Wa-shta-ge gens.

Xu-tha'-gthe-zhe, Speckled-eagle. The speckled eagle is an immature golden eagle whose tail feathers are speckled. The bird is one of the life symbols of this gens. Son of Hiⁿ-sha'-a-xthi and Xu-tha-'da-wiⁿ.

Xu-tha'-gthe-zhe. Son of Wa-ça'-be-wiⁿ of the Hoⁿ' I-ni-ḳa-shi-ga gens.

Xu-tha'-k'iⁿ, Eagle-carrier. (Don Dickinson.)

FEMALE

A'-ḳ'a-mi-ṭse-xi, South-wind-Mi-na-the-favored. Daughter of Ḳa'-wa-xo-dse and Wa-ṭoⁿ-i'-ça-e.

A'-ḳ'a-wiⁿ, South-wind-woman. (In the Hoⁿ'-ga gens of the Omaha tribe.) Daughter of Hiⁿ-sha'-a-xthi and Xu-tha'-da-wiⁿ.

A'-ḳ'a-wiⁿ. Wife of Ṭa-he'-ga-xe of the Ṭa' I-ni-ḳa-shi-ga gens.

Hoⁿ'-ga-mi-ṭse-xi, Hoⁿ'-ga-Mi-na-the-favored. Daughter of Ḳa'-wa-çi and Gia'-çoⁿ-ba.

Hoⁿ'-ga-mi-ṭse-xi. Daughter of Ḳa'-wa-çi and Gia'-çoⁿ-ba.

Hoⁿ'-ga-mi-ṭse-xi. Daughter of Hiⁿ-sha'-a-xthi and Xu-tha'-da-wiⁿ.

Hoⁿ'-ga-mi-ṭse-xi. (Ethel Brant.)

Hoⁿ'-ga-mi-ṭse-xi. Wife of Wa-noⁿ'-she-zhiⁿ-ga of the Hoⁿ'-ga gens.

Hoⁿ'-ga-wiⁿ, Eagle-woman.

Hoⁿ'-ga-wiⁿ. Wife of Xu-tha'-zhu-dse of the Ṭsi'-zhu Wa-shta-ge gens.

Iⁿ'-be-zhoⁿ-ḳa, Forked-tail-kite.

Iⁿ'-be-zhoⁿ-ḳa. Wife of Ni'-wa-the of the Ṭsi'-zhu Wa-shta-ge gens.

Iⁿ'-be-zhoⁿ-ḳa-wiⁿ, Forked-tail-kite-woman. Daughter of Hoⁿ'-ga.

Iⁿ'-be-zhoⁿ-ḳa-wiⁿ. Wife of Ga-hi'-ge-ṭoⁿ of the Ṭsi'-zhu Wa-shta-ge gens.

Iⁿ'-be-zhoⁿ-ḳa-wiⁿ. (Sylvia Wood.)

Wa-hiu'-çoⁿ-iⁿ, White-bones-woman. Refers, probably, to the story that at the beginning this gens controlled the winds, and by their use destroyed all animals, leaving their bones to whiten on the ground around the village.

Wa-hiu'-çoⁿ-iⁿ. Daughter of Ḳa'-wa-xo-dse and Wa-ṭoⁿ-i'-ça-e.

Wa-hiu-çoⁿ-iⁿ. Wife of Ṭa-he-ga-xe of the Ṭa' I-ni-ḳa-shi-ga gens.

## ṬSI'-ZHU DIVISION

### Ṭsi'-zhu Wa-noN Gens

#### MALE

ÇoN-dse-u'-gthiN, Dweller-in-upland-forest. (Not Ni'-ḳi-e.) Also We'-thiN-ga-xe, Maker-of-straps. Refers to the office of this gens of ceremonially making the captive straps for the warriors of a war party. Husband of MoN-zhoN-dsi-i-ṭa of the Ṭsi'-zhu Wa-shta-ge gens.

Ga-hi'-ga-zhi, Not-a-chief. A chief could not be chosen from this gens because its office has to do with war. Son of Mi'-ṭse-xi-hoN-ga, wife of O-ḳi'-ça.

Ho'-ça-zhiN-e, Young-strong-voice. (Married to a white woman.)

HoN'-ga-ha-bi, He-who-is-called-HoN'-ga.

HoN'-ga-ha-bi. Also Wa-xthi', Stingy.

HoN'-ga-ha-bi. Son of Pa'-zhi-hi of the HoN'-ga gens.

I'N'-do-ḳa-wa-da-iN-ga, Playful-wet-stone.

MoN'-hiN-çpe-we-ṭsiN, Battle-ax.

MoN-iN'-ḳa-u-ga-hni. (Meaning obscure.) Son of O'-tha-ha-moN-iN and MoN'-çi-ṭse-xi.

Ni'-ḳa-i-çi-wa-the, Hated-man. Refers to the aggressive character of this gens. Husband of Ḳi'-o of the Tho'-xe gens.

NoN-ba'-k'iu-e. (Meaning obscure.) Son of O'-tha-ha-moN-iN and MoN-çi-ṭse-xi.

NoN-xthoN'-zhe, Tramples-the-grass. Refers to the discovery of the tracks of buffalo by an official runner. Son of I'N'-do-ḳa-wa-da-iN-ga.

O-ça'-ḳi-e. (Meaning obscure.)

O'-tha-ha-moN-iN, The-follower. Husband of MoN'-çi-ṭse-xi of the Ṭsi'-zhu Wa-shta-ge gens.

Pa'-thiN-wa-we-xta, Annoyer-of-the-enemy. (War name.) Husband of Gthe-doN-mi-ṭse-xi of the Ni-ḳa-wa-ḳoN-da-gi gens.

Sha'-ge-wa-biN, Bloody-hands. Refers to the butchering of the buffalo, parts of which were dedicated to ceremonial use in the war rites. (See pp. 264 to 582, 36th Ann. Rept. Bur. Amer. Ethn.) Son of Gia'- çoN-ba of the PoN'-ḳa Wa-shta-ge gens.

Ṭse-wa'-hiu, Buffalo-bones. Husband of ÇoN-çi'-gthe of the Ṭa' I-ni-ḳa-shi-ga gens.

Wa-doN. (Meaning obscure.)

Wa'-i-noN-zhiN, Stands-over-them. (In the IN-gthe'-zhi-de gens of the Omaha tribe.)

Wa-stse'-e-doN, Good-doctor. Son of O'-tha-ha-moN-iN and MoN'-çi-ṭse-xi.

Wa'-ṭse-goN-tha. (Meaning obscure.) Wa-xthi'-zhi says that the real name of this man is Mi'-ga-xe, Sun-maker.

Wa-zha'-a-ḳi-pa, Met-the-Wa-zha'-zhe.  Refers to the first meeting
of the Ṭsi'-zhu division with the Wa-zha'-zhe.

We'-ṭsi$^n$, War-club.  Refers to the ceremonial war-club made by
this gens.  (See 36th Ann. Rept. Bur. Amer. Ethn., pp. 442–445.)
Son of I$^{n'}$-do-ḳa-wa-da-i$^n$-ga.

Xu-tha'-wa-ḳo$^n$-da, Mysterious-eagle.  Son of Gia'-ço$^n$-ba of the
Po$^{n'}$-ḳa Wa-shta-ge gens.

Xu-tha'-wa-ḳo$^n$-da.  Son of Ṭse-wa'-hiu and Ço$^n$-çi'-gthe.

Xu-tha'-wa-ḳo$^n$-da.  Husband of Mo$^{n'}$-çi-ṭse-xi of the Wa-ça'-be
gens.

Xu-tha'-wa-ḳo$^n$-da.  Son of O'-tha-ha-mo$^n$-i$^n$ and Mo$^{n'}$-çi-ṭse-xi.

Xu-tha'-wa-ḳo$^n$-da.  Son of Xu-tha'-wa-ṭo$^n$-i$^n$ and Hi$^{n'}$-i-ḳi-a-bi

Xu-tha'-wa-ṭo$^n$-i$^n$, Eagle-plainly-seen.

Zhi$^n$-ga'-wa-da-i$^n$-ga, Little-playful-one.

FEMALE

Do-ra Strike-ax.  Daughter of Zhi$^n$-ga'-wa-da-i$^n$-ga.

Lucy Ho$^{n'}$-ga-ha-bi.  Daughter of Ho$^{n'}$-ga-ha-bi or Wa-xthi'.

Mi'-gthe-do$^n$-wi$^n$, Sun-hawk-woman.  (In the Tha'-ṭa-da gens of
the Omaha tribe.)

Mi'-gthe-do$^n$-wi$^n$.  Daughter of Ṭse-wa'-hiu and Ço$^n$-çi'-gthe.

Mi'-gthe-do$^n$-wi$^n$.  Daughter of Zhi$^n$-ga'-wa-da-i$^n$-ga.

Mi'-gthe-do$^n$-wi$^n$.  Daughter of O'-tha-ha-mo$^n$-i$^n$ and Mo$^{n'}$-çi-ṭse-xi.

Mi'-ho$^n$-ga, Sacred-sun.  (Also used by the Omaha tribe.)  Daughter
of Gia-ço$^n$-ba of the Po$^{n'}$-ḳa Wa-shta-ge gens.

Mi'-ho$^n$-ga.  Wife of Do'-ba-mo$^n$-i$^n$ of the Tho'-xe gens.

Grace Miller.  Daughter of Ho'-ça-zhi$^n$-e.

Mo$^{n'}$-btho$^n$-ba, Corn-hill.

Mo$^{n'}$-btho$^n$-ba.  Wife of Mi-ḳa'-ḳ'e-zhi$^n$-ga of the Mi-ḳ'i$^{n'}$ gens.

Mo$^{n'}$-btho$^n$-ba.  Daughter of Xu-tha'-wa-ṭo$^n$-i$^n$ and Hi$^{n'}$-i-ḳi-a-bi.

Wa-ḳ'o'-ga-hi-ge, Woman-chief.  (Not Ni'-ḳi-e.)  Daughter of Zhi$^n$-
ga'-wa-da-i$^n$-ga.

Wa'-ḳo$^n$-ça-mo$^n$-i$^n$.  (Meaning obscure.)  Daughter of Ço$^n$-dse-u'-
gthi$^n$ and Mo$^n$-zho$^{n'}$-dsi-i-ṭa.

Wa-ḳo$^{n'}$-da-hi-tho$^n$-be, God-who-appears.  Refers to the rising sun.

Wa-ḳo$^{n'}$-da-hi-tho$^n$-be.  Wife of Mo$^{n'}$-xe-a-gthe of the Ho$^{n'}$-ga
U-ṭa-no$^n$-dsi gens.

Wa-ḳo$^{n'}$-da-hi-tho$^n$-be.  Wife of Wa-thi'-gtho$^n$-thi$^n$-ge of the Ṭsi'-
zhu Wa-shta-ge gens.

Wa-ḳo$^{n'}$-da-hi-tho$^n$-be.  Wife of Mi-hi-the of the Mi-ḳ'i$^{n'}$ gens.

Wa-xthe'-tho$^n$-ba, Two-standards.  Wife of Mi-ḳ'i$^{n'}$-wa-da-i$^n$-ga of
the Mi-ḳ'i$^n$ gens.

Wa-xthe'-tho$^n$-ba.  Wife of Ni'-ḳa-wa-zhi$^n$-ṭo$^n$-ga of the Po$^{n'}$-ḳa
Wa-shta-ge gens.

Wa-xthe'-tho$^n$-ba.  Wife of Ṭsi'-zhu-a-ḳi-pa of the Po$^{n'}$-ḳa Wa-
shta-ge gens.

Wa-xthe$'$-tho$^n$-ba.   Wife of Po$^{n\prime}$-ḳa-wa-da-i$^n$-ga of the Po$^{n\prime}$-ḳa Wa-shta-ge gens.

Wa-xthe$'$-tho$^n$-ba.   Daughter of Ṭse-wa$'$-hiu and Ço$^n$-çi$'$-gthe.

Wa-xthe$'$-tho$^n$-ba.   (Annie Kinney.)

Wa-xthe$'$-tho$^n$-ba.   Daughter of Ho$^{n\prime}$-ga-ga-bi or Wa-xthi$'$.

Wa-xthe-tho$^n$-ba.   Daughter of O$'$-tha-ha-mo$^n$-i$^n$ and Mo$^{n\prime}$-çi-ṭse-xi.

Wa-xthe$'$-xtho-xtho-wi$^n$, Standard-woman.

Wa-zha$'$-mi-ṭse-xi, Wa-zha$'$-zhe-Mi-na-the-favorite.   Daughter of Xu-tha$'$-wa-ṭo$^n$-i$^n$.

Wa-zha$'$-zhe-wi$^n$, Wa-zha-zhe-woman.   Daughter of Ni$'$-ḳa-i-çi-wa-the and Ḳi$'$-o.

Xu-tha$'$-da-wi$^n$, Good-eagle-woman.   Wife of Wa-çe$'$-ṭo$^n$-zhi$^n$-ga of the Ṭsi$'$-zhu Wa-shta-ge gens.

Xu-tha$'$-da-wi$^n$.   Wife of Hi$^n$-sha$'$-a-xthi or Zhi$^n$-ga$'$-ga-hi-ge of the I$'$-ba-ṭse gens.

Xu-tha$'$-da-wi$^n$.   Daughter of Pa$'$-zhi-hi of the Ho$^n$-ga gens.

### ÇI$^{N\prime}$-DSE-A-GTHE (WEARERS-OF-LOCKS)

#### MALE

Mo$^n$-i$^{n\prime}$-ḳa-u-ga-hni.   (Meaning obscure.)   Son of U-ho$^{n\prime}$-ge-u-zho$^n$ and Gia$'$-ço$^n$-ba.

Ni-o$^{n\prime}$-ba-giu-e.   (Meaning obscure.)   Son of U-ho$^{n\prime}$-ge-u-zho$^n$ and Gia$'$-ço$^n$-ba.

U-ho$^{n\prime}$-ge-u-zho$^n$, Lies-at-the-end.   Also Sho$^{n\prime}$-ge-thi-hi, Dog-scarer. Refers to the dog, one of the life symbols of the gens.

Wa-hiu$'$-tha-zhu, Bone-gnawer.   Refers to the habit of the dog. Son of U-ho$^{n\prime}$-ge-u-zho$^n$ and Gia$'$-ço$^n$-ba.

Wa-ḳo$^{n\prime}$-da-no$^n$-pa-i$^n$, The-god-who-is-feared.   Refers to the con-stellation, Canis Major, the life symbol of this gens.

#### FEMALE

Wa-xthe$'$-tho$^n$-ba, Two-standards.

Xu-tha$'$-da-wi$^n$, Good-eagle-woman.   Daughter of U-ho$^{n\prime}$-ge-u-zho$^n$ and Gia$'$-ço$^n$-ba.

Xu-tha$'$-da-wi$^n$.   Wife of Mo$^n$-i$^{n\prime}$-ḳa-mo$^n$-i$^n$ of the Po$^{n\prime}$-ḳa Wa-shta-ge gens.

### ṬSI$'$-ZHU WA-SHTA-GE

Special kinship terms and names of the first three sons and the first three daughters in a family of the Ṭsi$'$-zhu Wa-shta-ge gens, as given by Btho$'$-ga-hi-ge.

#### SONS

1. I$^n$-gtho$^{n\prime}$. Wa-ṭsi$'$-da.   (Meaning obscure.)
2. Ksho$^{n\prime}$-ga. Ni$'$-wa-the, Life-giver.   Refers to the office of the gens to give the word that a captive shall live and not be killed.
3. Ḳa$'$-zhi$^n$-ga. Mo$^{n\prime}$-ça-no$^n$-pa-i.   (Meaning obscure.)

## DAUGHTERS

1. Mi'-na.   Xi-tha'-da-wi$^n$, Good-eagle.
2. Wi'-he.   Mo$^{n'}$-çi-țse-xi, Sacred-arrowshaft.
3. A-çi$^{n'}$-ga.   Mo$^n$-zho$^{n'}$-dsi-i-ța.   (Meaning obscure.)

### OTHER NAMES

#### MALE

A'-hiu-zhi$^n$-ga, Little-wings.   Husband of E-no$^{n'}$-do$^n$-a-bi of the Ho$^{n'}$ I-ni-ķa-shi-ga gens.

A'-hiu-zhi$^n$-ga.   Son of O-tho'-xa-wa-the and Xu-tha'-da-wi$^n$.

Btho'-ga-hi-ge, Chief-of-all.   Refers to the sacred character of the position of the hereditary chief chosen from this gens to represent the Țsi'-zhu tribal division.   Husband of Wa'-dsi-u-hi-zhi of the Ni'-ķa-wa-ķo$^n$-da-gi gens.

Ga-hi'-ge-țo$^n$, Standing-chief.   Refers to the position of the hereditary chief of the Țsi'-zhu tribal division.

Ga-hi'-ge-țo$^n$.   Son of Mi-da'-i$^n$-ga and Do$^{n'}$-a-bi.

Ga-hi'-ge-țo$^n$.   Son of Pi-çi' and Ço$^n$-çi'-gthe.

Ga-hi'-ge-țo$^n$-ga, Big-chief.   Refers to the high position of the hereditary chief of the Țsi'-zhu tribal division.   Husband of I$^{n'}$-be-zho$^n$-ķa-wi$^n$ of the I'-ba-țse gens.

Gthe-do$^{n'}$-mo$^n$-çe, Iron-hawk.   Husband of Mi'-țse-xi of the Ho$^{n'}$ I-ni-ķa-shi-ga gens.

Gthe-do$^{n'}$-zhi$^n$-ga, Little-hawk.   Son of Gthe-do$^{n'}$-wi$^n$ of the Ni'-ķa-wa-ķo$^n$-da-gi gens.

Gthe-mo$^{n'}$-zhi$^n$-ga.   (Meaning obscure.)   Young Claremore.   Husband of Wa-xthe'-tho$^n$-ba of the Mi-ķ'i$^{n'}$ gens.

Ha-xi$^n$-u'-mi-zhe.   (Not a gentile name.)   Husband of Ho$^n$-be'-do-ķa of the Po$^{n'}$-ka Wa-shta-ge gens.

Ho$^{n'}$-ba-tha-gthi$^n$, Peaceful-day.   Refers to the office of the gens as Peacemaker.   (Used in the I$^n$-shta'-ço$^n$-da gens of the Omaha tribe as a woman's name.)   Son of Mo$^{n'}$-çe-no$^n$-p'i$^n$.

Ho-wa'-ça-e.   (Meaning obscure.)   Husband of Ni'-ķa-a-ça of the Tho'-xe gens.

Ķa'-xe-tho$^n$-ba, Two-crows.   The significance of this name is lost.   (In the Ho$^{n'}$-ga gens of the Omaha tribe refers to the feathers of two crows used in making the staff of authority in the buffalo hunt.)

Mi-da'-i$^n$-ga, Playful-sun.   Refers to the sun as one of the symbols of this gens.   Husband of Mo$^{n'}$-çi-țse-xi of the Mi-ķ'i$^n$ gens.

Mi-da'-i$^n$-ga.   Husband of Do$^{n'}$-a-bi of the Tho'-xe gens.

Mo$^{n'}$-ça-no$^n$-pa-i$^n$, Dreaded-arrow-shaft.   Son of Pa-ho$^n$-gthe-ga-xthi.

Mo$^{n'}$-çe-no$^n$-p'i$^n$, Iron-necklace.

Mo$^{n\prime}$-ce-no$^n$-p'i$^n$, Also Ṭsi'-zhu-wa-da-i$^n$-ga, Playful Ṭsi-zhu. Husband of Ho$^{n\prime}$-ga-wi$^n$ of the O'-po$^n$ gens.

Mo$^{n\prime}$-ha-u-gthi$^n$, Sits-under-a-bank. Husband of Mi$^n$-chu'-xa-ge of the Ni'-ḳa-wa-ḳo$^n$-da-gi gens.

Mo$^n$-zho$^n$-a'-ḳi-da, Watches-over-the-land. Husband of Ho$^n$-be'-do-ḳa of the Ṗo$^{n\prime}$-ḳa-wa-shta-ge gens.

Mo$^n$-sho$^n$-a'-shi$^n$-e, Travels-over-the-land. Son of Ga-hi'-ge-to$^n$ and I$^{n\prime}$-be zho$^n$-ḳa-wi$^n$.

Mo$^n$-to'-e. The-earth.

Ni-'wa-the, Giver-of-life. Refers to the authority of this gens to permit captives to live.

Ni'-wa-the. Son of Mo$^n$-zho$^n$-a'-ḳi-da and Ho$^n$-be'-do-ḳa.

Ni'-wa-the. Son of Gthe-mo$^{n\prime}$-zhin-ga and Wa-xthe'-tho$^n$-ba.

Ni'-wa-the. Husband of I$^{n\prime}$-be-zho$^n$-ka of the I'-ba-ṭse gens.

Ni'-wa-the. Son of O-tho'-xa-wa-the and Xu-tha'-da-wi$^n$.

No$^n$-be'-çi, Yellow-hands. Refers to the yellow feet of the eagle, one of the life symbols of this gens. Son of Btho-ga-hi-ge.

No$^n$-be'-çi. Son of Mo$^n$-zho$^n$-a'-ḳi-da and Ho$^n$-be'-do-ḳa.

No$^n$-be'-ci. Son of Ha-xi$^n$-u'-mi-zhe and Ho$^n$-be'-do-ḳa.

O-ḳi'-ça. (Meaning obscure.) Husband of Mi'-tse-xi-ho$^n$-ga of the Ho$^{n\prime}$-ga U-ṭa-no$^n$-dsi gens.

O-pa'-sho-e. (Meaning obscure.) Husband of Wa-ṭo$^n$-i'-ça-e of the Ṗo$^{n\prime}$-ḳa Wa-shta-ge gens.

O-tho'-xa-wa-the. (Meaning obscure.) Husband of Xu-tha'-da-wi$^n$ of the Mi-ḳ'i$^n$ gens.

Ṗa'-ba-wa-xo$^n$, Head-cutter. Refers to the custom of cutting off the heads of the enemy. Son of O-pa'-sho-e and Wa-ṭo$^n$i'-ça-e.

Ṗa-'ba-wa-xo$^n$. Son of Ni-ḳa'-shi-e of the Ṭa' I-ni-ḳa-shi-ga gens.

Ṗa'-ba-wa-xo$^n$. Son of Mo$^{n\prime}$-ce-no$^n$-p'i$^n$.

Ṗa'-ba-wa-xo$^n$. Son of Ṗi-çi' and Ço$^n$-çi'-gthe.

Ṗa'-ba-wa-xo$^n$. Son of Mo$^n$-zho$^n$-a'-ḳi-da and Ho$^n$-be'-do-ḳa.

Ṗa'-ha-wa-xo$^n$. Son of Wa-çe'-ṭo$^n$-zhi$^n$-ga. (Louis Pryor.)

Ṗa'-ba-wa-xo$^n$. Son of Gthe-do$^{n\prime}$-mo$^n$-çe and Mi'-ṭse-xi.

Ṗa-hiu'-çka, White-hair. (In the Ho$^{n\prime}$-ga gens of the Omaha tribe and refers to the sacred white buffalo.) Husband of Mi'-do$^n$-a bi of the Mi-ḳ'i$^{n\prime}$ gens.

Ṗi'-çi, Acorn-of-the-red-oak. Refers to the mythical story of the eagle causing the acorns to drop down in showers as he alighted on a red oak when he came down from the sky. Husband of Ço$^n$-çi'-gthe of the Ṗo$^{n\prime}$-ḳa Wa-shta-ge gens.

Sho$^{n\prime}$-ge-mo$^n$-i$^n$, Walking-dog. (War name.) This man belonged to the Ba'-po subgens of the Ṭsi'-zhu Wa-shta-ge gens. This subgens had the office of making the stem for the peace pipe. The stem was made from the elder tree, which was called ba-po, popper, because boys made popguns out of this tree. Ba'-po-zhi$^n$-ga, Little-ba-po, is one of the child names of this gens. Husband of Wa-ṭse'-wi$^n$ of the Mi-ḳ'i$^{n\prime}$ gens.

Tho$^n$-ba'-zhi. (Meaning obscure.) Son of Tho$^{n'}$-dse-wa-hi.

Tho$^{n'}$-dse-wa-hi, Bone-heart.

Ṭo$^{n'}$-wo$^n$-ga-xe, Village-maker. (In Mo$^n$-i$^n$-ḳa-ga-xe gens of the Omaha tribe.) Husband of Ço$^n$-çi'-gthe of the Ṭa' I-ni-ḳa-shi-ga gens.

Ṭo$^n$-wo$^{n'}$-i-hi, Arrives-at-the-village. Son of Ni'-wa-the.

Ṭo$^n$-wo$^{n'}$-i-hi. Husband of Ṭse-ço$^{n'}$-wi$^n$ of the Tho'-xe gens.

Ṭo'-thi-xtho-dse, Potato-peeler. Husband of Pa'-xpi-ço$^n$-dse of the Ṭa' I-ni-ḳa-shi-ga gens.

Ṭs'e-mo$^{n'}$-i$^n$, Walks-in-death. Son of Wa-thi'-gtho$^n$-thi$^n$-ge.

Ṭsi'-zhu-ga-hi-ge, Ṭsi-zhu-chief. Son of Wa-çe'-ṭo$^n$-zhi$^n$-ga and Xu-tha-da-wi$^n$.

Ṭsi'-zhu$^n$-ho$^n$-ga, Sacred-Ṭsi-zhu. Refers to the sacred character of the office of the gens. Husband of Gthe-do$^{n'}$-ço$^n$-wi$^n$ of the Ni'-ḳa-wa-ḳo$^n$-da-gi gens.

Ṭsi'-zhu-zhi$^n$-ga, Young-Ṭsi-zhu. Husband of Ṭse'-mi-ṭse-xi of the Tho'-xe gens.

Ṭsi'-zhu-zhi$^n$-ga. Husband of Xu-tha'-da-wi$^n$ of the Ho$^{n'}$-ga gens.

Wa-çe'-ṭo$^n$-zhi-$^n$ga. (Meaning obscure.) Husband of Xu-tha'-da-wi$^n$ of the Ṭsi'-zhu Wa-no$^n$ gens.

Wa-çe'-ṭo$^n$-zhi-$^n$ga. (Louis Pryor.)

Wa-ḳo$^{n'}$-da-i-e, One-who-saw-wa-ḳo$^n$-da. Son of Wa-thi'-gtho$^n$-thi$^n$-ge.

Wa-ḳo$^{n'}$-da-i-e. Son of Pi-çi' and Ço$^n$-çi'-gthe.

Wa-ḳo$^{n'}$-da-i-e. Son of Mo$^n$-zho-a'-ḳi-da and Ho$^n$-be'-do-ḳa.

Wa-ḳo$^{n'}$-da-i-e. Son of Mi-da'-i$^n$-ga and Do$^{n'}$-a-bi.

Wa-ḳo$^{n'}$-da-i-e. Son of O-tho'-xa-wa-the and Xu-tha'-da-wi$^n$.

Wa-ni'-e-to$^n$, Giver-of-life. Refers to the office of this gens as a peace-maker. Son of Mi-da-'i$^n$-ga and Mo$^{n'}$-çi-ṭse-xi.

Wa-ni'-e-ṭo$^n$. Son of Gthe-do$^{n'}$-wi$^n$ of the Ni'-ḳa-wa-ḳo$^n$-da-gi gens.

Wa-ni'-e-ṭo$^n$. Son of Ha-xi$^n$-u'-mi-zhe and Ho$^n$-be'-do-ḳa.

Wa-ni'-e-ṭo$^n$. Husband of Wa'-ḳo$^n$-ça-mo$^n$-i$^n$ of the Po$^{n'}$-ḳa Wa-shta-ge gens.

Wa-stse'-e-do$^n$, Good-doctor. Refers to the practice of the people of bringing their sick to some member of this gens to be fed ceremonially so that they may get well. Son of Pa-ho$^{n'}$-gthe-ga-xthi and Xu-tha'-da-wi$^n$.

Wa-stse'-e-do$^n$. Son of A-hiu'-zhi$^n$-e and E-no$^{n'}$-do$^n$-a-bi.

Wa-stse'-e-do$^n$. Son of Btho'-ga-hi-ge.

Wa-stse'-e-do$^n$. Husband of Wa-xthe'-tho$^n$-ba of the Ṭsi'-zhu Wa-no$^n$ gens.

Wa-stse'-e-do$^n$. Son of Ṭsi'-zhu-ho$^n$-ga.

Wa-stse'-e-do$^n$. Son of Mo$^n$-zho$^n$-a'-ḳi-da and Ho$^n$-be'-do-ḳa.

Wa-stse'-e-do$^n$. Son of No$^n$-be'-çi and Wa-zha'-zhe-mi-ṭse-xi.

Wa-stse'-e-do$^n$. Son of Ha-xi$^n$-u'-mi-zhe and Ho$^n$-be'-do-ka.

Wa-stse'-e-do$^n$. Son of To'-thi-xtho-dse‾and Pa'-xpi-co$^n$-dse.

Wa-stse'-e-do$^n$. Son of Mo$^{n'}$-çe-no$^n$-p'i$^n$ and Ho$^{n'}$-ga-wi$^n$.

Wa-thi'-gtho$^n$-thi$^n$-ge, No-mind. (Not Ni-ki-e.) (In Mo$^{n'}$-thi$^n$-ka-ga-xe gens of the Omaha tribe.) Also Ha'-ba-zhu-dse, Red-corn, a name which refers to a life symbol of the gens. Husband of Wa-ko$^{n'}$-da-hi-tho$^n$-be of the Tsi'-zhu Wa-no$^n$ gens.

Wa'-thu-xa-ge, Clutches-them-till-they-cry. Refers to the attack of the eagle on its prey. Husband of Xu-tha'-mi-tse-xi of the Ho$^{n'}$-ga gens.

Wa-zhi$^{n'}$-ga-ça-be, Black-bird. (In the Mo$^n$-i$^{n'}$-ka-ga-xe gens of the Omaha tribe.) Husband of Do$^{n'}$-a-bi of the Tho'-xe gens.

Wa-zhi$^{n'}$-ga-hi$^n$, Bird-feathers. Refers to the eagle, one of the life symbols of the gens. Son of Sho$^{n'}$-ge-mo$^n$-i$^n$.

Xu-tha'-ts'a-ge, Aged-eagle. Refers to the eagle as a symbol of long life. Son of Tsi-zhu-ho$^n$-ga and Gthe-do$^{n'}$-ço$^n$-wi$^n$.

Xu-tha'-ts'a-ge. Son of Gthe-do$^{n'}$-wi$^n$ of the Ni'-ka-wa-ko$^n$-da-gi gens.

Xu-tha'-zhu-dse, Red eagle. Refers to the life symbol of the gens.

Xu-tha'-zhu-dse. Son of Pi-çi' and Çon-çi'-gthe.

Xu-tha'-zhu-dse. Husband of Ho$^{n'}$-ga-wi$^n$ of the I'-ba-tse gens.

FEMALE

Mary Cox. Daughter of A-hiu'-zhi$^n$-e and E-no$^{n'}$-do$^n$-a-bi.

E-no$^{n'}$-do$^n$-a-bi, One-only-seen-by-all. Refers to the sun, one of the life symbols of the gens. Daughter of Tsi'-zhu-ho$^n$-ga and Gthe-do$^{n'}$-ço$^n$-wi$^n$.

E-no$^{n'}$-do$^n$-a-bi. Daughter of No$^n$-be-'çi and Wa-zha'-zhe-mi-tse-xi.

E-no$^{n'}$-do$^n$-a-bi. Daughter of Gthe-do$^{n'}$-mo$^n$-çe and Mi'-tse-xi.

E-no$^{n'}$-do$^n$-a-bi. Daughter of O-tho'-xa-wa-the and Xu-tha'-da-wi$^n$.

Gthe-do$^{n'}$-wi$^n$, Hawk-woman. (Ni'-ka-wa-ko$^n$-da-gi name.) Daughter of Pa'-hiu-çka and Mi'-do$^n$-a-bi. (In Mo$^{n'}$-thi$^n$-ka-ga-xe gens of the Omaha tribe.)

Gthe-do$^{n'}$-wi$^n$. Daughter of Ni'-ka-zhu-e of the Ta' I-ni-ka-shi-ga gens.

Hi'-ga-mo$^n$-ge, Eagle-down. Refers to the use of the eagle down in the tribal ceremonies.

Hi'-ga-mo$^n$-ge. Daughter of Mi-da'-i$^n$-ga and Do$^{n'}$-a-bi.

Hi'-ga-mo$^n$-ge. Daughter of O-tho'-xa-wa-the and Xu-tha'-da-wi$^n$.

Hi$^{n'}$-i-ki-a-bi, Eagle-down. Refers to the eagle, a symbol of long life. Wife of Gthi'-kshe of the Mi-k'i$^n$ gens.

Hi$^{n'}$-i-ki-a-bi. Daughter of Mi-da'-i$^n$-ga and Mo$^{n'}$çi-tse-xi.

Hi$^{n'}$-i-ḳi-a-bi.   Granddaughter of Wa-ḳo$^{n'}$-da-hi-o$^{n}$-be, wife of Mo$^{n}$-xe-a-gthe.

Hi$^{n'}$-i-ḳi-a-bi.   Daughter of Ṭsi'-zhu-ho$^{n}$-ga and Gthe-do$^{n'}$-ço$^{n}$-wi$^{n}$.

Hi$^{n'}$-i-ḳi-a-bi.   Wife of Ṭse-do'-a-ṭo$^{n}$-ga of the Tho'-xe gens.

Hi$^{n'}$-i-ḳi-a-bi.   Daughter of Mi-da-i$^{n}$-ga and Do$^{n'}$-a-bi.

Hi$^{n'}$-i-ḳi-a-bi.   Wife of Wa-ḳo$^{n'}$-da-ṭsi-e of the Ṭa' I-ni-ḳa-shi-ga gens.

Hi$^{n'}$-i-ḳi-a-bi.   Wife of Xu-tha'-wa-ṭo$^{n}$-i$^{n}$ of the Ṭsi'-zhu Wa-no$^{n}$ gens.

I'-ga-mo$^{n}$-ge, same as Hi'-ga-mo$^{n}$-ge.   Daughter of Ṗa-hiu'-çka and Mi'-do$^{n}$-a-bi.

I'-ga-mo$^{n}$-ge.   Wife of John Lookout of the Ho$^{n'}$-ga gens.

I'-ni-a-bi, Protector.   Refers to the duty of this gens to protect those who flee to the house of refuge, in the keeping of this gens, for protection.   Daughter of Ṗa-ho$^{n'}$-ga-ga-xthi and Xu-tha'-da-wi$^{n}$.

I'-ni-a-bi, Annie Daniels.

I'-ni-a-bi.   Daughter of Btho'-ga-hi-ge.

I'-ni-a-bi.   Daughter of Mi-da'-i$^{n}$-ga and Do$^{n'}$-a-bi.

I'-ni-a-bi.   Wife of A'-hiu-çka of the Ho$^{n'}$-ga gens.

I'-ni-a-bi.   Daughter of Xu-tha'-zhu-dse and Ho$^{n'}$-ga-wi$^{n}$.

Mo$^{n'}$-çi-ṭse-xi, Sacred-arrow-shaft.   Wife of Mo$^{n}$-shi-ṭa-mo$^{n}$-i$^{n}$. (This is an I$^{n}$-gtho$^{n'}$-ga name.)

Mo$^{n'}$-çi-tse-xi.   Wife of Wa-sho'-she of the Ho$^{n'}$-ga gens.

Mo$^{n'}$-çi-ṭse-xi.   Wife of Gi'-thi-ḳo$^{n}$-bi of the Ṗo$^{n'}$-ḳa Wa-shta-ge gens.

Mo$^{n'}$-çi-ṭse-xi.   Daughter of Mo$^{n'}$-çe-no$^{n}$-p'i$^{n}$.

Mo$^{n'}$-çi-ṭse-xi.   Wife of Ho$^{n'}$-mo$^{n}$-ça of the O'-po$^{n}$ gens.

Mo$^{n'}$-çi-ṭse-xi.   Wife of O-tha'-ha-mo$^{n}$-i$^{n}$ of the Ṭsi'-zhu Wa-no$^{n}$ gens.

Mo$^{n'}$-çi-ṭse-xi.   Daughter of O-ḳi'-ça and Mi-ṭse'-xi-ho$^{n}$-ga.

Mo$^{n'}$-zho$^{n}$-dsi-i-ṭa.   Born-on-the-earth.   Daughter of Ṗi-çi' and Ço$^{n}$-çi-gthe.

Mo$^{n}$-zho$^{n'}$-dsi-i-ṭa.   Daughter of Wa-çe'-ṭo$^{n}$-zhi$^{n}$-ga and Xu-tha'-da-wi$^{n}$.

Mo$^{n}$-zho$^{n'}$-dsi-i-ṭa.   Wife of Wa-zhi$^{n'}$-wa-xa of the Ṗo$^{n'}$-ḳa Wa-shta-ge.

Mo$^{n}$-zho$^{n'}$-dsi-i-ṭa.   Wife of Ço$^{n}$-dse-u'-gthi$^{n}$ or We'-i$^{n}$-ga-xe.

Ṗa-hiu'-thi-sho$^{n}$.   (Meaning obscure.)   Daughter of Mo$^{n}$-zho$^{n}$-a'-ḳi-da.

Wa-ça'-a-ba.   (Meaning obscure.)   Daughter of Mo$^{n'}$-çe-no$^{n}$-p'i$^{n}$.

Wa-ça'-be-wi$^{n}$, Black-bear-woman.   Daughter of No$^{n}$-be'-çi and Wa-zha'-zhe-mi-ṭse-xi.

Wa-k'o'-ga-hi-ge, Woman-chief.   (Not a gentile name.)

Wa-k'o'-ga-hi-ge.   Wife of Xu-tha'-xtsi of the Ṗo$^{n'}$-ḳa Wa-shta-ge gens.

Daisy Ware.  Daughter of Ha-xi$^n$-u'-mi-zhe and Ho$^n$-be'-do-ḳa.

Wa-zha'-xe-i$^n$  (Meaning obscure.)  Wife of Ṭse-do'-ga-i$^n$-dse of the Ṭse-do'-ga-i$^n$-dse gens.

Wa-zha'-xe-i$^n$.  Wife of Mi'-she-ṭsi-the of the Ho$^{n'}$-ga gens.

Xu-tha'-da-wi$^n$, Good-eagle-woman.  Daughter of Ṗa-hiu'-çka and Mi'-do$^n$-a-bi.

Xu-tha'-da-wi$^n$.  Wife of Ço$^n$-dse'-ḳo$^n$-ha of the Ṭa' I-ni-ḳa-shi-ga gens.

Xu-tha'-da-wi$^n$.  Wife of Wa-xthi'-zhi of the I$^n$-gtho$^{n'}$-ga gens.

Xu-tha'-da-wi$^n$.  Wife of No$^{n'}$-ḳa-ṭo-ho of the Ni'-ḳa-wa-ḳo$^n$-da-gi gens.  (Daughter of Sho$^{n'}$-ge-mo$^n$-i$^n$.)

Xu-tha'-da-wi$^n$.  Wife of Ṗo$^{n'}$-ḳa-zhi$^n$-ga of the Ṗo$^{n'}$-ḳa Wa-shta-ge gens.

Xu-tha'-da-wi$^n$.  Daughter of Ho-wa'-ça-e and Ni'-ḳa-a-ça.

Xu-tha'-da-wi$^n$.  Daughter of Ṭo$^{n'}$-wo$^n$-ga-xe and Ço$^n$-çi'-gthe.

Xu-tha'-da-wi$^n$.  Daughter of No$^{n'}$-ḳo$^n$-çe-wi$^n$ of the Ho$^{n'}$-ga gens.

Xu-tha'-da-wi$^n$.  Daughter of Ni'-wa-the.

Xu-tha'-da-wi$^n$, Augustine Crow.

Xu-tha'-da-wi$^n$.  Wife of Ni'-ḳa-wa-da-i$^n$-ga of the Mi-ḳ'i$^{n'}$ gens.

Xu-tha'-da-wi$^n$.  Daughter of Mo$^n$-zho$^n$-a'-ḳi-da and Ho$^n$-be'-do-ḳa.

Xu-tha'-da-wi$^n$.  Daughter of Mi-da'-i$^n$-ga and Do$^{n'}$-a-bi.

Xu-tha'-da-wi$^n$.  Daughter of Ha-xi$^n$-u'mi-zhe and Ho$^n$-be'-do-ḳa.

Xu-tha'-da-wi$^n$.  Daughter of Wa-ni'-e-ṭo$^n$ and Wa'-ḳo$^n$-ça-mo$^n$-i$^n$.

Xu-tha'-da-wi$^n$.  Daughter of Ni'-wa-the and I$^{n'}$-be-zho$^n$-ḳa.

Xu-tha'-da-wi$^n$.  Wife of Ḳo'-zhi-çi-gthe of the Ṗo$^{n'}$-ḳa Wa-shta-ge gens.

Xu-tha'-da-wi$^n$.  Wife of Tho$^{n'}$-dse-ṭo$^n$-ga of the Ṗo$^{n'}$-ḳa Wa-shta-ge gens.

Xu-tha'-da-wi$^n$.  Daughter of Ṭo'-thi-xtho-dse and Ṗa'-xpi-ço$^n$-dse.

Xu-tha'-da-wi$^n$.  Wife of Ga-hi'-ge-no$^n$-zhi$^n$ of the Ṭa' I-ni-ḳa-shi-ga gens.

Xu-tha'-da-wi$^n$.  Wife of A'-ḳi-da-zhi$^n$-ga of the Ṭa' I-ni-ḳa-shi-ga gens.

## ṬSE-DO'-GA I$^N$-DSE GENS

### MALE

Ho$^{n'}$-ga-ha-bi, Taken-for-a-Ho$^{n'}$-ga. ˙ Refers to a mythical story in which it is said that the Wa-zha'-zhe mistook the Ṭsi'-zhu for the Ho$^{n'}$-ga on their first meeting.

Ho$^{n'}$-ga-ha-bi.  Son of Ṭse-do'-ga-i$^n$-dse and Wa-zha'-xe-i$^n$.

Ṭse-do'-ga-i$^n$-dse, Buffalo-bull-face.  Refers to the description given by the tribal messenger of the first buffalo he found.  Husband of Wa-zha'-xe-i$^n$ of the Ṭsi'-zhu Wa-shta-ge gens.

Ṭse-ṗa-u'-thi$^n$-ga, Holder-of-the-buffalo-head.  Refers to the butchering of the first buffalo found.

Wa'-ḳi-a-shke, Tied-together. Refers to the tying of two pieces of meat by the hunter for convenience of carrying.

Wa-ṭo-ge', Active. Husband of I'-ni-a-bi of the Ṭsi'-zhu Wa-shta-ge gens.

Wa-zha'-a-ḳi-pa, Met-the-Wa-zha'-zhe. Son of Wa-ṭo-ge' and I'-ni-a-bi.

Xu-tha'-wa-ḳo$^n$-da, Mysterious-eagle. Son of Ho$^n$-be'-do-ḳa of the Po$^{n'}$-ḳa Wa-shta-ge gens.

### FEMALE

Gia'-ço$^n$-wi$^n$. (Meaning obscure.) Daughter of Ho$^n$-be'-do-ḳa of the Po$^{n'}$-ḳa Wa-shta-ge gens.

Xu-tha'-da-wi$^n$, Good-eagle-woman. Daughter of Ho$^n$-be'-do-ḳa of the Po$^{n'}$-ḳa Wa-shta-ge gens.

Xu-tha'-da-wi$^n$. Daughter of Ṭse-do'-ga-i$^n$-dse and Wa-zha'-xe-i$^n$.

## Ṭse Tho$^{N'}$-ḳa Gens

### (Only one of this gens survives)

Ṭse'-mi-ṭse-xi, Sacred-buffalo-woman. (In the I$^n$-ḳe'-ça-be gens of the Omaha tribe.) Wife of Xu-tha'-pa of the Ho$^{n'}$-ga gens.

## Mi-ḳ'i$^{N'}$ Gens

Special kinship terms and personal names of the first three sons and the first three daughters in a family of the Mi-ḳ'i$^{n'}$, Sun-carrier gens, as given by E-hiu'-gthe, a member of the gens.

### SONS

1. I$^n$-gtho$^{n'}$. Ho$^{n'}$-ga-ha-bi, Mistaken-for-a-Ho$^{n'}$-ga.
2. Ksho$^{n'}$-ga. Gthe-do$^{n'}$-ga-xe, Hawk-maker.
3. Ḳa'-zhi$^n$-ga. Mi'-hi-the, Sun-down; also, Mi'-hi-the-zhi$^n$-ga, Little-sun-down.

### DAUGHTERS

1. Mi'-na. Xu-tha'-da-wi$^n$, Good-eagle-woman.
2. Wi'-he. Mi'-do$^n$-a-bi, Sun-that-is-looked-at.
3. Çi'-ge or A-çi$^n$-ga. Mi-ḳ'i$^{n'}$-wi$^n$, Mi-ḳ'i$^{n'}$-woman.

### OTHER NAMES

#### MALE

George. Son of Mi'-hi-the and Wa-ḳo$^{n'}$-da-tho$^n$-be.

Gthe-do$^n$-a-xe, Hawk-maker.

Gthe-do$^{n'}$-wa-ḳo$^n$, Mystery-hawk. Son of I'-ṭo$^n$-mo$^n$-i$^n$ and Wa-ṭo$^n$-i'-ça-e.

Gthi'-kshe, The returned. Refers to the new moon. Husband of Hi$^{n'}$-i-ḳi-a-bi of the Ṭsi'-zhu Wa-shta-ge gens.

Ho$^n$'-ga-ha-bi, Mistaken-for-a-Ho$^n$'-ga.

Ho$^n$'-ga-ha-bi. Son of Mi-ķa'-ķ'e-zhi$^n$-ga and Mo$^n$'-btho$^n$-ba.

Ho$^n$'-ga-ha-bi. Son of Mi'-hi-the and Wa-ķo$^n$'-da-hi-tho$^n$-be.

Ho$^n$'-ga-ha-bi. Son of Mi-tho-ţo$^n$'-mo$^n$-i$^n$-zhi$^n$-ga and Pa-hiu'-e-çe.

Ho$^n$'-i-ķa-zhi. (Meaning obscure.) Son of Mi-ķa'-ķ'e-zhi$^n$-ga and Mo$^n$'-btho$^n$-ba.

I'-gi-a-ba-zhi, Lost. Refers to the waning of the moon. Son of I'-ţo$^n$-mo$^n$-i$^n$ and Wa-ţo$^n$'-i-ça-e.

I'-ţo$^n$-mo$^n$-i$^n$. (Meaning obscure.) Husband of Wa-ţo$^n$'-i-ça-e of the Po$^n$'-ķa Wa-shta-ge gens.

John. Son of Mi'-hi-the and Wa-ķo$^n$'-da-hi-tho$^n$-be.

Mi'-hi-the, Sunset. Refers to the sun, one of the life symbols of this gens. Husband of Wa-ķo$^n$'-da-hi-tho$^n$-be of the Ţsi'-zhu Wa-no$^n$ gens.

Mi-ķa'-ķ'e-zhi$^n$-ga, Little-star. Husband of Mo$^n$'-btho$^n$-ba of the Ţsi'-zhu Wa-no$^n$ gens.

Mi-ķ'i$^n$'-wa-da-i$^n$-ga, Playful-Mi-ķ'i$^n$. Husband of Wa-xthe'-tho$^n$-ba of the Ţsi'-zhu Wa-no$^n$ gens.

Mi-ķ'i$^n$'-wa-da-i$^n$-ga. Also E-hiu-gthe, Elm-creek, given to him in honor of his father, who was killed in battle on a creek by that name. Also Be-ga-xa-zhi, Never-beaten. Husband of Xu-tha'-da-wi$^n$ of the Ţsi'-zhu Wa-shta-ge gens.

Mi-tho-ţo$^n$'-mo$^n$-i$^n$-zhi$^n$-ga, Young-mid-day. Refers to the sun, one of the life symbols of this gens. Husband of Pa-hiu'-e-çe.

Ţo$^n$'-i$^n$-kshe, Moon-returned-to-sight. Refers to the new moon. Son of Mi-ķ'i$^n$-wa-da-i$^n$-ga and Wa-xthe-tho$^n$-ba.

Wa-zha'-a-ķi-pa, Met-the-Wa-zha'-zhe. Refers to the first meeting of the Ţsi'-zhu and the Wa-zha'-zhe divisions. Son of Mi-tho'-ţo$^n$-mo$^n$-i$^n$ and Wa-ţo$^n$-i-ça-e.

Wa-zhi$^n$-ga-tha-gthi$^n$, Good-bird.

Wa'-zho$^n$-gi-the, Met-them-by-chance. (Hall Good.)

Zho$^n$-i'-ni-tha, Clings-to-tree-for-safety. Also Ķa'-xe-a-gtho$^n$, Crow-head-dress.

### FEMALE

Do$^n$'-a-bi, Looked-upon. Refers to the sun, one of the life symbols of the gens. Daughter of I'-ţo$^n$-mo$^n$-i$^n$ and Wa-ţo$^n$'-i-ça-e.

Mi'-do$^n$-a-bi, Sun-looked-upon. Wife of Pa-hiu'-çka of the Ţsi'zhu Wa-shta-ge gens.

Mi'-do$^n$-a-bi. Daughter of Mi-ķ'i$^n$'-wa-da-i$^n$-ga and Wa-xthe'-tho$^n$-ba.

Mi'-ga-sho$^n$-i$^n$, Sun-that-travels. (In the Ho$^n$'-ga gens of the Omaha tribe.) Daughter of Mi-tho'-ţo$^n$-mo$^n$-i$^n$ and Wa-ţo$^n$'-i-ça-e.

Mo$^n$'-çi-ţse-xi, Sacred-arrow-shaft.

Mo$^n$'-çi-ţse-xi. Wife of Mi-da'-i$^n$-ga of the Ţsi'-zhu Wa-shta-ge gens.

Ni'-ḳa, Person.  Wife of Kshi'-zhi of the Ho$^n$'-ga gens.

Wa'-ṭse-wi$^n$, Star-woman.  (In the Tha'-ṭa-da gens of the Omaha tribe.)  Wife of Sho$^n$-ge-mo$^n$-i$^n$ of the Ṭsi'-zhu Wa-shta-ge gens.

Wa-xthe'-tho$^n$-ba, Two-standards.  Wife of Gthe-mo$^n$'-zhi$^n$-ga of the Ṭsi'-zhu Wa-shta-ge gens.

Xu-tha'-da-wi$^n$, Good-eagle-woman.  Wife of Mo$^n$'-ge-ça-be of the O'-po$^n$ gens.

Xu-tha'-da-wi$^n$.  Wife of I$^n$-shta'-mo$^n$-çe of the I$^n$-gtho$^n$'-ga gens.

Xu-tha'-da-wi.  Wife of O-tho'-xa-wa-the of the Ṭsi'-zhu Wa-shta-ge.

### Ho$^N$' I-ni-ḳa-shi-ga (Night-people)

Special kinship terms and personal names of the first three sons and the first three daughters in a fanily of the Ho$^n$' I-ni-ḳa-shi-ga gens, as given by Ni'-ḳa-tho$^n$-ba, a member of the gens.

#### sons

1. I$^n$-gtho$^n$'.  Ho$^n$'-mo$^n$-i$^n$, Moves-in-the-night.
2. Kshon'-ga.  Ṭsi'-zhu-u-thu-ha-ge, Last-in-the-order-of-the-Ṭsi'-zhu.
3. Ka'-zhi$^n$-ga.  Ho$^n$'ga-i-ṭa-zhi, Not-of-the-Ho$^n$'-ga.  Also Ho$^n$'-ba-hiu, Day-comes.

#### daughters

1. Mi'-na.  Mi'-ṭse-xi, Mi'-na-the-favorite.
2. Wi'-he.  Ho$^n$-wa'-k'u, Night-woman.
3. Çi'-ge or A-çi$^n$'-ga, E-no$^n$'-do$^n$-a-bi, Only-one-that-is-seen.

#### other names

##### Male

Çi$^n$'-dse-thi$^n$-ge, No-tail.  Refers to the red black bear, the symbol of the Black bear gens of the Ṭsi'-zhu division.  (Hayes Little-bear.)

Ho$^n$'-ba-hiu, Day-comes.  Refers to the passing of night, the life symbol of this gens.  Husband of Ho$^n$-be'-do-ḳa of the Ṭa' I-ni-ḳa-shi-ga gens.

Ho$^n$'-ba-hiu.  Husband of Ço$^n$-çi'-gthe of the Po$^n$'-ḳa Wa-shta-ge gens.

Ho$^n$'-ga-a-ḳa-zhi.  (Meaning obscure.)  Son of Wa-zha'-zhe-mi-ṭse-xi, wife of No$^n$-be-çi.

Ho$^n$'-ga-a-ḳa-zhi.  Son of Tho-ṭa-a-ça of the Ni'-ḳa-wa-ḳo$^n$-da-gi gens, wife of Ḳi'-mo$^n$-ho$^n$ of the O'-po$^n$ gens.

Ho$^n$'-mo$^n$-i$^n$, Traveling-night.  (In the I$^n$-ḳe'-ça-be gens of the Omaha tribe.)  Son of Ni'-ḳa-tho$^n$-ba.

Ho$^n$'-mo$^n$-i$^n$.  (Andrew Jackson.)

Ni'-ḳa-a-ḳi-ba-no$^n$, Runs-to-meet-men.  Also E'-zhi-ga-xthi, Slew-the-wrong-man.  (War name.)  Husband of Gthe-do$^n$'-wi$^n$-ṭse-xi of the Ni-ḳa-wa-ḳo$^n$-da-gi gens.

Ni'-ka-tho$^n$-ba, Two-men.

Pe'-dse-mo$^n$-i$^n$, Fire-walker. Refers to the finding of the red bear, the life symbol of this gens. He was found walking in the night, a light like that of fire shining from his breast. Husband of We'-tsi$^n$-thu-ça of the Ho$^n$'-ga U-ṭa-no$^n$-dsi gens.

Sho'-dse, Smoke. Refers to the duty of this gens to light the ceremonial pipe. Son of Ni'-ka-a-ḳi-ba-no$^n$ and Gthe-do$^n$-wi$^n$-ṭse-xi.

We'-ça-ba-zhi. (Meaning obscure.) Son of Ni'-ka-a-ḳi-ba-no$^n$ and Gthe-do$^n$'-wi$^n$-ṭse-xi.

Xo$^n$'-dse-u-mo$^n$-i$^n$, Walks-among-cedars. Refers to the habit of the bears. Husband of Xu-tha'-wi$^n$ of the Ho$^n$'-ga gens.

FEMALE

E-no$^n$'-a-bi, Only-one-seen-by-all. Refers to the sun. Wife of A-hiu-zhi$^n$-e of the Ṭsi'-zhu Wa-shta-ge gens.

Ho$^n$'-do$^n$-wa-ḳ'u, Woman-of-the-night.

Mi-do$^n$'-be, Sees-the-sun. Daughter of Ni'-ka-a-ḳi-ba-no$^n$ and Mi'-ṭse-xi, Mi'-na-the-favorite. (In I$^n$-ḳe'-ça-be gens of the Omaha tribe.) Wife of Tha-çiu'-e of the I'-ba-ṭse gens.

Mi'-ṭse-xi. Wife of Gthe-do$^n$'-mo$^n$-çe of the Ṭsi'-zhu Wa-shta-ge gens.

Mi'-ṭse-xi. Daughter of Tho'-ṭa-a-ça of the Ni'-ka-wa-ḳo$^n$-da-gi gens, wife of Ḳi'-mo$^n$-ho$^n$ of the O'-po$^n$ gens.

Mi'-ṭse-xi. Wife of Thi-hi'-bi of the Ṭa' I-ni-ka-shi-ga gens.

Ni'-ka-shi-ṭsi-the. (Meaning obscure.) Wife of Chi-zhe'-wa-the of the Ṭa' I-ni-ka-shi-ga gens.

Wa-ça'-be-wi$^n$, Black-bear-woman. Refers to the symbol of the Black Bear gens of the Ṭsi'-zhu division. (Lucy H. Bangs.)

The following are special kinship terms and personal names of the first three sons and the first three daughters in a family of this gens, as given by Ho$^n$'-mo$^n$-i$^n$, a member. This man told the following story of the origin of this gens:

When the Ho$^n$' I-ni-ka-shi-ga, People of the Night, were made they had fire. They wandered about upon the earth, but saw no people. At the beginning of day, when night had passed, they suddenly came upon the Ṭsi'-zhu Wa-no$^n$, a warlike people. The Ho$^n$' I-ni-ka-shi-ga offered their services to these strangers, which were accepted. The Ṭsi'-zhu Wa-no$^n$ gave to the Ho$^n$' I-ni-ka-shi-ga the office of Sho'-ḳa, which carried with it the duty of filling the ceremonial pipe and lighting it with the mystic fire of the People of the Night.

SONS

1. I$^n$-gtho$^n$'. Ho$^n$'-mo$^n$-i$^n$, Traveling-night.
2. Ksho$^n$'-ga'. Sho'-dse, Smoke. Referring to the sacred fire.
3. Ka'-zhi$^n$-ga. Ṭa-ḳo$^n$'-i$^n$-ge, No-sinews. The black bear are said to have no sinew.

## DAUGHTERS

1. Mi'-na.  Mi'-na-the-favorite.
2. Wa-ça'-be-wi$^n$, Black-bear-woman.
3. Çi'-ge.  E-no$^{n'}$-do$^n$-a-bi, Seen-by-all.  All living creatures see the sun.

### OTHER NAMES

#### MALE

Çi-gthe'-wa-thi-ṭa, Crosses-trail.  The bear in his wanderings crosses the trails of other animals.

Çi-the'-dse-xo-dse, Gray-heels.

Da'-ḳo$^n$-mo$^n$-i$^n$, Walks-as-in-fire-light.

Ho$^{n'}$-ga-thi-ḳa-zhi.  (Meaning obscure.)

Ho$^n$-gthi', Night-has-returned.

Mo$^n$-ḳo$^{n'}$, Medicine.

O-ḳo$^{n'}$-dsi-wa-shko$^n$, Struggles-by-himself.  No one to help him fight.

O-pa'-stse-dse, Long-body.

Ṗa-çi', Brown-nose.

Sha'-ge-btha-çka, Flat-hands.

Tho'-ṭo$^n$-gthi-no$^n$-zhi$^n$, Stands-upright.

Wa-ça'-e-wa-ḳo$^n$-da-gi, Mysterious-bear.

Wa-ça'-e-zhi$^n$-ga, Little-bear.

Wa-shi$^{n'}$-shto$^n$-ga, Soft-fat.

Wa-xa'-xa-do$^n$, Shaggy-hair.

Xo'-ga-hi$^n$-e-go$^n$, Hair-like-badger's.

#### FEMALE

Ho$^n$-wa'-k'u, Night-woman.

Mi'-zho$^n$-çka.  (Meaning obscure.)

Ni'-ḳa-shi-ṭsi-the, Person-passes-by.

Wa-xthe'-tho$^n$-ba, Two-standards.

### NI'-ḲA-WA-ḲO$^N$-DA-GI (MEN OF MYSTERY)

Special kinship terms and personal names of the first three sons and first three daughters in a family of this gens.  The thunder is the life symbol of this gens.

#### SONS

1. I$^n$-gtho$^{n'}$.  Gthe-do$^{n'}$-ṭse-ga, New-hawk.  Refers to the reconsecration of the hawk, the symbol of courage of the warrior.  Also Gthe-do$^n$-xo-e, Gray-hawk.  Refers to the grayish appearance of the hawk when it is painted afresh at a ceremony.
2. Ksho$^{n'}$-ga.  Gthe-do$^{n'}$-çka, White-hawk.  Refers to the whitish appearance of the hawk when freshly painted.

3. Ḳa'-zhiⁿ-ga. Ni-uⁿ'-ṭsi-gthe, Rumbling-in-the-distance. Refers to the low rumbling of the thunder in an approaching storm. Also Hu'-ṭoⁿ-moⁿ-iⁿ, Roars-as-he-comes.

DAUGHTERS

1. Mi'-na. Gthe-doⁿ'-mi-ṭse-ga, New-hawk-woman. Refers to the reconsecration of the symbolic hawk.
2. Wi'-he. Tho'-ṭa-a-ça. (Meaning obscure.)
3. Çi'-ge. Gthe-doⁿ'-wiⁿ-zhiⁿ-ga, Little-hawk-woman. Refers to the smallest of the hawks.

OTHER NAMES
MALE

A'-gthi-he-the, Returns-to-his-place. Refers to the returning of the symbolic hawk to its place after a ceremony.

A'-ḳi-da-ga-hi-ge, Chief-protector. Title of one of the protectors of the chiefs.

Ba'-çiu-ṭoⁿ-ga, Big-hail.

Çe'-ça-gi-da, Returns-trotting.

Gthe-doⁿ'-çka, White-hawk. (Kshoⁿ-ga name.) Son of Noⁿ'-ḳa-ṭo-ho and Xu-tha'-da-wiⁿ of the Ṭsi'-zhu Wa-shta-ge gens.

Gthe-doⁿ'-çka. Husband of Mi'-ga-shoⁿ-iⁿ of the Poⁿ'-ḳa Wa-shta-ge gens.

Gthe-doⁿ'-çka. Son of Gthe-doⁿ'-çka and Mi'-ga-shoⁿ-iⁿ.

Gthe-doⁿ'-çka. Son of We-ṭoⁿ'-ha-iⁿ-ga and Hoⁿ-be'-do-ḳa.

Gthe-doⁿ'-çka. Son of Noⁿ'-pe-wa-the and Hoⁿ'-ga-wiⁿ.

Gthe-doⁿ'-ṭse-ga, New-hawk. (Iⁿ-gthoⁿ' name.)

Gthe-doⁿ'-ṭsi-e, Hawk-passing-by. Refers to a hawk attacking its prey. Son of Ṭoⁿ'-woⁿ-ga-she and Xu-tha'-da-wiⁿ.

Gthi-noⁿ'-zhiⁿ, Returns-and-stands. Refers to the return of the war-hawk after a successful attack upon the enemy.

Ḳe-noⁿ'-xu-xe, Cracks-the-turtle-with-his-foot.

Ḳe'-tha-moⁿ-iⁿ, Clear-day-approaching. Refers to the oncoming of the clear sky after a thunderstorm.

Ḳi-xi'-tha-ba-zhi, Self-confident. Refers to the warlike spirit of this gens.

Mi-ḳa'-wa-da-iⁿ-ga, Playful-raccoon.

Mi-ḳa'-zhiⁿ-ga, Little-raccoon.

Mi-tsiu'-zhiⁿ-ga, Little-grizzly-bear.

Moⁿ-ge'-çi, Yellow-breast. A swallow. A bird that is closely associated with thunderstorms.

Moⁿ-xpi'-moⁿ-iⁿ, Traveling-cloud. (In the Iⁿ-shta'-çoⁿ-da gens of the Omaha tribe.)

Ni-zhiu'-ça-ge, Violent-rain.

Ni-zhiu'-moⁿ-iⁿ, Traveling-rain.

Ni-zhiu'-ṭoⁿ-ga, Big-rain.

No$^{n}$-ka-ṭo-ho, Blue-back. Refers to the sacred hawk whose back is painted blue. (In the I$^{n}$-gthe'-zhi-de gens of the Omaha tribe.) Also, Mi-ka'-zhi$^{n}$-ga. Refers to the raccoon-skin robe of this gens used in ceremonies. Husband of Xu-tha'-da-wi$^{n}$ of the Ṭsi'-zhu Wa-shta-ge gens.

No$^{n}$-pe-wa-the, Fear-inspiring. Refers to the fear inspired by the thunder. (In the Tha'-ṭa-da gens of the Omaha tribe.) Husband of Ho$^{n}$-ga-wi$^{n}$ of the O'-po$^{n}$ gens.

O-pa'-the-e. (Meaning obscure.) Saucy-calf thinks it is a valor name.

Pa-thi$^{n}$'-wa-xpa-thi$^{n}$, Poor-Pawnee. Refers to the killing of a half-starved Pawnee by an Osage.

Pratt, Charles. Son of No$^{n}$-pe-wa-the and Ho$^{n}$-ga-wi$^{n}$.

Sha'-wa-bi$^{n}$, Bloody-hands. Refers to the talons of a hawk.

Shi-tho$^{n}$'-dse-we-tsi$^{n}$, Strikes-with-the-knee.

Ṭo$^{n}$'-wo$^{n}$-ga-she, Taker-of-towns. This man has the office of renewing of the sacred hawks. Husband of Xu-tha'-da-wi$^{n}$ of the Ṭsi'-zhu Wa-no$^{n}$ gens.

Wa-hiu'-ga-xthi, Strikes-the-bones. Valor name.

Wa'-thu-da-çe, Crashing-sound. Refers to the thunder.

We'-ṭo$^{n}$-ha-i$^{n}$-ge. (Meaning obscure.) Husband of Ho$^{n}$-be'-do-ka of the Ṭa' I-ni-ka-shi-ga gens.

Wa-xo'-be-zhi$^{n}$-ga, Little-shrine. Refers to the small portable shrine containing the hawk and other symbolic articles.

Wa-zhi$^{n}$'-ni-ka, Bird-man.

Xo'-ka, Initiator. (Not gentile name.) Husband of Gtho$^{n}$-zho$^{n}$-ba of the O'-po$^{n}$ gens.

Xo$^{n}$'-dse-u-mo$^{n}$-i$^{n}$, Dwell-among-the-cedars. The thunder and the lightning are said to live among the cedars.

Xu-e'-gi-da, Comes-roaring. Refers to the coming of the storm with roaring winds.

Xu-e'-no$^{n}$-zhi$^{n}$, Stands-soughing. Refers to the murmuring of the cedar tree as the wind passes through its branches.

Zho$^{n}$'-ga-xthi, Tree-killer. Refers to the habit of the lightning of striking trees.

Zho$^{n}$'-u-thi-stse-ge, Tree-splitter. Refers to the splitting of a tree by lightning.

FEMALE

Gthe-do$^{n}$'-ço$^{n}$-wi$^{n}$, White-hawk-woman. Refers to the white paint put upon some of the sacred hawks. Wife of Ṭsi'-zhu-ho$^{n}$-ga of the Ṭsi'-zhu Wa-shta-ge gens.

Gthe-do$^{n}$'-mi-ṭse-xi, Hawk-Mi-na-the-favorite.

Gthe-do$^{n}$'-mi-ṭse-xi. Wife of Zhi$^{n}$-ga'-wa-ça of the Ho$^{n}$'-ga gens.

Gthe-do$^{n}$'-mi-ṭse-xi. Wife of Pi'-zhi-ṭo$^{n}$-ga of the Tho'-xe gens.

Gthe-do$^{n}$'-mi-ṭse-xi. Daughter of No$^{n}$-pe-wa-the and Ho$^{n}$-ga-wi$^{n}$.

Gthe-do$^n$'-win, Hawk-woman. Refers to the sacred hawks. (In the Mo$^n$'-thi$^n$-ka-ga-xe gens of the Omaha tribe.)

Gthe-do$^n$'-wi$^n$-tse-xi, Hawk-Mi-na-the favorite. (In the Ta-pa' of the Omaha tribe.) Daughter of We-to$^n$'-ha-i$^n$-ga and Ho$^n$-be'-do-ka.

I'$^n$'-sho$^n$-ba. (Meaning obscure.) Daughter of Mo$^n$'-çi-tse-xi of the I$^n$-gtho$^n$'-ga gens.

Mi$^n$-tsiu'-xa-ge. (Meaning obscure.) Wife of Mo$^n$-ha-u-gthi$^n$ of the Tsi'-zhu Wa-shta-ge gens.

Tho-ta'-a-ça. (Meaning obscure.) (In the Tha'-ta-da gens of the Omaha tribe.) Daughter of Wa'-ko$^n$-ça-mo$^n$-i$^n$ of the Pon'-ka Wa-shta-ge gens.

Tho-ta'-ta-ça. Daughter of Ki-xi'-tha-ba-zhi and Mi'-ço$^n$-i$^n$.

Tho'-ta-a-ça. Wife of Ki'-mo$^n$-ho$^n$ of the O'-po$^n$ gens.

Wa'-dsi-u-hi-zhi. (Meaning obscure.) Wife of Btho'-ga-hi-ge of the Tsi'-zhu Wa-shta-ge gens.

Xo$^n$'-dse-wi$^n$, Cedar-woman. The cedar is a tree that is closely associated with thunder.

Xo'-ta-wi$^n$, Blackbird-woman. The blackbird is one of the war symbols of the Ni'-ka-wa-ko$^n$-da-gi gens. Daughter of Wa'-ko$^n$-ça-mo$^n$-i$^n$ of the Po$^n$'-ka Wa-shta-ge gens.

## THO'-XE GENS

Special kinship terms and personal names of the first three sons and the first three daughters in a family of the Tho'-xe gens, as given by Saucy-calf.

### SONS

1. I$^n$-gtho$^n$'. Ko$^n$'-çe-wa-e. (Meaning obscure.)
2. Ksho$^n$'-ga. Hi$^n$-ba'-sda, Sheds-his-hair. Refers to the shedding of hair by the buffalo.
3. Ka'-zhi$^n$-ga. Tse-zhi$^n$'-ho$^n$-ga, Sacred-calf.

### DAUGHTERS

1. Mina. Do$^n$'-a-bi, Gazed-upon. Also Tho'-xe-wi$^n$, Tho'-xe-woman.
2. Wi'-he. Pa-hiu'-thi-sho$^n$, Shaggy-head.
3. Çi'-ge, or A-çi$^n$'-ga. Tse-mi'-çi, Brown-buffalo-woman. Also Bo$^n$-gi'-da, The-lowing-herd. Also Tse-mi'-xtsi, Real-buffalo-woman.

### OTHER NAMES

#### MALE

A'-ga-ha-mo$^n$-i$^n$, Walks-outside. Refers to the bulls, that are in the habit of walking outside of the herd.

A'-ga-zho$^n$, Bushy. Refers to the bushy hair on the front legs of the buffalo bull.

A'-hi$^n$-u-ha-zhi-hi, Red-forelegs. Refers to the reddish-brown legs of the buffalo.

Çi-ha', Soles. Refers to the footprints of the buffalo. (In the Tha'-ṭa-da gens of the Omaha tribe.)

Çi-ha', Son of Tho'-xe-zhi$^n$-ga and Gia'-ço$^n$-ba.

Çi$^{n'}$-dse-ço-ṭa, Slender-tail. Refers to the slender tail of the buffalo.

Çi$^{n'}$-dse-wa-ḳo$^n$-da, Mystic-tail. Refers to the scalps attached to the tail of the sacred hawk.

Çi$^{n'}$-dse-wa-ḳo$^n$-da. Son of Ṭse'-çe-ṭo$^n$-ga and Wa'-ḳo$^n$-ça-mo$^n$-i$^n$.

Çi$^{n'}$-dse-wa-ḳo$^n$-da. Son of No$^{n'}$-ba-mo$^n$-thi$^n$ and Xu-tha'-mi-ṭse-xi.

Çi$^{n'}$-dse-wa-ḳo$^n$-da. Son of Mi'-ga-sho$^n$-i$^n$, wife of Mo$^{n'}$-zhi-çka-ḳ'i$^n$-ga-xthi.

Çi$^{n'}$-dse-zhi$^n$-ga, Little-tail. Refers to the tail of the buffalo.

Çi'-ṭo$^n$-ga, Big-feet. Refers to the great size of the buffalo's feet. (In the Tha'-ṭa-da gens of the Omaha tribe.)

Da'-ba-dsi$^n$, Swollen. Refers to the wounded buffalo found dead in a state of decomposition.

Do'-ba-mo$^n$-thi$^n$, Walk-by-fours. Refers to the habit of the bulls of walking by fours. (In the In-ḳe'-ça-be gens of the Omaha tribe.) Husband of Mi'-ho$^n$-ga of the Ṭsi-'zhu Wa-no$^n$ gens.

Do'-ba-mo$^n$-thi$^n$. Son of Tho'-xe-zhi$^n$-ga and Gia'-ço$^n$-ba.

Fletcher, Francis. Son of Tho'-xe-zhi$^n$-ga and Mi'-ço$^n$-e.

Ga-dsi$^{n'}$-gthi-tho$^n$, Crosses. Refers to the hungry calf that runs in front of its mother to stop her. (In the I$^n$-ḳe'-ça-be gens of the Omaha tribe.)

Gthe-do$^{n'}$-stse-dse, Long-hawk. Refers to the long scalp locks attached to the sacred hawks. Son of Tho'-xe-zhi$^n$-ga and Gia'-ço$^n$-ba.

He-ba'-ṭo$^n$-he, Stubby-horns. Refers to the old bull who had worn his horns down to stumps.

Hiu'-gthe-ṭo$^n$-ga, Big-legs. Refers to the great size of the legs of the buffalo bull.

Hi$^n$-çi'-mo$^n$-i$^n$, Brown-hair-walker. Refers to the brown color of the calf. Also Çi-ha, Soles.

I'-hi$^n$-u-ba-do$^n$, Pointed-beard. Refers to the beard of the buffalo.

I'-shka-da-bi, Playful. Refers to the sport afforded the hunter by the herds of buffalo. (In the I$^n$-ḳe'-ça-be gens of the Omaha tribe.)

I-tha'-no$^n$-ça, Head-them-off. Refers to the heading off of the buffalo trying to escape the hunter.

I'-wa-shko$^n$, Dependable. Valor name. A man returned from the warpath discouraged. On approaching the village he heard the Herald singing his praises. He went back, attacked the enemy, and won a big victory. Also Sho$^n$-ha-u-ḳi-pa-ṭse, Wolf-robe. He thought a great deal of this robe, but when he attacked the enemy he threw it away and lost it. These two names the warrior won in this fight.

Ḳi-no$^{n\prime}$-do$^n$, Springs-forth. Valor name. Also Ṭse-mo$^{n\prime}$-gi-u-e. (Meaning obscure.) Son of Mi$^\prime$-ho$^n$-ga of the Ṭsi-'zhu Wa-no$^n$ gens.

Louis. Son of Ṗa-çi$^\prime$-do-ba and Mi$^\prime$-ço$^n$-e.

Mi$^{n\prime}$-dse-ḳo$^n$, Bow-string. The bow-string is made of buffalo sinew and is of great value to the hunter and warrior. Son of Ṭse-do$^\prime$-a-ṭo$^n$-ga and Hi$^{n\prime}$-i-ḳi-a-bi.

Mo$^n$-ga$^\prime$-shu-dse or Mo$^n$-ga$^\prime$-shu-e, Dust-makers. Refers to the dust raised by the herds of buffalo. Also Ṗe$^\prime$-zhe-u-tha-ha, Grass-clings-to-him. Husband of Wa-ṭo$^{n\prime}$-i-ça-e of the Ṭa$^\prime$ I-ni-ḳa-shi-ga gens.

Mo$^n$-i$^{n\prime}$-gthe-do$^n$, Walks-home. Son of Ṭse-do$^\prime$-a-ṭo$^n$-ga and Hi$^n$-i-ḳi-a-bi.

Mo$^n$-zho$^{n\prime}$-u-ga-sho$^n$, Wanderer. Refers to the buffalo that roams over the land.

Ni-ga$^\prime$-xu-e, Roaring-waters. Refers to the waters disturbed by a herd of buffalo crossing a stream. (In the I$^n$-ḳe$^\prime$-ça-be gens of the Omaha tribe.)

No$^n$-ba$^\prime$-mo$^n$-thi$^n$, Two-walking. Refers to two buffalo walking side by side. (In the Tha$^\prime$-ṭa-da gens of the Omaha tribe.) Husband of Xu-tha$^\prime$-mi-ṭse-xi of the Ho$^{n\prime}$-ga gens.

No$^{n\prime}$-ḳa-a-ba-zha-ṭa, Straddles-the-back. Refers to the packing of the buffalo meat on the back of the horse by the hunter.

No$^{n\prime}$-pe-wa-the, Fear-inspiring. This name is used by both this and the Ni-ḳa-wa-ḳo$^n$-da-gi gens. (In the Tha$^\prime$-ṭa-da gens of the Omaha tribe.)

No$^n$-zhi$^{n\prime}$-tsi-e, Rises-suddenly. Refers to the alertness of the buffalo.

O$^{n\prime}$-be-çu-zhi$^n$-ga, Small-hips. Refers to the smallness of the hips of the buffalo.

Ṗa-çi-do-ba, Four-hills. Refers to the descent of a herd of buffalo from a hilltop in four lines. (In the Ḳo$^{n\prime}$-çe gens of the Omaha tribe.) Husband of Wa-zha$^\prime$-zhe-mi-ṭse-xi of the Ṭa$^\prime$ I-ni-ḳa-shi-ga gens.

Ṗa-çi$^\prime$-do-ba. Husband of Mi$^\prime$-ço$^n$-e of the Ho$^{n\prime}$-ga gens.

Ṗa$^\prime$-ṭa-hi$^n$-shku-e, Hairy-head. Refers to the hairy head of the buffalo.

Ṗe$^\prime$-zhe-a-ṭse, Grass-eater. Refers to the eating of grass by the buffalo.

Ṗi$^\prime$-zhi-gthi-no$^n$-zhi$^n$, Returns-to-fight. Refers to the enraged bull standing to fight the hunter.

Ṗi$^\prime$-zhi-ṭo$^n$-ga, Big-bad-one. Refers to the big bull that is always ready to fight. Husband of Gthe-do$^{n\prime}$-mi-ṭse-xi of the Ni-'ḳa-wa-ḳo$^n$-da-gi gens.

Ṗi$^\prime$-zhi-ṭo$^n$-ga, Husband of Mary of the O$^\prime$-po$^n$ gens.

Sha'-be-no$^n$-zhi$^n$, Stands-dark. The lone buffalo standing still against the horizon. (In the Ho$^{n\prime}$-ga gens of the Omaha tribe.)

The'-çe-xa-ga, Rough-tongue. The tongue of the buffalo is rough.

Thi-xa'-ba-zhi, Not-chased. Refers to the little calf the hunter allows to escape.

Thi-xa'-bi-a-ķi-zhi$^n$, Thinks-himself-chased. Refers to the fleeing of a buffalo even when he is not pursued by the hunter.

Tho$^{n\prime}$-dse-ṭo$^n$-ga, Big-heart.

Tho'-xe-ga-hi-ge, Tho-xe-chief.

Tho'-xe-wa-ķo$^n$-da, The-mystic-Tho-xe.

Tho'-xe-zhi$^n$-ga, Young-Tho-xe. Also Wa-ṭo$^{n\prime}$-i$^n$-ķi-the, Comes-to-view. (A Mi-ķ'i$^{n\prime}$ name.) Refers to the new moon. Husband of Mi'-ço$^n$-e of the Wa-ça'-be gens.

Tho'-xe-zhi$^n$-ga. Husband of Gia'-ço$^n$-ba of the Po$^{n\prime}$-ķa Wa-shta-ge gens.

Tho'-xe-wa-da-i$^n$-ga, Mischievous-Tho-xe.

Ṭse'-çe-ṭo$^n$-ga, Big-belly. Refers to the great size of the bull. Husband of Wa'-ķo$^n$-ça-mo$^n$-i$^n$ of the Po$^{n\prime}$-ķa Wa-shta-ge gens.

Ṭse-çi$^{n\prime}$-dse, Buffalo-tail. (The name of a gens in the Omaha tribe.)

Ṭse-do'-a-mo$^n$-i$^n$, Walking-bull.

Ṭse-do'-a-ṭo$^n$-ga, Big-bull. Husband of Hi$^{n\prime}$-i-ķi-a-bi of the Ṭsi'-zhu Wa-shta-ge gens.

Ṭse-do'-a-zhi$^n$-ga, Little-bull. (In the Ṭse-çi$^{n\prime}$-dse gens of the Omaha tribe.)

Ṭse-do'-ga, Buffalo-bull. (In the Ho$^{n\prime}$-ga gens of the Omaha tribe.)

Ṭse-mo$^{n\prime}$-gi-the. (Meaning obscure.)

Ṭse-pa'-zhi$^n$-ga, Little-buffalo-head. Husband of Wa-ça'-be-wa-ķ'u of the Wa-ça'-be gens.

Ṭse'-thi-ṭsi, Buffalo-ribs. (In the Tha'-ṭa-da gens of the Omaha tribe.)

Ṭse-zhi$^{n\prime}$-ga-wa-da-i$^n$-ga, Playful-calf. Refers to the playfulness of the buffalo calf. Akso Xa-ge'-wa-the, Makes-them-weep. (In the Ķo$^{n\prime}$-çe gens of the Omaha tribe.)

U-ga'-ha-xpa, Bushy-head.

U-ķo$^{n\prime}$-dsi-no$^n$-zhi$^n$, Stands-alone. Refers to the solitary buffalo that stands alone, apart from the herd.

U-mi'-zhe, Bedding. Refers to the use of the buffalo hide for bedding.

U-ķi'-pa-to$^n$, Rolls-himself. Refers to the rolling of the buffalo on the ground. (In the I$^n$-gthe'-zhi-de gens of the Omaha tribe.)

U-tha'-ga-bi, Famed. Valor name.

Wa-no$^{n\prime}$-ge, Stampede. Refers to the stampeding of a buffalo herd.

Wa'-stse-ge, Strip-of-meat.

Wa'-u-wi-çi, Jumper. Refers to the leaps of the buffalo when charging on the hunter.

We'-zhi-u-gi-pi, Trench-full. Refers to the fullness of the fire trench used in jerking meat.

FEMALE

Bo$^n$-giu'-da, Lowing. Refers to the lowing of the herd as heard in the distance.

Bo$^n$-giu'-da, same as above. Daughter of Ṭse-do'-a-ṭo$^n$-ga, this gens, and Hi$^n$'i-ḳi-a-bi of the Ṭsi'-zhu Wa-shta-ge gens.

Bo$^n$-giu-da, same as above. Wife of Ḳo$^n$'-çe-ho$^n$-ga of the Ho$^n$'-ga U-ṭa-no$^n$-dsi gens.

Do$^n$'-a-bi, Gazed-upon. Name applied to first daughter.

Do$^n$'-a-bi, same as above. Wife of Mi'-da-i$^n$-ga of the Ṭsi'-zhu Wa-shta-ge gens.

Do$^n$'-a-bi, same as above. Wife of Wa-zhi$^n$'-ga-ça-be of the Ṭsi'-zhu Wa-shta-ge gens.

I'-ṭo$^n$-mo$^n$-i$^n$, meaning uncertain. A Mi'ḳ'i$^n$ name. Daughter of Tho'-xe-zhi$^n$-ga, this gens, and Mi'-çi$^n$-e of the Wa-ça'-be gens.

I'-ṭo$^n$-wo$^n$-gtho$^n$-bi, One-for-whom-villages-are-built. Daughter of Ṭse-pa'-zhi$^n$-ga, this gens, and Wa-ça'-be wa-ḳ'o of the Wa-ça-be gens.

Ḳi'-o, wounded. Wife of Ni'-ḳa-i-çi-wa-the of the Ṭsi'-zhu Wa-no$^n$ gens.

Ni'-ḳa-a-ça, meaning uncertain.

Ni'-ḳa-a-ça, wife of Ho-wa'-ça-e of the Ṭsi'-zhu Wa-shta-ge gens.

Ni'-ḳo$^n$-a-ça, daughter of Ṭse-çe-ṭo$^n$-ga, this gens, and Wa'-ḳo$^n$ mo$^n$-i$^n$ of the Po$^n$'-ḳa Wa-shta-ge gens.

Pa-hiu'-thi-sho$^n$, Shaggy-head. Name of second daughter in the gens.

Pa-hiu'-thi-sho$^n$, same as above. Daughter of Pa-çi'-do-ba, this gens, and Mi'-ço$^n$-e of the Ho$^n$-ga gens.

Tho'-xe-wi$^n$, Tho'-xe-woman.

Ṭse-ço$^n$'-wi$^n$, White-buffalo-woman. Wife of To$^n$'-wo$^n$-i-hi of the Ṭsi-zhu Wa-shta-ge gens. Appears in Ho$^n$'-ga gens of Omaha tribe.

Ṭse-ço$^n$'-wi$^n$, same as above. Daughter of Tho'-xe-zhi$^n$-ga, this gens, and Gia'-ço$^n$-ba of the Po$^n$'-ḳa Wa-shta-ge gens.

Ṭse'-ho$^n$-ga-wi$^n$, Sacred-buffalo-woman. Daughter of Ṭse-do-a-ṭo$^n$-ga, this gens, and Hi$^n$'-i-ḳi-a-bi of the Ṭsi'-zhu Wa-shta-ge gens.

Ṭse-i'-ḳo$^n$-tha, meaning uncertain.

Ṭse-mi'-çi, Brown-buffalo-woman. Name of third daughter in gens.

Ṭse-mi'-çi, daughter of Hi$^n$-çi'-mo$^n$-i$^n$, this gens.

Ṭse-mi-çi, same as above. Daughter of Tho'-xe-zhi$^n$-ga, this gens, and Gia'-ço$^n$-ba of the Po$^n$'-ḳa Wa-shta-ge gens.

Ṭse-wi'-ho$^n$-ga, Buffalo-sacred-cow. Wife of Ho$^n$'-ga-tha-ghti$^n$ of the Ho$^n$'-ga gens.

Ṭse-mi'-xtsi, Red-buffalo-woman. Wife of Ṭsi'-zhu-zhi$^n$-ga of the Ṭsi'-zhu Wa-shta-ge gens.

Wa-shi$^n$'-wi$^n$, Fat-woman. Daughter of Pa-çi'-do-ba, this gens, and Mi'-ço$^n$-e of the Ho$^n$'-ga gens.

Printed in the USA
CPSIA information can be obtained
at www.ICGtesting.com
LVHW080345261023
761875LV00031B/49

9 781169 269736